In cooperation with

NorthStar

Building Skills for the TOEFL® iBT

Intermediate

John Beaumont

Series Editors
Frances Boyd
Carol Numrich

D1511739

PEARSON
Longman

NorthStar: Building Skills for the TOEFL iBT, Intermediate

Pearson Education, 10 Bank Street, White Plains, NY 10606

Vice president, multimedia and skills: Sherry Preiss
Project manager: Debbie Sistino
Production coordinator: Melissa Leyva
Senior production editor: Robert Ruvo
Director of manufacturing: Patrice Fraccio
Senior manufacturing buyer: Dave Dickey
Photo research: Shana McGuire
Cover design: Rhea Banker
Cover art: Der Rhein bei Duisburg, 1937, 145(R 5) Rhine near Duisburg
  19 × 27.5 cm; water-based on cardboard; The Metropolitan Museum of
  Art, N.Y. The Berggruen Klee Collection, 1984. (1984.315.56)
  Photograph © 1985 The Metropolitan Museum of Art. © 2003 Artists
  Rights Society (ARS), New York / VG Bild-Kunst, Bonn
Text composition: Anthology, Inc.
Text font: 11/13 Sabon
Credits: see page xii

Library of Congress Cataloging-in-Publication Data

Beaumont, John, 1964-
  Northstar. Building skills for the TOEFL iBT intermediate / John
Beaumont.
    p. cm.
  Includes bibliographical references and index.
  ISBN 0-13-193706-5 (pbk. : alk. paper) — ISBN 0-13-198576-0 (pbk. :
alk. paper)
  1. Test of English as a Foreign Language—Study guides. 2. English
language—Textbooks for foreign speakers. 3. English
language—Examinations—Study guides. I. Title. II. Title: Building
for the TOEFL iBT intermediate.
PE1128.B407 2006
428'.0076—dc22

2005023551

ISBN: 0-13-193706-5 (Student Book)
       0-13-198576-0 (Student Book with Audio CDs)

LONGMAN ON THE **WEB**

Longman.com offers online resources for
teachers and students. Access our Companion
Websites, our online catalog, and our local
offices around the world.

Visit us at **longman.com.**

Printed in the United States of America
1 2 3 4 5 6 7 8 9 10—VHG—09 08 07 06 05

Contents

Welcome to **NorthStar**

Building Skills for the TOEFL® iBT

In Cooperation with ETS®

Pearson Longman and *ETS* combine their expertise in language learning and test development to create an innovative approach to developing the skills assessed in the new TOEFL Internet-based test (iBT). *NorthStar Building Skills for the TOEFL iBT*, a new three-level series, links learning and assessment with a skill-building curriculum that incorporates authentic test material from the makers of the TOEFL iBT.

Each book in the series has 10 thematic units that are organized like the TOEFL iBT into listening, reading, speaking and writing sections. Each unit includes focused integrated skill practice to develop critical thinking and communicative competence. Authentic TOEFL iBT practice sets developed by ETS offer practice and further assessment.

Purpose

The TOEFL test has changed, so preparation for it must change, too. *NorthStar: Building Skills for the TOEFL iBT* takes a new approach—an instructional approach—to test preparation. In this approach, students develop academic skills in English, while building test-taking confidence.

The TOEFL iBT requires students to show their ability to use English in a variety of campus and academic situations such as listening to lectures on unfamiliar topics, orally paraphrasing and integrating information that they have just read and listened to, and writing a well-organized essay with detailed examples, correct grammar, and varied vocabulary. The speaking and writing tasks require clear and confident expression. With these books, students move progressively, sharpening language skills *and* test-taking abilities.

The three *Building Skills* texts are intended as stepping stones from classroom instruction in English to TOEFL and academic readiness. In language instruction, students will benefit most from an integrated-skills, content-based curriculum, with a focus on critical thinking. In instructional test preparation with these books, students will encounter the same content-rich material, tasks, and question types that appear on the test. Using these books in the classroom will improve students' communicative skills, keep their interest, sharpen awareness of their skills, and build their confidence.

Extensive Support to Build the Skills Assessed on the TOEFL iBT

The *Building Skills* books strengthen English language skills while they familiarize students with the type of content, questions and tasks on the *TOEFL iBT*. Practice and mastery of these skills can help learners build confidence to communicate successfully in an academic environment.

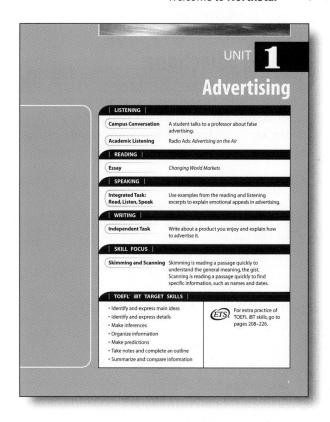

High-Interest Listening Selections

Campus conversations introduce students to practical vocabulary, conversations, and situations encountered in everyday life in a college or university.

Academic listenings present lectures, reports, and interviews, helping students understand a wide variety of styles and topics.

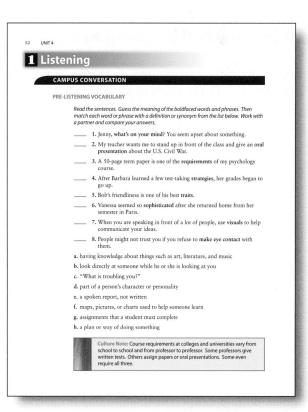

High-Interest Academic Reading Selections

Through engaging readings from many different academic disciplines, students sharpen critical reading skills such as categorizing, summarizing, and analyzing.

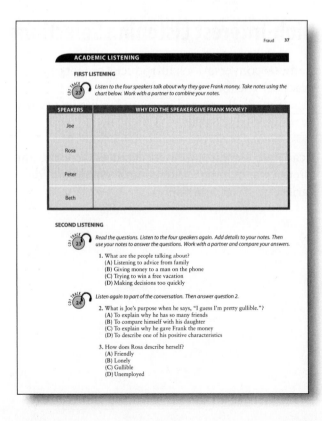

READING

Read the passage and answer the questions. Then work with a partner and compare your answers. When you disagree, go back to the text to find helpful information.

The Organic Health Center

1 Do you have cancer? Have the doctors given you no hope? I can help you. My name is Benjamin Harrison. I am the founder of the Organic Health Center. My health center offers the most advanced treatments for curing cancer and other diseases.

2 After traveling around the world for nine years looking for a cure for myself, I was able to learn the causes of cancer. Now, I can help others by offering them a cure. This cure is available only at the Organic Health Center.

3 As a result of my experiences, I realized that Western doctors are just frauds who are unqualified to help their patients. I, on the other hand, have learned how to use the best herbs and organic foods to heal people, and I am qualified to help you. That's why doctors will tell you not to trust me. They know that I can do something they can't do.

4 My program focuses on the whole body. It works on the cause of the cancer. I will put you on the healthiest diet available. This diet uses the best herb and plant products I gathered from my travels around the world. All of the products I use are natural, so they won't make you feel sick. After one to six months on this diet, you will be cured of cancer.

5 Here are some of the programs my center offers:

PROGRAM A:	PROGRAM B:	PROGRAM C:
For all types of cancers	*For cancer found early*	*For all other diseases*
Stay at my clinic for one month of treatment. Then continue the treatment in your home for two more months.	Complete a sixty-day program in your home. Eat a special diet with herbs and other healthy foods. Also follow an exercise schedule.	Complete a ninety-day program in your home. Eat a special diet with herbs and other healthy foods.

6 I am willing to travel to your home to teach you how to follow the program. And, if you would like, I have testimonials for you to read. These letters are filled with words of praise and thanks to me from my patients.

7 I offer a money-back guarantee if the program fails. If my treatments don't work, you will get back 100% of your money. How can I do this? It is my guarantee to you that my treatment works. A doctor will tell you that cancer can't be cured. It's the doctors who are the frauds.

Extensive Note-taking Practice

Students practice structured and semi-structured note-taking. These kinds of activities not only enhance comprehension of both listening and reading selections, but they also teach students how to organize information for speaking and writing responses.

ACADEMIC LISTENING

FIRST LISTENING

CD1 TRACK 23   *Listen to the four speakers talk about why they gave Frank money. Take notes using the chart below. Work with a partner to combine your notes.*

SPEAKERS	WHY DID THE SPEAKER GIVE FRANK MONEY?
Joe	
Rosa	
Peter	
Beth	

SECOND LISTENING

CD1 TRACK 23   *Read the questions. Listen to the four speakers again. Add details to your notes. Then use your notes to answer the questions. Work with a partner and compare your answers.*

1. What are the people talking about?
    (A) Listening to advice from family
    (B) Giving money to a man on the phone
    (C) Trying to win a free vacation
    (D) Making decisions too quickly

CD1 TRACK 24   *Listen again to part of the conversation. Then answer question 2.*

2. What is Joe's purpose when he says, "I guess I'm pretty gullible."?
    (A) To explain why he has so many friends
    (B) To compare himself with his daughter
    (C) To explain why he gave Frank the money
    (D) To describe one of his positive characteristics

3. How does Rosa describe herself?
    (A) Friendly
    (B) Lonely
    (C) Gullible
    (D) Unemployed

New TOEFL-Type Items and Item Analysis

Extensive TOEFL-type practice items familiarize students with the kinds of
questions and tasks they will encounter in the TOEFL iBT. Analysis activities
help them understand the purpose of each item.

---

98   UNIT 6

6. What is the best way of describing Nai Soi?
   (A) A tradition from Myanmar
   (B) A hotel for tourists in Thailand
   (C) A woman with coils on her neck
   (D) A village with long-necked women

7. What can be inferred about Sandra Miller?
   (A) She thinks that the tradition of wearing coils is dead.
   (B) She is going to visit a village of long-necked women.
   (C) She traveled to Thailand to help long-necked women.
   (D) She believes the coils are physically dangerous to the women.

8. In paragraph 8, which of the following is NOT an opinion expressed by
   Frederick Johnson?
   (A) The tradition of the long-necked women ended when they left Myanmar.
   (B) The long-necked women are hurting themselves physically.
   (C) Tourists are treating the long-necked women like animals.
   (D) The long-necked women are good entertainment for tourists.

9. In paragraph 8, the word *degrading* is closest in meaning to
   (A) entertaining.
   (B) disrespectful.
   (C) interesting.
   (D) disappointing.

10. How does the author present this topic?
    (A) By arguing one opinion on the issue
    (B) By comparing groups in Myanmar
    (C) By presenting both sides of the argument
    (D) By explaining the origins of the tradition

11. Look at the four squares ☐ that indicate where the following sentence could
    be added to the passage. Where would the sentence best fit? Circle the letter
    that shows the point where you would insert this sentence.

    According to tradition, these coils are a sign of wealth and beauty.

    Each year around 10,000 tourists visit three small villages along the
    Thai/Myanmar border to see the famous long-necked women. ☐A☐ The attraction
    is a tradition which requires women to stretch their necks by wearing brass
    coils, or rings. ☐B☐ Originally from the Padaung tribe, the women and their
    families have been running from Myanmar to Thailand since the 1980s to
    escape poverty and war. ☐C☐ Their new lives are very different from their lives as
    farmers in Myanmar. Now they spend their days talking with tourists, posing
    for pictures, and selling handmade souvenirs. ☐D☐

---

42   UNIT 3

ANALYSIS

It is helpful to know the purpose of a test item. There are four types of questions
in the reading section.

1. Basic Comprehension
   • main ideas
   • details
   • the meaning of specific sentences

2. Organization
   • the way information is structured in the text
   • the way ideas are linked between sentences or between paragraphs

3. Inference
   • ideas are not directly stated in the text
   • author's intention, purpose, or attitude not explicitly stated in the text

4. Vocabulary and Reference
   • the meaning of words
   • the meaning of reference words such as *his, them, this,* or *none*

*Go back to the reading questions and label each question with 1, 2, 3, or 4. Then work
with another student to see if you agree. Check the Answer Key for the correct answers.
Which questions did you get right? Which did you get wrong? What skills do you need
to practice?*

3 Speaking

INTEGRATED TASK: READ, LISTEN, SPEAK

In this section, you will read a short excerpt and listen to an excerpt on the same
topic. Then you will speak about the relationship between the two.

Guided Practice in Integrated and Independent Tasks

Integrated tasks require students to synthesize information from two sources and then speak or write a response. Students practice critical thinking, as well as note-taking and other practical steps for producing a quality response.

Independent tasks help students build the skills they need to express and support opinions.

---

12   UNIT 1

LISTENING

Listen to the excerpt. Use the outline to take notes as you listen. The main idea has been done for you.

Main Idea: Advertisers use different techniques to persuade us to buy.

Effective Technique: _____

Most Popular: _____

Example of An Ad: _____

SPEAKING

Speak on the following topic. Follow the steps below to prepare.

Discuss the ideas about emotional appeals in ads. Use the example of Jacko in Australia and in the U.S. to explain emotional appeal.

Step 1

Work with a partner. Skim the reading and your notes from the reading and the listening tasks on pages 11–12. Complete this outline to help you organize your ideas.

Ideas

Emotional Appeals: _____

Examples

Jacko in Australia: _____

Jacko in the U.S.: _____

Energizer Bunny® in the U.S.: _____

Step 2

Work with a partner. Take turns practicing a one-minute oral response. Use the information in your outline to help you.

Step 3

Change partners. Take turns giving a one-minute response to the topic again.

To evaluate your partner's response, use the Speaking Evaluation Form on page 180.

Fraud   45

4 Writing

INDEPENDENT TASK

Write on the following topic. Follow the steps below to prepare.

Write about an experience you have had with fraud or dishonesty, such as lying or cheating. What happened? What were the results or consequences?

Step 1

• Think of experiences with fraud and cheating you have had. Make a list.

• Choose one experience that you find the most interesting. Use the chart to take notes about what happened before, during, and after this experience.

BEFORE	DURING	AFTER

Step 2

• Work with a partner. Take turns telling your stories. Tell your partner what happened before, during, and after this experience.

• Give your partner feedback on his or her story. What was the best part of the story? How could your partner improve or change the story?

Step 3

Write for 20 minutes. Leave the last 5 minutes to edit your work.

To evaluate a partner's writing, use the Writing Evaluation Form on page 179.

Essential Academic Skills for TOEFL iBT Success

The Skill Focus section in each book raises students' awareness of a key academic language skill. At each level of the series, students deepen and broaden mastery of these ten essential skills:

- Skimming and Scanning
- Identifying and Using Main Ideas and Details
- Making Inferences
- Identifying and Using Rhetorical Structure
- Using Context Clues
- Paraphrasing
- Summarizing
- Using Detailed Examples
- Comparing and Contrasting
- Identifying and Using Cohesive Devices

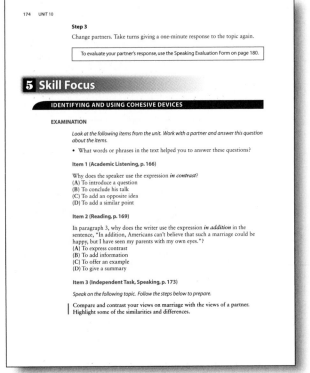

ETS Practice Section

Developed by ETS especially for this new series,
TOEFL iBT tasks offer authentic practice and
further assessment.

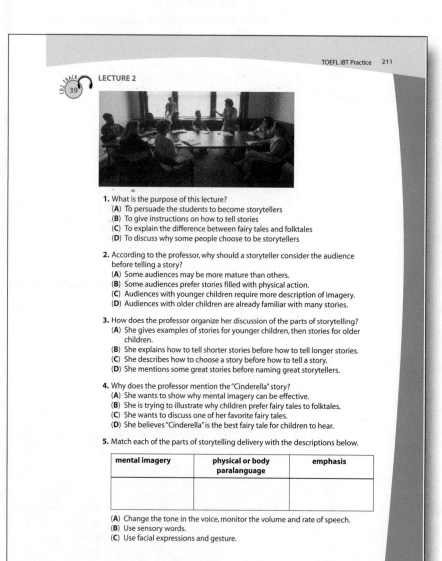

LECTURE 2

CD2 TRACK 39

1. What is the purpose of this lecture?
   (A) To persuade the students to become storytellers
   (B) To give instructions on how to tell stories
   (C) To explain the difference between fairy tales and folktales
   (D) To discuss why some people choose to be storytellers

2. According to the professor, why should a storyteller consider the audience
   before telling a story?
   (A) Some audiences may be more mature than others.
   (B) Some audiences prefer stories filled with physical action.
   (C) Audiences with younger children require more description of imagery.
   (D) Audiences with older children are already familiar with many stories.

3. How does the professor organize her discussion of the parts of storytelling?
   (A) She gives examples of stories for younger children, then stories for older
       children.
   (B) She explains how to tell shorter stories before how to tell longer stories.
   (C) She describes how to choose a story before how to tell a story.
   (D) She mentions some great stories before naming great storytellers.

4. Why does the professor mention the "Cinderella" story?
   (A) She wants to show why mental imagery can be effective.
   (B) She is trying to illustrate why children prefer fairy tales to folktales.
   (C) She wants to discuss one of her favorite fairy tales.
   (D) She believes "Cinderella" is the best fairy tale for children to hear.

5. Match each of the parts of storytelling delivery with the descriptions below.

mental imagery	physical or body paralanguage	emphasis

   (A) Change the tone in the voice, monitor the volume and rate of speech.
   (B) Use sensory words.
   (C) Use facial expressions and gesture.

Measuring Skills

To develop fluency and accuracy in English, students need practice and feedback. Students can complete Writing and Speaking Evaluation Forms to assess each other's written and spoken responses.

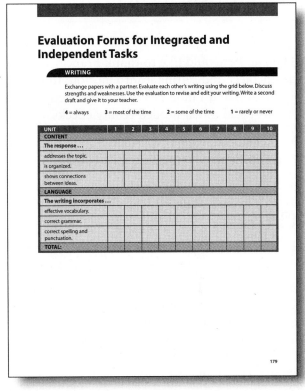

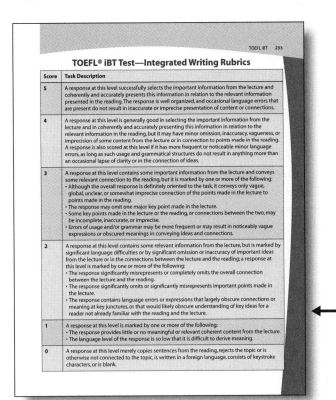

Teachers can use the authentic TOEFL iBT Scoring Rubrics developed by ETS to assess student responses to Integrated and Independent Tasks.

Teachers' Manuals

Teachers' Manuals for each level provide unit-by-unit suggestions as well as evaluation tools to track students' progress. The Teachers' Manuals also include actual student responses to speaking and writing tasks at all score levels. Provided by ETS, these authentic samples enable teachers to assess proficiency.

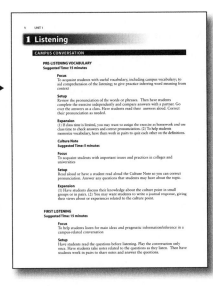

Acknowledgments

The author would like to thank Frances Boyd, Carol Numrich and Sherry Preiss for conceiving of this project and setting it into motion, to Debbie Sistino for getting us to the finish line, Helen Solórzano and Linda Fellag for their generous input, and, finally, Kam Chan for his continuous support and much-needed reality checks.

Many people at ETS contributed to this project, but Longman would especially like to thank Phil Everson, Matt Chametzky, Kate Kazin, Will Jared, and Frank Heron.

Credits

pages 27, 30, 31 "An Interview with Tony Hawk" created using published information from *Hawk Occupation: Skateboarder* by Tony Hawk with Sean Mortimer, copyright 2001, Regan Books; **page 54** "An Interview with Jackie Torrence" "Storytelling: Torrence Describes Her Craft." The text and audio of a news interview by NPR's Frank Stasio was originally broadcast on National Public Radio's *Weekend Edition Sunday*® on June 28, 1998, and is used with the permission of National Public Radio, Inc. Any unauthorized duplication is strictly prohibited; **page 113** Information for this passage was taken from *Love, Lucy* by Lucille Ball, copyright 1997, Berkley Publishing Group.

We acknowledge Helen S. Solorzano and Jennifer P.L. Schmidt for use of their material from *Northstar: Listening and Speaking Intermediate*, Second Edition and Laurie Barton and Carolyn Dupaquier Sardinas for use of their material from *Northstar: Reading and Writing Intermediate*, Second Edition.

Photo Credits

page 3, © Don Mason/Corbis; **page 11**, © Eveready Battery Company, Inc.; **page 19** left; © Reuters/Corbis; **page 19** right; © David Madison/The Image Bank/Getty Images; **page 21**, © Gunter Marx Photography/Corbis; **page 35**, © David Young-Wolff/PhotoEdit; **page 53**, © Charles Gupton/Corbis; **page 57**, © Raymond A. Mendez/Animals Animals; **page 67**, © Asian Art & Archaeology, Inc./Corbis; **page 71**, © Gary Conner/PhotoEdit; **page 76**, © Wartenberg/Picture Press/Corbis; **page 91**, © Neil Rabinowitz/Corbis; **page 97**, © Karen Su/Corbis; **page 99**, © Roger Mear/Getty Images; **page 109**, © Jim Cummins/Corbis; **page 111**, © Photofest; **page 114**, © Photofest; **page 127**, © Elena Rooraid/PhotoEdit; **page 132**, © Courtesy of David Schmidt; **page 145**, © Spencer Grant/PhotoEdit; **page 149**, © Dusan Petricic; **page 163**, © Tom Stewart/zefa/Corbis; **page 165**, © AP/Wide World Photos; **page 171**, © Bettmann/Corbis; **page 207**, © Royalty-Free/Corbis; **page 211**, © Ron Chapple/Taxi/Corbis; **page 213**, © Owen Franken/Corbis; **page 223**, © Brooks Kraft/ Corbis.

PART ONE

NorthStar Practice Units for the TOEFL® iBT

Advertising

| LISTENING |

Campus Conversation   A student talks to a professor about false advertising.

Academic Listening   Radio Ads: *Advertising on the Air*

| READING |

Essay   *Changing World Markets*

| SPEAKING |

Integrated Task:
Read, Listen, Speak   Use examples from the reading and listening excerpts to explain emotional appeals in advertising.

| WRITING |

Independent Task   Write about a product you enjoy and explain how to advertise it.

| SKILL FOCUS |

Skimming and Scanning   Skimming is reading quickly to understand the general meaning, the gist. Scanning is reading quickly to find specific information, such as names and dates.

| TOEFL® iBT TARGET SKILLS |

- Identify and express main ideas
- Identify and express details
- Make inferences
- Organize information
- Make predictions
- Take notes and complete an outline
- Summarize and compare information

 For extra practice of TOEFL iBT skills, go to pages 208–226.

1 Listening

CAMPUS CONVERSATION

PRE-LISTENING VOCABULARY

Read the sentences. Guess the meaning of the boldfaced words and phrases. Then match each word or phrase with a definition or synonym from the list below. Work with a partner and compare your answers.

_____ 1. Gena was watching **infomercials** on TV. She ordered a frying pan that was being advertised, but when she received it, she said it didn't work very well.

_____ 2. She thinks the advertisers made **false claims** about the product. It certainly doesn't work the way they said it would.

_____ 3. The company can be **held liable** if the product doesn't work.

_____ 4. The new **ab machines** at the gym are effective. I've got a flatter stomach.

_____ 5. The company can even **be sued** if the product is dangerous in some way and someone gets hurt.

_____ 6. "You paid $25.00 for that beautiful watch? **Come on!** It looks so expensive."

_____ 7. Sarah said she watched 10 hours of TV yesterday. I know she **exaggerated** because I saw her go to work in the morning and come home late.

_____ 8. Before you take any medicine, **read the fine print** on the label. There might be important information you need to know.

_____ 9. "Let's **vary** the workout today by starting with stretching instead of running exercises, OK?"

a. be taken to court for money

b. long TV commercials designed to provide information about a product or service

c. exercise machines to make the abdominal (stomach) muscles stronger

d. tell the truth

e. make slightly different

f. considered legally responsible

g. made a fact bigger or greater than it really is

h. dishonest statements

i. read the details

> **Culture Note:** Students can make appointments to meet their professors during their office hours, but often they just stop by a professor's office to ask questions about an assignment.

FIRST LISTENING

Read the questions. Listen to the conversation between a student and a professor. Take notes after each question. Share your notes with a partner. Then use your notes to answer the questions.

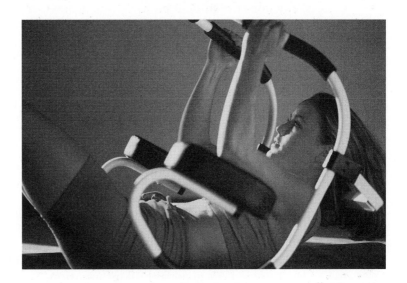

1. What is the subject of the conversation? _____

_____

_____

2. What question does the student have? _____

_____

_____

3. What example does the student use? _____

_____

_____

SECOND LISTENING

Read the questions. Listen to the conversation again. Add details to your notes. Then use your notes to answer the questions. Work with a partner and compare your answers.

1. What is the conversation mainly about?
   (A) The truth in infomercials
   (B) The false claims in many ads
   (C) The effectiveness of ab machines
   (D) The meaning of *caveat emptor*

2. Why does the student go to see his professor?
   (A) To disagree with the professor's opinion about a topic
   (B) To add information to a point made in the professor's lecture
   (C) To discuss a personal problem
   (D) To ask the professor if he could get a refund

3. Why is the student's friend unhappy with her ab machine?
   (A) She paid too much for the machine.
   (B) She didn't see any changes.
   (C) She didn't get the results she expected.
   (D) She only lost 2 inches.

Listen again to part of the conversation. Then answer question 4.

4. What does the professor mean when he says, "Well, as far as I know, companies can't make false claims about their products."?
   (A) Infomercials give truthful information.
   (B) We can't tell whether infomercials are truthful or not.
   (C) Infomercials tend to make false claims about their products.
   (D) It's my understanding that infomercials have to be truthful.

Listen again to part of the conversation. Then answer question 5.

5. What is the student's attitude when he says, "Well, that may be so, but in my experience, the product isn't always what it appears to be."?
   (A) He is doubtful about what the professor says.
   (B) He is surprised by what the professor says.
   (C) He is annoyed by what the professor says.
   (D) He is opposed to what the professor says.

ACADEMIC LISTENING

FIRST LISTENING

Listen to the two ads. Take notes using the chart below. Fill in the missing information. Work with a partner to combine your notes.

	PRODUCT NAME	PROBLEM	EFFECT OF THE PRODUCT
Ad 1	•	•	• *thief touches car and an alarm rings* •
Ad 2	•	• *dandruff, white, powdery flakes* • •	• *your dandruff will go away* •

SECOND LISTENING

Read the questions. Listen to the ads again. Add details to your notes. Then use your notes to answer the questions. Work with a partner and compare your answers.

1. How are the two ads similar?
   (A) They both present embarrassing situations.
   (B) They both present frightening situations.
   (C) They both present negative situations.
   (D) They both present humorous situations.

2. What two products are advertised in these ads? Choose TWO answers.
   (A) Cars
   (B) A security system
   (C) Jackets
   (D) Shampoo
   (E) Cornflakes

3. In the first ad, what technique does the ad use to sell the product?
   (A) It tells a personal story.
   (B) It compares different car alarms.
   (C) It explains a two-step process.
   (D) It describes its many features.

Listen again to part of the conversation. Then answer question 4.

4. In the first ad, why does the announcer say, "So why put your car at risk any longer? Get a Thief Buster Security System today!"?
(A) To ask listeners to answer the question
(B) To introduce a solution to the problem
(C) To invite listeners to discuss the topic
(D) To make listeners feel that they don't know anything

Listen again to part of the conversation. Then answer question 5.

5. In the second ad, what is the speaker's attitude toward his problem when he says this?
(A) He is embarrassed.
(B) He is angry.
(C) He is frustrated.
(D) He is confused.

6. What does Rinse Away stop?
(A) Itchy shoulders
(B) White hair
(C) Dandruff
(D) Headaches

2 Reading

CHANGING WORLD MARKETS

PRE-READING

Read the title and skim the first and last sentences of each paragraph of the passage on the next page. Underline them. Then, with a partner, predict what the text will be about. List the ideas that might be discussed.

- _____
- _____
- _____

READING

Read the passage and answer the questions. Then work with a partner and compare your answers. When you disagree, go back to the text to find helpful information.

Changing World Markets

1   As companies try to grow and introduce their products in other countries, they need to see the important differences among international markets. It is becoming more and more important for companies to create products and advertising strategies that fit different cultures.

2   Consider TV advertising in the United States, for example. When someone in the U.S. watches a movie on TV, he or she might be waiting for "the good guy" to get "the bad guy," but then suddenly a TV commercial interrupts the action. There is a break for three—sometimes as much as ten—minutes. Eventually the commercials end, and the movie continues. However, a few minutes later—just when "the good guy" is in serious trouble—the movie is interrupted again by another set of TV commercials. People in the U.S. are used to this, and they might think that it is the same all over the world. In fact, it is not. In places like France and Spain, a viewer can watch at least a half hour of a program before a commercial interruption.

3   The situation in China is a completely different story. For many years, all commercial advertising was illegal in China. Government advertising was everywhere, but business advertising was nonexistent. Then Sony came along and changed things. Sony and other Japanese companies were the first businesses to start advertising in China. They also led the way for other companies to enter the country.

4   Companies wishing to enter international markets can learn something from the Chinese market. In China, it is important for a company not to go in overnight and start advertising right away because this can lead to serious mistakes. Advertisers must take their time and plan their campaigns carefully. For example, because there are millions of people in China who don't know what a "Big Mac" is, a company would not want to rush over there and try to sell Big Macs to the Chinese. Instead, a company must plan ahead five or ten years. It pays to be patient in China.

5   If a company is interested in introducing a product in Russia, it should carefully think about its product and whether or not there is really a market for it. Fast food, for example, was a very strange idea in Russia. In Russian restaurants, a customer usually sits down and the waiter brings the soup, salad, meat, and potatoes—one thing at a time. Traditionally, Russians think people should take their time and enjoy their food.

6   The case of pizza in Russia is an interesting example of introducing a product in an international market. Before the restaurant called "Pizzeria" opened there, the company first had to convince Russian people to try its product. To do this, they explained that pizza was similar to Russian *vatrushka*. The Russians liked it, but the restaurant was

not so popular with foreign visitors because the pizza did not always have enough tomato sauce and cheese. Another problem was that if customers wanted to take the pizza home with them, the chef would not allow it. He did not want it to get cold.

7   World markets are changing every day, and new ones are opening up all the time. Companies and advertisers have to look at the big picture before they start planning a marketing campaign. They need to consider: Will people buy the product? Will they understand the marketing plan? Companies should remember that for years in China and Russia, people had a hard time buying things. The best advertisement of all was a long line in front of a store. That is how people knew which store was the place to go. So, businesses that want to expand into international markets must think about how things are changing if they expect to be successful.

1. What is the main idea of this text?
   (A) Changing world markets require a change in advertising strategy.
   (B) There are certain world markets where you should not advertise.
   (C) Advertising in China is different from advertising in Russia.
   (D) These days most American products are easy to advertise around the world.

2. In paragraph 2, the word *interruption* is closest in meaning to
   (A) correction
   (B) break
   (C) ad
   (D) product

3. What can be inferred from paragraph 2 about advertising in the U.S.?
   (A) There is too much advertising on American TV.
   (B) American advertisements do not sell products well.
   (C) Other countries should follow American advertising strategies.
   (D) There is too much violence on American TV.

4. All of the following are mentioned in paragraph 3 as examples of the Chinese situation EXCEPT
   (A) commercial advertising used to be illegal
   (B) government advertising was nonexistent
   (C) business advertising was not seen anywhere
   (D) the Japanese changed advertising in China

5. In paragraph 6, the key to selling pizza in Russia was that
   (A) it was similar to *vatrushka*
   (B) it was sold in Moscow
   (C) foreign visitors loved it
   (D) you could take it home

6. In paragraph 7, the expression *big picture* is closest in meaning to
   (A) a large photo
   (B) the worst situation
   (C) the whole context
   (D) the most important point

7. Why does the author make the comment, "Companies should remember that for years in China and Russia, people had a hard time buying things."?
   (A) To contrast them with other countries
   (B) To remind the reader of difficult markets
   (C) To give an example of how things change
   (D) To explain how countries can become successful

8. In paragraph 7, what does the word *that* refer to in the sentence, "That is how people knew which store was the place to go."?
   (A) China
   (B) Advertisement
   (C) Long line
   (D) Store

9. Look at the four squares ☐ that indicate where the following sentence could be added to the passage. Where would the sentence best fit? Circle the letter that shows the point where you would insert this sentence.

   In many parts of the world, advertisements in the middle of a program are rare.

   Consider TV advertising in the United States, for example. When someone in the U.S. watches a movie on TV, he or she might be waiting for "the good guy" to get "the bad guy," but then suddenly a TV commercial interrupts the action. ⒶThere is a break for three—sometimes as much as ten—minutes. ⒷEventually the commercials end, and the movie continues. However, a few minutes later—just when "the good guy" is in serious trouble—the movie is interrupted again by another set of TV commercials. People in the U.S. are used to this, and they might think that it is the same all over the world. ⒸIn fact, it is not. ⒹIn places like France and Spain, a viewer can watch at least a half hour of a program before a commercial interruption.

10. Which of the following expresses the essential information in this sentence from the passage?

    The Russians liked it, but the restaurant was not so popular with foreign visitors because the pizza did not always have enough tomato sauce and cheese.

    (A) Even though the Russians liked Pizzeria pizza, the foreign visitors did not.
    (B) Because the pizza did not have enough tomato sauce and cheese, the foreign visitors did not like it.
    (C) The Russians and the foreign visitors both liked the pizza.
    (D) The Russians liked the pizza, but it did not have enough sauce and cheese.

11. Read the first sentence of a summary of the passage. Then complete the summary by circling the THREE answer choices that express the most important ideas of the passage. Some sentences do not belong in the summary because they express ideas that are not presented in the passage or are minor ideas in the passage.

> Changing world markets require companies to adapt their advertising strategies.

(A) The frequency of commercial advertising varies from country to country.
(B) Getting into the country before your competitors is important.
(C) Fast food is not common in other countries.
(D) It takes time to get to know your new market.
(E) It is important to respect the customs of the new market.
(F) In some cases, people have to stand in line to buy a new product.

ANALYSIS

It is helpful to know the purpose of a test item. There are four types of questions in the reading section.

1. Basic Comprehension

- main ideas
- details
- the meaning of specific sentences

2. Organization

- the way information is structured in the text
- the way ideas are linked between sentences or between paragraphs

3. Inference

- ideas are not directly stated in the text
- author's intention, purpose, or attitude not explicitly stated in the text

4. Vocabulary and Reference

- the meaning of words
- the meaning of reference words such as *his, them, this,* or *none*

Go back to the reading questions and label each question with 1, 2, 3, or 4. Then work with a partner to see if you agree. Check the Answer Key for the correct answers. Which questions did you get right? Which did you get wrong? What skills do you need to practice?

3 Speaking

INTEGRATED TASK: READ, LISTEN, SPEAK

In this section, you will read a short excerpt and listen to an excerpt on the same topic. Then you will speak about the relationship between the two.

READING

Read the excerpt. Then, with a partner, discuss your ideas about the following topic:

Summarize the relationships among Jacko, Australia, the Energizer Bunny®, and the United States.

Advertising All over the World

1   How can a rabbit be stronger than a football hero? How can a rabbit be more powerful than a big, strong man? In the world of advertising, this is quite possible. Consider the example of Jacko. This great Australian football hero recently appeared on TV and yelled at the audience to buy products. Jacko's angry campaign worked well in Australia, so Energizer® batteries invited him north to sell their product in the United States. But Jacko's yelling did not convince the American audience to buy batteries. So, good-bye, Jacko. Hello, Energizer Bunny®, the little toy rabbit that has sold far more batteries than Jacko.

2   In the world of advertising, selling products is the most important goal.

As companies are becoming more global, they are looking for new ways to sell their products all over the world. It is true that because of global communication, the world is becoming smaller today.

LISTENING

Listen to the excerpt. Use the outline to take notes as you listen. The main idea has been done for you.

Main Idea: *Advertisers use different techniques to persuade us to buy.*

　　　Effective Technique: _____

　　　Most Popular: _____

　　　Example of An Ad: _____

SPEAKING

Speak on the following topic. Follow the steps below to prepare.

Discuss the ideas about emotional appeals in ads. Use the example of Jacko in Australia and in the U.S. to explain emotional appeal.

Step 1

Work with a partner. Skim the reading and your notes from the reading and the listening tasks on pages 11–12. Complete this outline to help you organize your ideas.

Ideas

　　　Emotional Appeals: _____

Examples

　　　Jacko in Australia: _____

　　　Jacko in the U.S.: _____

　　　Energizer Bunny® in the U.S.: _____

Step 2

Work with a partner. Take turns practicing a one-minute oral response. Use the information in your outline to help you.

Step 3

Change partners. Take turns giving a one-minute response to the topic again.

To evaluate your partner's response, use the Speaking Evaluation Form on page 180.

4 Writing

INDEPENDENT TASK

Write on the following topic. Follow the steps below to prepare.

Think of a product that you enjoy. Explain how you would advertise this product. What would be the message? What would be the emotional appeal? How would you convince people to buy the product?

Step 1

- Think of a product you like. Write some notes explaining why you like it. To advertise it, what would be the message and the emotional appeal? How would you convince people to buy it?

- Work in groups. Take turns describing the ads you would make for your products.

- React to what you have heard. What is the emotional appeal of each ad? Which ads do you think would convince people to buy the product?

Step 2

Write for 20 minutes. Leave the last 5 minutes to edit your work.

To evaluate a partner's writing, use the Writing Evaluation Form on page 179.

5 Skill Focus

SKIMMING AND SCANNING

EXAMINATION

Look at the following items on the next page from the unit. Work with a partner and answer these questions about the two items.

- Did you reread the text to answer the question?

- If so, exactly how much of the text did you reread? Go back to the text and mark it. Show it to your partner and discuss your selection.

- Did you reread it quickly or slowly?

Item 1 (Reading, page 10)

Read the first sentence of a summary of the passage. Then complete the summary by circling the THREE answer choices that express the most important ideas of the passage. Some sentences do not belong in the summary because they express ideas that are not presented in the passage or are minor ideas in the passage.

> Changing world markets require companies to adapt their advertising strategies.

(A) The frequency of commercial advertising varies from country to country.
(B) Getting into the country before your competitors is important.
(C) Fast food is not common in other countries.
(D) It takes time to get to know your new market.
(E) It is important to respect the customs of the new market.
(F) In some cases, people have to stand in line to buy a new product.

Item 2 (Reading, p. 9)

In paragraph 7, the expression *big picture* is closest in meaning to
(A) a large photo
(B) the worst situation
(C) the whole context
(D) the most important point

Tips

To do well on the TOEFL, it is essential to learn how to skim and scan. When you *skim* a text, you are reading quickly to understand the general meaning, the gist. When you *scan* a text, you are reading quickly to find specific information, such as facts, names, and dates.

Skimming Tips

- Go back to the text and reread it quickly.

- Read the first and last sentences of paragraphs.

Scanning Tips

- It is not necessary to read each word.

- Look at the text quickly to find key word(s).

In **Item 1**, you probably skimmed the whole text to answer the question. When you skim, you want to get the main ideas. Therefore, the best choices are "The frequency of commercial advertising varies from country to country," "It takes time to get to know your new market," and "It is important to respect the customs of the new market."

In contrast, in **Item 2**, you probably scanned paragraph 7 to find the specific phrase *the big picture.* Then you probably skimmed the nearby sentences to help you find the best answer, which is (C) the whole context.

PRACTICE

1 *Read the two paragraphs, which continue the text on pages 7-8. Then, use the strategies for skimming and scanning to answer the questions.*

1   But it is also true that the problems of global advertising—problems of language and culture—have become larger than ever. For example, Braniff Airlines wanted to advertise its fine leather seats. But when its advertisement was translated from English to Spanish, it told people that they could fly naked! Another example of incorrect translation is how Chevrolet tried to market the Chevy Nova in Latin America. In English, the word *nova* refers to a star. But in Spanish, it means "doesn't go." Would you buy a car with this name?

2   To avoid these problems of translation, most advertising firms are now beginning to write completely new ads. In writing new ads, global advertisers consider the different styles of communication in different countries. In some cultures, the meaning of an advertisement is usually found in the exact words that are used to describe the product and to explain why it is better than the competition. This is true in such countries as the United States, Britain, and Germany. But in other cultures, such as Japan's, the message depends more on situations and feelings than it does on words. For this reason, the goal of many TV commercials in Japan will be to show how good people feel at a party or other social situation. The commercial will not say that a product is better than others. Instead, its goal will be to create a positive mood or feeling about the product.

1. Write down the main idea of the two paragraphs.

_____

2. In which paragraph does the author compare several countries?

_____

(continued on next page)

3. What does the word *nova* refer to in English?

_____

4. What does the phrase *the competition* refer to?

_____

2 *Discuss your answers with a partner. How did you use skimming or scanning to find your answers?*

Extreme Sports

LISTENING	
Campus Conversation	A student talks to a professor about her parents' expectations concerning her plan of study.
Academic Listening	Lecture: *Sensation Seekers*

READING	
Newspaper Article	*High School Star Hospitalized for Eating Disorder*

WRITING	
Integrated Task: Read, Listen, Write	Relate the different meanings of the word *obsession* to the experience of Tony Hawk, the skateboarder.

SPEAKING	
Independent Task	Describe a time in your life when you did something obsessively.

SKILL FOCUS	
Making Inferences	Inferences are guesses, predictions, or conclusions about information that is not stated directly.

TOEFL® iBT TARGET SKILLS

- Identify and express main ideas
- Identify and express details
- Take notes and complete an outline
- Relate an abstract idea to concrete information
- Infer a speaker's or writer's intention or purpose

 For extra practice of TOEFL iBT skills, go to pages 208–226.

1 Listening

CAMPUS CONVERSATION

PRE-LISTENING VOCABULARY

Read the sentences. Guess the meaning of the boldfaced words and phrases. Then match each word or phrase with a definition or synonym from the list below. Work with a partner and compare your answers.

_____ 1. I'm feeling a lot of **pressure** to do well in my classes because my parents expect me to get all A's.

_____ 2. Baseball, baseball, baseball! My little brother is **obsessed** with baseball. That's all he cares about.

_____ 3. This **semester** I am taking algebra, and next semester I plan to take calculus.

_____ 4. Linda wasn't sure how to solve the math problem, but she decided to **give it a shot** anyway.

_____ 5. Jennifer did not study for two weeks. As a result, her grades began to **suffer**.

_____ 6. I was a student at Harvard University in Cambridge, Massachusetts for one year. Then I **transferred** to Columbia University because I wanted to live in New York City.

_____ 7. Without a full **scholarship**, Elizabeth can't go to college. She doesn't have enough money.

_____ 8. I **am sick of** watching TV every night. Tonight, let's go dancing instead.

_____ 9. Bob **failed out of** high school. Now it is difficult for him to find a good job.

a. money given to someone to pay for education

b. had to leave a school because of very poor grades

c. go down, become worse

d. negative feelings or stress

e. one half of the school year

f. unable to stop thinking about or doing something

g. try

h. tired of something because it has been going on for a long time

i. changed from one school to another

> **Culture Note:** Students usually receive letter grades in their classes. An A+ is the highest grade. Other grades, in order, include: A, A-, B+, B, B-, C+, C, C-, D+, D, and F. If a student gets an F, or failing grade, he/she receives no credit for the course. Even though C's and D's are passing grades, they are very low. Some colleges and universities require students to have a B average in their major subject in order to graduate.

FIRST LISTENING

Read the questions. Listen to the conversation between a student and a professor. Take notes after each question. Share your notes with a partner. Then use your notes to answer the questions.

1. What are the student and the professor discussing? _____

_____

2. What does the student want to do? _____

_____

SECOND LISTENING

Read the questions. Listen to the conversation again. Add details to your notes. Then use your notes to answer the questions. Work with a partner and compare your answers.

1. What is the conversation mainly about?
(**A**) Dealing with parental pressure
(**B**) Finding out about medical school
(**C**) Looking for a college scholarship
(**D**) Getting information about transferring

2. Why does Susan go to see her professor?
   (A) To talk about getting a scholarship
   (B) To find out about transferring
   (C) To discuss her low grades
   (D) To ask for some advice about her stress

3. What are Susan's parents obsessed with?
   (A) Her starting a career in sports
   (B) Her not failing out of school
   (C) Her going to medical school
   (D) Her not being able to sleep

Listen again to part of the conversation. Then answer question 4.

4. What does the professor imply when she says, "Perhaps your parents aren't the only ones with an obsession."?
   (A) Susan's parents are obsessed with her going to medical school.
   (B) Susan is obsessed with going to medical school.
   (C) Susan is obsessed with having a career in sports.
   (D) Susan's parents are obsessed with her going to the Olympics.

Listen again to part of the conversation. Then answer question 5.

5. What is Susan's attitude when she says, "Well . . . I'll give it a shot, but they're not going to like it."?
   (A) Relieved
   (B) Doubtful
   (C) Angry
   (D) Relaxed

Listen again to part of the conversation. Then answer question 6.

6. What does the professor mean when she says, "Give them a chance. They might surprise you."?
   (A) They might give you a gift.
   (B) They might change their minds.
   (C) They might be worried about you.
   (D) They might praise you.

ACADEMIC LISTENING

FIRST LISTENING

Listen to the excerpt. Take notes using the chart on the next page. Fill in the missing information. Work with a partner to combine your notes.

The passage is about people called _____

These people like
- *strong emotions*
- *hard rock music*
- •
- •
- •

SECOND LISTENING

Read the questions. Listen to the excerpt again. Add details to your notes. Then use your notes to answer the questions. Work with a partner and compare your answers.

1. This passage is mainly about
   (**A**) sensation seekers
   (**B**) emergency room doctors
   (**C**) mountain climbers
   (**D**) psychologists

2. Sensation seekers enjoy
   (**A**) flying in airplanes
   (**B**) a regular schedule
   (**C**) strong feelings
   (**D**) finding jobs

3. What is the speaker's attitude toward sensation seekers?
   (**A**) Sympathetic
   (**B**) Neutral
   (**C**) Impatient
   (**D**) Critical

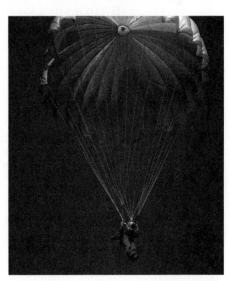

Listen again to part of the conversation. Then answer question 4.

4. Why does the speaker ask, "As psychologists, we need to ask ourselves, why is this person doing this?"
   (A) To show his lack of understanding
   (B) To get an answer from his listeners
   (C) To introduce the ideas he will discuss
   (D) To express his concern about these people

5. What job would be most appropriate for a sensation seeker?
   (A) Dentist
   (B) Firefighter
   (C) Teacher
   (D) Musician

6. According to the passage, why would a sensation seeker want to be an emergency room doctor?
   (A) To do something new every day
   (B) To make a lot of money
   (C) To repeat the same thing every day
   (D) To help other people

ANALYSIS

It is helpful to know the purpose of a test item. There are three types of questions in the listening section.

1. Basic Comprehension

- main ideas
- details
- the meaning of specific sentences

2. Organization

- the way information is structured
- the way ideas are linked

3. Inference

- ideas are not directly stated
- speaker's intention, purpose, or attitude not explicitly stated

Go back to the listening questions and label each question with 1, 2, or 3. Then work with a partner to see if you agree. Check the Answer Key for the correct answers. Which questions did you get right? Which did you get wrong? What skills do you need to practice?

2 Reading

HIGH SCHOOL STAR HOSPITALIZED FOR EATING DISORDER

PRE-READING

Read the title of the passage and skim the first line of each paragraph. Work with a partner and predict the answers to the following questions. You may have more than one answer for each question.

1. What kind of "star" is this high school student? _____

_____

2. Is the student a boy or a girl? _____

_____

3. What are the possible causes of the student's eating disorder? _____

_____

READING

Read the passage and answer the questions. Then, work with a partner and compare your answers. When you disagree, go back to the text to find helpful information.

High School Star Hospitalized for Eating Disorder

1   Sierra High School gymnast Ashley Lindermann was hospitalized Tuesday for complications related to anorexia nervosa. Her coach, Dianne Coyle, says that she will not be returning to the gymnastics team this season.

2   "It's really a loss—not only to the team but also to Ashley personally," says Coyle. "She had hopes of qualifying for the Olympics. But her health comes first, of course. Once she is better, I'm sure she can get back into the sport and go for the gold ."

3   Dr. Paula Kim, director of the Eating Disorders Clinic at Baldwin Hospital, explains that it is not unusual for athletes, especially gymnasts, to become obsessed with their weight. One reason for this is that, in gymnastics, the lighter the body, the more skillfully it can perform. She explains that an obsession with

(continued on next page)

weight can lead to extreme dieting, which affects not only the body but also the mind.

4   "For the anorexic, the mental focus becomes very small: food and weight. In a way, it's easy to see how this helps the anorexic manage the fear of living in the big, uncontrollable world out there. You may not be able to control how other people feel about you, but you can control what you put in your mouth. You can also control how many hours you spend at the gym. Soon you get hooked on controlling your weight."

5   High school counselor Lisa Rodriguez has expressed concern that Lindermann's illness is related to pressure.

6   "There's an enormous amount of pressure that goes along with training for the Olympics," she says. "I know that she comes from an athletic family—I think that's why she felt she had to accomplish so much in sports. Also, when you talk about the Olympics, you're talking about being the best of the best. I think that added to Ashley's feeling of pressure."

7   Since joining the Sierra High gymnastics team as a sophomore two years ago, Ashley has broken all school records and led the team to three regional championships.

8   Coach Coyle says, "As soon as I met Ashley, I could tell right away that she was obsessed with the sport. And that's not the kind of athlete that you have to push. My goal with Ashley was to try and help her have more of a balanced life. I talked to her about how she was doing in her classes, what she might want to study in college. I also told her and all the members on the team to take at least one or two days a week just to let their bodies rest. I know there's some controversy about her situation, but all I can say is that I'm very, very sorry that Ashley got sick."

9   Coyle's concern for Lindermann's health is shared by her teammates and friends. Some of them recall how the tiny gymnastics star worked out at the health club in addition to hours of regular practice with the team. They describe how the walls of her bedroom are covered with photos of Olympic winners—Mary Lou Retton and Nadia Comaneci—to name a few.

10   Lindermann, who currently weighs only 72 pounds (32.6 kg), is expected to remain in the hospital for at least a few months.

1. What is the reading mainly about?
   (A) Why students should participate in sports
   (B) An athlete who developed anorexia nervosa
   (C) A coach who works hard to help young athletes
   (D) How gymnastics influences a high school education

2. In paragraph 2, what does the word *it* refer to when Coach Coyle says, "It's really a loss—not only to the team but also to Ashley personally."?
   (A) Ashley's failing out of high school
   (B) Ashley's going to the hospital
   (C) Ashley's qualifying for the Olympics
   (D) Ashley's not returning to the team this season

3. In paragraph 2, what does Coach Coyle mean by *go for the gold*?
   (A) Leave Baldwin Hospital
   (B) Become a stronger student
   (C) Get accepted at a good college
   (D) Try to win at the Olympics

4. In paragraph 4, what does Dr. Kim imply about Ashley?
   (A) Ashley was trying to manage her world.
   (B) Ashley wanted to control how others felt about her.
   (C) Ashley's mental focus became very large.
   (D) Ashley spent too much time at the gym.

5. In paragraph 4, how does Dr. Kim explain the problem of anorexia?
   (A) By summarizing Ashley's case
   (B) By comparing Ashley to other anorexics
   (C) By giving examples about girls in general
   (D) By identifying the physical effects of anorexia

6. In paragraph 8, what does Coach Coyle mean when she says, "As soon as I met Ashley, I could tell right away that she was obsessed with the sport. And that's not the kind of athlete that you have to push."?
   (A) She disliked Ashley's attitude.
   (B) She thought Ashley was talented.
   (C) She was angry with Ashley.
   (D) She was concerned about Ashley.

7. In paragraph 8, all of the following were Coach Coyle's goals EXCEPT
   (A) to encourage Ashley to relax.
   (B) to ask Ashley about her classes.
   (C) to push Ashley as a gymnast.
   (D) to talk to Ashley about going to college.

8. In paragraph 9, why does the author mention Mary Lou Retton and Nadia Comaneci?
   (A) To show that Ashley was serious about gymnastics
   (B) To compare Ashley to famous Olympic gymnasts
   (C) To point out Ashley's problem with losing weight
   (D) To emphasize that Ashley's teammates respected her

9. Look at the four squares ☐ that indicate where the following sentence could be added to the passage. Where would the sentence best fit? Circle the letter that shows the point where you would insert this sentence.

   However, there are also risks for gymnasts who want a lighter body.

   ☐A Dr. Paula Kim, director of the Eating Disorders Clinic at Baldwin Hospital, explains that it is not unusual for athletes, especially gymnasts, to become obsessed with their weight. ☐B One reason for this is that, in gymnastics, the lighter the body, the more skillfully it can perform. ☐C She explains that an obsession with weight can lead to extreme dieting, which affects not only the body but also the mind. ☐D

10. Which of the following expresses the essential information in this sentence from the passage?

> You may not be able to control how other people feel about you, but you can control what you put in your mouth.

(A) Anorexics try to control everyone and everything, including their food.
(B) Anorexics control other people's feelings by controlling their food.
(C) Anorexics control their food, but they can't control other people.
(D) Anorexics worry more about other people's feelings than about eating.

11. Read the first sentence of a summary of the passage. Then complete the summary by circling the THREE answer choices that express the most important ideas of the passage. Some sentences do not belong in the summary because they express ideas that are not presented in the passage or are minor ideas in the passage.

> Pressures in Ashley Lindermann's life led to her being hospitalized for anorexia.

(A) Ashley felt pressure because she came from an athletic family.
(B) Ashley was an average student academically.
(C) Her coach supported her athletically.
(D) Her Olympic dreams caused her to work harder.
(E) Her teammates were very concerned about her family.
(F) She wanted control over her world perhaps most of all.

3 Writing

INTEGRATED TASK: READ, LISTEN, WRITE

In this section, you will read a short excerpt and listen to an excerpt on the same topic. Then you will write about the relationship between the two.

READING

*Read the following definitions of the word **obsession**. Then, with a partner, discuss the answer to the following question:*

How do the definitions of the word *obsession* apply to sensation seekers and people suffering from anorexia nervosa?

> **obsession** [1] /əb'sɛʃən/ *n.* **1.** something or someone you think about all the time or almost all the time; **2.** a strong motivation to do something, such as to reach a goal; **3.** something you do or want to do repeatedly because it causes a strong emotional reaction
>
> **obsession** [2] /əb'sɛʃən/ *n.* **1.** something or someone you can't stop thinking about; **2.** a thought or action that is the cause of anxiety or the result of anxiety; **3.** an extreme, unhealthy interest in something or a worry about something, which stops a person from thinking about anything else

LISTENING

Listen to the excerpt of an imaginary interview with Tony Hawk, a professional skateboarder. Use the outline to take notes as you listen. The main idea has been done for you.

Main Idea: _Tony Hawk's obsession turned into something positive_

Support:

High point of his career: _____

1999 Summer X Games: _____

Problems in school: _____

WRITING

Write on the following topic. Follow the steps below to prepare.

Look at the definitions of the word *obsession* again. Which definition is closer to Hawk's experience? Give specific support from the reading and the listening.

Step 1

Work with a partner. Skim the reading and your notes from the listening task above. Then discuss these questions with your partner:

• What is Tony Hawk's obsession?

• How are the two definitions of *obsession* different?

• Which definition has a positive meaning? Which has a negative meaning?

• What positive things happened to Tony Hawk? What negative things happened?

Step 2

Write for 20 minutes. Leave the last 5 minutes to edit your work.

To evaluate a partner's writing, use the Writing Evaluation Form on page 179.

4 Speaking

INDEPENDENT TASK

Speak on the following topic. Follow the steps below to prepare.

Talk about a specific time when you did something obsessively. For example, did you "go to extremes" playing video games, worrying about an exam, or practicing a sport or music? What did you do? What were the good and bad results? Explain.

Step 1

Think of a time when you obsessed about something. Use this outline to help you organize your ideas.

Your Obsession (an activity or a thought): _____

Details: _____

_____

_____

Results:

Good: _____

_____

Bad: _____

_____

Step 2

Work with a partner. Take turns practicing a one-minute oral response. Use the information in your outline to help you.

Step 3

Change partners. Take turns giving a one-minute response to the topic again.

To evaluate your partner's response, use the Speaking Evaluation Form on page 180.

5 Skill Focus

MAKING INFERENCES

EXAMINATION

Look at the following items from the unit. Work with a partner and answer this question about the items.

- What information or clues in the passages helped you find the answers?

Item 1 (Campus Conversation, page 20)

What is Susan's attitude when she says, "Well . . . I'll give it a shot, but they're not going to like it."?
(A) Relieved
(B) Doubtful
(C) Angry
(D) Relaxed

Item 2 (Campus Conversation, page 20)

What does the professor mean when she says, "Give them a chance. They might surprise you."?
(A) They might give you a gift.
(B) They might change their minds.
(C) They might be worried about you.
(D) They might praise you.

Item 3 (Reading, page 25)

In paragraph 4, what does Dr. Kim imply about Ashley?
(A) Ashley was trying to manage her world.
(B) Ashley wanted to control how others felt about her.
(C) Ashley's mental focus became very large.
(D) Ashley spent too much time at the gym.

Tips

To do well on the TOEFL, it is essential to learn how to make **inferences**. An inference is a conclusion based on reasoning from something you know or think. The answer to an inference question is *not* directly stated in the passage.

There are two verbs that are common in inference questions: *imply* and *infer*. A speaker or writer may *imply*, or suggest, something in a passage

(continued on next page)

without stating it directly. Listeners or readers *infer*, or come to a conclusion, based on the information they hear or read. The word *infer* can be a synonym of *suggest*.

Inference questions ask about the speaker's or writer's purpose for speaking or writing. These questions may ask about the speaker's or writer's attitude or reason for stating an idea.

To answer an inference question:

- **Focus on the content of the text.**
  Are there facts that are not directly stated in the text?

- **Focus on the words.**
  Does the speaker or writer use words that give clues to his or her attitude or intended meaning?

- **Pay attention to the speaker's intonation in a speaking text.**
  Does the speaker's intonation give a clue to his or her attitude or intended meaning?

To answer **Item 1** correctly, you should notice that Susan is not sure that her parents will support her because they want her to go to medical school. You "hear" that she is doubtful; she uses rising intonation. Therefore, the best answer is (B).

To answer **Item 2** correctly, you should notice the professor's optimistic attitude when speaking to Susan. The professor encourages Susan to speak with her parents because she expects that Susan's parents will support their daughter. You can also hear the professor's optimism in her intonation. Therefore, the best choice is (B).

To answer **Item 3** correctly, you should notice that when the doctor mentions in general how anorexics try to "manage the fear of living in the big, uncontrollable world," she is also referring to Ashley. Therefore, the best answer is (A).

PRACTICE

 CD1 TRACK 16

1 *Listen to an excerpt of the imaginary interview with Tony Hawk. Then, use the strategies for making inferences to answer the questions.*

1. What does Tony imply about his parents?
   (A) They supported his interest in skateboarding.
   (B) They also skateboarded in the house.
   (C) They were too old to care about Tony.
   (D) They cared very little about the family.

Listen again to part of the interview. Then answer question 2.

2. Why does the interviewer ask, "Your parents let you skate in the house?"?
   (A) To make sure she understood Tony
   (B) To get Tony to say more about it
   (C) To show how much Tony practiced
   (D) To illustrate how large Tony's house was

Listen again to part of the interview. Then answer question 3.

3. What is the interviewer's attitude when she says, "That couldn't stop you from skating!"?
   (A) She is angry.
   (B) She is excited.
   (C) She is disappointed.
   (D) She is surprised.

Listen again to part of the interview. Then answer question 4.

4. Why does Tony ask, "What class did I create?"?
   (A) To confuse the interviewer
   (B) To surprise the interviewer
   (C) To stop the interviewer's questions
   (D) To check the interviewer's understanding

2 *Read the excerpt of the imaginary interview with Tony Hawk. Then, use the strategies for making inferences to answer the questions.*

INTERVIEWER: As an occupation, it has rewarded you pretty well, wouldn't you say?

TH: Yeah, there were some great benefits along the way—like being able to buy my own home when I was still in high school. And later, being able to buy another home out in the desert—and build my own skate park. But now that I think about it, you know what I'm really proud of accomplishing?

INTERVIEWER: Making skateboard history when you landed the 900?

TH: Nope. It was having Disney animators use some of my tricks in the Tarzan movie. When my son watched Tarzan swinging through the trees, he realized that it had something to do with me. And he thought I was awesome! Now that's the greatest feeling you can get, believe me.

1. What can be inferred about Tony Hawk?
   (A) Tony made a lot of money when he was a teenager.
   (B) Tony's son likes skateboarding.
   (C) Tony is most proud of landing the 900.
   (D) Tony was the star of the Disney movie *Tarzan*.

2. What is "the 900" that the interviewer asks Tony about?
   (A) The size of his skateboard park
   (B) The cost of one of his houses
   (C) The name of one of his skateboard moves
   (D) The distance that Tarzan traveled

3. Why does Tony ask the interviewer, "But now that I think about it, you know what I'm really proud of accomplishing?"?
   (A) To introduce something unexpected
   (B) To give an example of his tricks
   (C) To agree with the interviewer
   (D) To see if the interviewer knows the answer

3 *Discuss your answers with a partner. What clues helped you to make inferences and answer the questions?*

Fraud

| **LISTENING** |

Campus Conversation   A student talks to a financial aid advisor about scholarships.

Academic Listening   Interviews: *Victims of Fraud*

| **READING** |

An Advertisement   *The Organic Health Center*

| **SPEAKING** |

Integrated Task: Read, Listen, Speak   Role play a situation that supports the points of view described in the listening and reading excerpts.

| **WRITING** |

Independent Task   Describe an experience with fraud or dishonesty.

| **SKILL FOCUS** |

Using Context Clues   Using context clues means using surrounding information in a written or spoken text to determine the meaning of unknown words or phrases.

| **TOEFL® iBT TARGET SKILLS** |

- Identify and express main ideas
- Identify and express details
- Make inferences
- Organize information in a chart
- Skim text to make predictions
- Outline information in a timeline

 For extra practice of TOEFL iBT skills, go to pages 208–226.

1 Listening

CAMPUS CONVERSATION

PRE-LISTENING VOCABULARY

Read the sentences. Guess the meaning of the boldfaced words and phrases. Choose the best definition or synonym. Work with a partner and compare your answers.

1. Henry decided to go to a local college because the **tuition** was a lot less. He knew he could get a good education without spending too much money.
   a. quality of education
   b. money a student pays for courses

2. The governor of California promised to work harder to help **minorities** such as African-Americans, Asians, and Latinos find jobs in the state.
   a. a small part of the population that is different from the rest
   b. small groups of people who don't have jobs

3. When choosing a doctor, you should **keep in mind** that you need to find one who will accept your medical insurance.
   a. decide
   b. remember

4. I read about an insurance **scam** in the newspaper. A company promised to help old people who were sick, but the company just took their money and didn't help them.
   a. dishonest plan to make money
   b. honest offer of assistance

5. You can't believe everyone. If a stranger offers you a chance to make a lot of money quickly, be very **suspicious**.
   a. accepting
   b. doubtful

6. When you go to the doctor, you usually don't have to pay **up front**. Just ask the doctor to send you a bill.
   a. in advance
   b. afterwards

7. Tom was sick for two weeks last month. His wife said, "You'll be **better off** if you see the doctor." He took her advice, and soon he was healthy again.
   a. having more advantages than before
   b. taking advice from someone

8. If you want to find a **reputable** doctor, you should ask your friends for the names of doctors they like.
   a. respected
   b. inexpensive

9. It might **take a while** to find a good doctor, but when you finally do find one, you will feel more confident when you get sick.
   a. take a long time
   b. take a little time

> **Culture Note:** It is common for students at colleges and universities to pay for their education with scholarships and loans. Students do not have to pay anyone back when they receive a scholarship. However, loans come from banks, and loans must be paid back with an extra interest charge.

FIRST LISTENING

Read the questions. Listen to the conversation between a student and a financial aid advisor. Take notes after each question. Share your notes with a partner. Then use your notes to answer the questions.

1. What is the topic of the conversation? _____

   _____

2. What question does the student have? _____

   _____

SECOND LISTENING

Read the questions. Listen to the conversation again. Add details to your notes. Then use your notes to answer the questions. Work with a partner and compare your answers.

1. What is the conversation mainly about?
   (A) A guide to getting scholarships
   (B) A college offering the student a scholarship
   (C) A description of the services of this office
   (D) A student who wants to find a scholarship

2. Why does the student go into the office?
   (A) He needs money to pay his tuition.
   (B) He is lost and looking for another office.
   (C) He wants to transfer to another school.
   (D) He did not pay his tuition this semester.

3. Why is the student going to return to the Student Financial Services office the following day?
   (A) He has another appointment to go to.
   (B) He wants to speak to another employee.
   (C) He needs more time to look for scholarships.
   (D) The office will have additional information for him then.

4. What does the woman tell the student about scholarship search agencies?
   (A) Scholarship search agencies are scams.
   (B) Some are reputable but others are just scams.
   (C) Many colleges have scholarship search agencies.
   (D) Using such an agency is easier than doing it yourself.

Listen again to part of the conversation. Then answer question 5.

5. After he looks at the computer screen, what is the student's attitude when he says, "Wow. All these?"?
   (A) Surprise
   (B) Anger
   (C) Happiness
   (D) Relief

Listen again to part of the conversation. Then answer question 6.

6. Why does the student say, "OK, I'll come back tomorrow after my class."?
   (A) He knows that the office is going to close soon.
   (B) He has to go to his next class.
   (C) He is too tired to look for scholarships that day.
   (D) He wants to contact a scholarship search agency instead.

ACADEMIC LISTENING

FIRST LISTENING

Listen to the four speakers talk about why they gave Frank money. Take notes using the chart below. Work with a partner to combine your notes.

SPEAKERS	WHY DID THE SPEAKER GIVE FRANK MONEY?
Joe	
Rosa	
Peter	
Beth	

SECOND LISTENING

Read the questions. Listen to the four speakers again. Add details to your notes. Then use your notes to answer the questions. Work with a partner and compare your answers.

1. What are the people talking about?
   (A) Listening to advice from family
   (B) Giving money to a man on the phone
   (C) Trying to win a free vacation
   (D) Making decisions too quickly

Listen again to part of the conversation. Then answer question 2.

2. What is Joe's purpose when he says, "I guess I'm pretty gullible."?
   (A) To explain why he has so many friends
   (B) To compare himself with his daughter
   (C) To explain why he gave Frank the money
   (D) To describe one of his positive characteristics

3. How does Rosa describe herself?
   (A) Friendly
   (B) Lonely
   (C) Gullible
   (D) Unemployed

Listen again to part of the conversation. Then answer question 4.

4. What is the Peter's attitude when he says, "I guess I got too excited about the free vacation and didn't think carefully."?
   (A) Regret
   (B) Satisfaction
   (C) Anger
   (D) Excitement

5. How did Beth feel while speaking with Frank?
   (A) Sad
   (B) Satisfied
   (C) Confident
   (D) Uncomfortable

6. How is the passage organized?
   (A) By examples
   (B) In time order
   (C) In order of importance
   (D) By comparison and contrast

2 Reading

THE ORGANIC HEALTH CENTER

PRE-READING

Read the title and skim the passage on the next page. As you skim, notice the words in the chart below. The paragraph number for each word is given. Guess the meaning of each of the words and write your definitions in the chart. Work with a partner and compare your answers.

PARAGRAPH	WORD IN PASSAGE	YOUR DEFINITION
1	founder	
2	cure	
3	qualified	
6	testimonials	

READING

Read the passage and answer the questions. Then work with a partner and compare your answers. When you disagree, go back to the text to find helpful information.

The Organic Health Center

1   Do you have cancer? Have the doctors given you no hope? I can help you. My name is Benjamin Harrison. I am the founder of the Organic Health Center. My health center offers the most advanced treatments for curing cancer and other diseases.

2   After traveling around the world for nine years looking for a cure for myself, I was able to learn the causes of cancer. Now, I can help others by offering them a cure. This cure is available only at the Organic Health Center.

3   As a result of my experiences, I realized that Western doctors are just frauds who are unqualified to help their patients. I, on the other hand, have learned how to use the best herbs and organic foods to heal people, and I am qualified to help you. That's why doctors will tell you not to trust me. They know that I can do something they can't do.

4   My program focuses on the whole body. It works on the cause of the cancer. I will put you on the healthiest diet available. This diet uses the best herb and plant products I gathered from my travels around the world. All of the products I use are natural, so they won't make you feel sick. After one to six months on this diet, you will be cured of cancer.

5   Here are some of the programs my center offers:

PROGRAM A:	PROGRAM B:	PROGRAM C:
For all types of cancers	*For cancer found early*	*For all other diseases*
Stay at my clinic for one month of treatment. Then continue the treatment in your home for two more months.	Complete a sixty-day program in your home. Eat a special diet with herbs and other healthy foods. Also follow an exercise schedule.	Complete a ninety-day program in your home. Eat a special diet with herbs and other healthy foods.

6   I am willing to travel to your home to teach you how to follow the program. And, if you would like, I have testimonials for you to read. These letters are filled with words of praise and thanks to me from my patients.

7   I offer a money-back guarantee if the program fails. If my treatments don't work, you will get back 100% of your money. How can I do this? It is my guarantee to you that my treatment works. A doctor will tell you that cancer can't be cured. It's the doctors who are the frauds.

1. What is the main idea of this passage?
   (A) Cancer and other diseases can be cured by Harrison's treatments.
   (B) Harrison traveled around the world to find a cure for cancer.
   (C) Harrison's program focuses on the whole body.
   (D) Western doctors do not trust Harrison.

2. In paragraph 1, the word *founder* is closest in meaning to
   (A) doctor
   (B) creator
   (C) patient
   (D) employee

3. Which of the following is true of Benjamin Harrison?
   (A) He says that he is a medical doctor.
   (B) He thinks that cancer can be cured with herbs alone.
   (C) He believes that Western doctors are well qualified.
   (D) He claims that he knows the causes of cancer.

4. In paragraph 2, what can be inferred about Harrison?
   (A) He spoke with many Western doctors.
   (B) He successfully treated his own cancer.
   (C) He discovered a cure for cancer at his clinic.
   (D) He attended medical schools around the world.

5. In paragraph 3, Harrison states, "They know that I can do something they can't do." What does Harrison mean by *something*?
   (A) Cure cancer and other diseases
   (B) Make false claims about cancer
   (C) Offer a money-back guarantee
   (D) Recommend a healthy diet

6. In paragraph 3, what is the author's primary purpose?
   (A) To compare Eastern and Western doctors
   (B) To explain how natural foods cure cancer
   (C) To convince the readers that he is qualified
   (D) To teach the readers about Western medicine

7. Which of the following is NOT one of Harrison's claims?
   (A) Cancer and other diseases can be cured.
   (B) He is a trained medical doctor.
   (C) Western doctors are frauds.
   (D) His treatments work.

8. In paragraph 7, the word *guarantee* is closest in meaning to
   (A) argument
   (B) promise
   (C) disease
   (D) cure

9. In paragraph 7, what does the word *this* refer to in the sentence, "How can I
do this?"
(A) Believe other doctors are frauds
(B) Say that my treatments work
(C) Cure cancer and other illnesses
(D) Give back all of your money

10. Look at the four squares ☐ that indicate where the following sentence could
be added to the passage. Where would the sentence best fit? Circle the letter
that shows the point where you would insert this sentence.

> On the contrary, they will make you feel better.

> My program focuses on the whole body. It works on the cause of the cancer.
> [A] I will put you on the healthiest diet available. [B] This diet uses the best herb
> and plant products I gathered from my travels around the world. [C] All of the
> products I use are natural, so they won't make you feel sick. [D] After one to six
> months on this diet, you will be cured of cancer.

11. Which of the following expresses the essential information in this sentence
from the passage?

> I, on the other hand, have learned how to use the best herbs and organic
> foods to heal people, and I am qualified to help you.

(A) Unlike Western doctors, I can cure your cancer with natural treatments.
(B) In contrast to Western doctors, I can cure any disease you have.
(C) Unlike the treatments used by Western doctors, mine are natural.
(D) Like Western doctors, I can cure your cancer with natural treatments.

12. Read the first sentence of a summary of the passage. Then complete the
summary by circling the THREE answer choices that express the most
important ideas of the passage. Some sentences do not belong in the
summary because they express ideas that are not presented in the passage or
are minor ideas in the passage.

> Benjamin Harrison, founder of the Organic Health Center, claims to know
> the truth about treating cancer and other diseases.

(A) Cancer can be cured with herbs, diet, and exercise.
(B) Harrison traveled around the world for nine years.
(C) Western doctors are frauds who tell patients that cancer cannot be cured.
(D) Harrison guarantees that his programs work.
(E) Harrison is willing to visit your home to teach you about his programs.
(F) Some patients stay at Harrison's clinic at the Organic Health Center.

ANALYSIS

It is helpful to know the purpose of a test item. There are four types of questions in the reading section.

1. Basic Comprehension

- main ideas

- details

- the meaning of specific sentences

2. Organization

- the way information is structured in the text

- the way ideas are linked between sentences or between paragraphs

3. Inference

- ideas are not directly stated in the text

- author's intention, purpose, or attitude not explicitly stated in the text

4. Vocabulary and Reference

- the meaning of words

- the meaning of reference words such as *his*, *them*, *this*, or *none*

Go back to the reading questions and label each question with 1, 2, 3, or 4. Then work with another student to see if you agree. Check the Answer Key for the correct answers. Which questions did you get right? Which did you get wrong? What skills do you need to practice?

3 Speaking

INTEGRATED TASK: READ, LISTEN, SPEAK

In this section, you will read a short excerpt and listen to an excerpt on the same topic. Then you will speak about the relationship between the two.

READING

Read the excerpt. Then, with a partner, discuss the answers to the following questions.

- What is a quack?
- What are some problems with a treatment from a quack?

A Miracle Cure

from *Healthier You* magazine

1   Many people don't realize how unsafe it is to use unproven treatments. First of all, the treatments usually don't work. They may be harmless, but if someone uses these products instead of proven treatments, he or she may be harmed. Why? Because during the time the person is using the product, his or her illness may be getting worse. This can even cause the person to die.

2   So why do people trust quacks? People want the "miracle cure." They want the product that will solve their problem . . . quickly, easily, and completely. A patient may be so afraid of pain, or even of dying, that he or she will try anything. The quack knows this and offers an easy solution at a very high price.

3   Quacks usually sell products and treatments for illnesses that generally have no proven cure. This is why we often hear about clinics that treat cancer or AIDS. Treatments for arthritis are also popular with quacks. Other common quackeries are treatments to lose weight quickly, to make hair grow again, and to keep a person young.

LISTENING

Listen to the excerpt. Complete this timeline of events as you listen. Use the events in the list on the next page.

ONE YEAR AGO   *One year ago Matt found out he had cancer.*

_____

A FEW MONTHS LATER   _____

THEN   _____

_____

_____

TODAY   *Today Matt is going to see a doctor who is a quack.*

- His doctors decided to treat his cancer immediately.

- A few months later, Matt found out that the cancer was still growing.

- He became sick and depressed.

- Matt found out he had cancer.

- Doctors gave him more medicine, but it didn't help.

- Doctors told him that they were unable to do anything more; he had only six months to live.

- Matt is going to see a doctor who is a quack.

SPEAKING

Speak on the following topic. Follow the steps below to prepare.

Create a role play of a conversation, with one partner playing the role of Matt Bloomfield and the other partner playing the role of his friend. Matt has decided to see a doctor who has developed an unproven cure for cancer. Matt's friend is trying to convince Matt NOT to see this doctor. He says this doctor is a quack. Use examples from the reading and listening excerpts to support the points of view.

Step 1

Work with a partner. Skim the reading and your notes from the reading and the listening tasks on pages 43-44. Complete this outline to help you organize your ideas.

Matt's reasons FOR going to a quack:

1. _____

2. _____

3. _____

Matt's friend's reasons AGAINST going to a quack:

1. _____

2. _____

3. _____

Step 2

Practice your role play. Use the information in your outline to help you.

Step 3

Change partners. Practice your role play again.

To evaluate your partner's response, use the Speaking Evaluation Form on page 180.

4 Writing

INDEPENDENT TASK

Write on the following topic. Follow the steps below to prepare.

> Write about an experience you have had with fraud or dishonesty, such as lying or cheating. What happened? What were the results or consequences?

Step 1

- Think of experiences with fraud and cheating you have had. Make a list.

- Choose one experience that you find the most interesting. Use the chart to take notes about what happened before, during, and after this experience.

BEFORE	DURING	AFTER

Step 2

- Work with a partner. Take turns telling your stories. Tell your partner what happened before, during, and after this experience.

- Give your partner feedback on his or her story. What was the best part of the story? How could your partner improve or change the story?

Step 3

Write for 20 minutes. Leave the last 5 minutes to edit your work.

To evaluate a partner's writing, use the Writing Evaluation Form on page 179.

5 Skill Focus

USING CONTEXT CLUES

EXAMINATION

Look at the following items from the unit. Work with a partner and answer this question about the items:

- What information or clues in the passages helped you answer each question?

Item 1 (Reading, page 40)

In paragraph 7, the word *guarantee* is closest in meaning to
(A) argument
(B) promise
(C) disease
(D) cure

Item 2 (Reading, page 41)

In paragraph 7, what does the word *this* refer to in the sentence, "How can I do this?"?
(A) Believe other doctors are frauds
(B) Say that my treatments work
(C) Cure cancer and other illnesses
(D) Give back all of your money

Item 3 (Reading, page 41)

Look at the four squares ☐ that indicate where the following sentence could be added to the passage. Where would the sentence best fit? Circle the letter that shows the point where you would insert this sentence.

On the contrary, they will make you feel much better.

My program focuses on the whole body. It works on the cause of the cancer. ⒜ I will put you on the healthiest diet available. ⒝ This diet uses the best herb and plant products I gathered from my travels around the world. ⒞ All of the products I use are natural, so they won't make you feel sick. ⒟ After one to six months on this diet, you will be cured of cancer.

Item 4 (Academic Listening, page 37)

What is Joe's purpose when he says, "I guess I'm pretty gullible."?
(A) To explain why he has so many friends
(B) To compare himself with his daughter
(C) To explain why he gave Frank the money
(D) To describe one of his positive characteristics

Tips

To do well on the TOEFL, it is essential to learn how to use context clues to understand meaning. Context clues may help you to understand words and ideas in a passage. Context clues may be stated directly in the passage or they may be implied, that is, not directly stated in the passage. Context clues include: key ideas as well as words and nonverbal clues that convey meaning or attitude, such as punctuation (in writing) or intonation (in speaking).

Use context clues to answer the following types of items:

Vocabulary

Vocabulary items ask about the meaning of specific words or phrases.

If the question is about vocabulary, ask yourself: Is there a context clue that tells me the definition?

This kind of context clue usually comes *after* the word or phrase in the question.

Item 1 is a vocabulary question. To answer Item 1 correctly, you should notice the sentence after the word **guarantee**: *If my treatments don't work, you will get back 100% of your money.* This context clue gives the definition of the word **guarantee**. Therefore, the best choice is (B).

Reference

Reference questions often ask about a pronoun *(it, that, this)*. For example, *"In the following sentence, what does the word it / that / this refer to?"*

For reference questions, ask yourself: What does this word or phrase refer back to? These context clues come *before* the word or phrase in the question.

Item 2 is a reference question. To answer Item 2 correctly, you should see the connection between **this** and the phrase *"you will get back 100% of your money."* Therefore, the best choice is (D).

(continued on next page)

Item 3 is also a reference question. To answer Item 3 correctly, you should notice that the word *they* in the new sentence refers to the word *products* in the sentence *"This diet uses the best herb and plant products I gathered from my travels around the world."* The new sentence is a detail that supports the sentence before it. Therefore, the best choice is (D).

Inference

Inference questions (see Skill Focus, Unit 2) can be answered with the help of context clues. Inference questions ask about the speaker's or writer's intention, purpose, or attitude for stating an idea. Note that a context clue may not be directly stated. In reading passages you will use context clues to answer vocabulary and reference items. In both reading and listening passages you will use context clues to answer certain types of inference items that convey a speaker's or writer's purpose or attitude.

Item 4 is an inference question from the Academic Listening. To answer Item 4 correctly, you need to use context clues. You should recall the sentence after the word *gullible*: "If someone tells me something, I usually believe them." This sentence provides an explanation of the word *gullible* and a clue to the speaker's intended meaning. In this context, you can see that Joe's purpose for saying "I guess I'm pretty gullible" is to explain why he gave Frank the money: He believes people too easily. Therefore, the best choice is (C).

Additional tips for using context clues:

- **Notice words or phrases after the verb *be*.**
  Fraud *is an illegal action of deceiving people in order to get their money.*

- **Notice words or phrases between commas.**
  Fraud, *an illegal action of deceiving people in order to get their money,* is a growing problem.

- **Notice examples.**
  Fraud, *such as cheating on income taxes and false insurance claims,* costs the government millions of dollars every year.

PRACTICE

1 *Read the following text on the next page. Then, use the strategies for using context clues to answer the questions.*

1   Many people don't realize how unsafe it is to use unproven treatments. First of all, the treatments usually don't work. They may be harmless, but if someone uses these products instead of proven treatments, he or she may be harmed. Why? Because during the time the person is using the product, his or her illness may be getting worse. This can even cause the person to die.

2   So why do people trust quacks? People want the "miracle cure." They want the product that will solve their problem . . . quickly, easily, and completely. A patient may be so afraid of pain, or even of dying, that he or she will try anything. The quack knows this and offers an easy solution at a very high price.

3   Quacks usually sell products and treatments for illnesses that generally have no proven cure. This is why we often hear about clinics that treat cancer or AIDS. Treatments for arthritis are also popular with quacks. Other common quackeries are treatments to lose weight quickly, to make hair grow again, and to keep a person young.

4   How can you recognize a quack? Sometimes it's easy because he or she offers something we know is impossible. A drink to keep you young is an example of this. But many times, these people lie, saying that their product was made because of a recent scientific discovery. This makes it more difficult to know if the product is real or a fraud. Another way to recognize quackery is that many quacks will say their product is good for many different illnesses, not just for one thing. They usually like to offer money-back guarantees if their treatment doesn't work. Unfortunately, the guarantee is often also a lie. Finally, the fraudulent clinic will often be in another country. Laws in the United States make it illegal for a quack to have a clinic in the United States because the quack doesn't have the proper medical training.

5   Quacks try to sell their products in similar ways. They will invite you to read testimonials, letters written by satisfied customers. These frauds will also promise quick, exciting cures. Often they say the product is made in a secret way or with something secret in it which can only be bought from a particular company. Quacks will also say that doctors and the rest of the medical community are against them.

6   You are not powerless. There are things you can do to protect yourself from health fraud. Before you buy a product or treatment, check to see if it's the real thing. Talk to a doctor, pharmacist, or another health professional. If you've been the victim of health fraud, you can complain to certain organizations. In the United States, the Better Business Bureau, the Food and Drug Administration (FDA), the Federal Trade Commission, or the National Council against Health Fraud will help you.

7   Don't make the mistake of letting yourself or anyone you know become a victim of health fraud. It could cost you a lot of money or, worse yet, your life.

1. According to the text, what is a "miracle cure"?

2. In paragraph 2, what does the word *this* refer to in the sentence "The quack knows *this* and offers an easy solution at a very high price"?

3. In paragraph 3, the word *quackeries* is most similar to
   (A) clinics
   (B) doctors
   (C) diseases
   (D) treatments

4. Look at the four squares ☐ that indicate where the following sentence could be added to the passage. Where would the sentence best fit? Circle the letter that shows the point where you would insert this sentence.

   > One newspaper advertisement offered a product that cured headaches *and* skin problems at the same time.

   How can you recognize a quack? [A] Sometimes it's easy because he or she offers something we know is impossible. A drink to keep you young is an example of this. But many times, these people lie, saying that their product was made because of a recent scientific discovery. This makes it more difficult to know if the product is real or a fraud. [B] Another way to recognize quackery is that many quacks will say their product is good for many different illnesses, not just for one thing. [C] They usually like to offer money-back guarantees if their treatment doesn't work. Unfortunately, the guarantee is often also a lie. Finally, the fraudulent clinic will often be in another country. [D] Laws in the United States make it illegal for a quack to have a clinic in the United States because the quack doesn't have the proper medical training.

5. What does the word *testimonials* mean, as it is used in paragraph 5?

6. In paragraph 6, *doctor* and *pharmacist* are two kinds of
   (A) quacks
   (B) fraud victims
   (C) organizations
   (D) health professionals

7. In the last sentence, what does the word *it* refer to?

2 *Discuss your answers with a partner. How did you use context clues to understand meaning?*

Storytelling

| LISTENING |

Campus Conversation — A student talks to a professor about making an oral presentation.

Academic Listening — Interview: *Jackie Torrence*

| READING |

Review — *Behind the Story of* "The Metamorphosis"

| WRITING |

Integrated Task: Read, Listen, Write — Synthesize the information in the listening and reading excerpts to convey how the author, Franz Kafka, uses anthropomorphism to describe the man, Gregor Samsa.

| SPEAKING |

Independent Task — Using the concept of anthropomorphism, compare yourself to an animal, plant, or non-living thing and describe your traits and abilities.

| SKILL FOCUS |

Identifying and Using Rhetorical Structure — Identifying and using rhetorical structure means you understand the relationships among facts and ideas in different parts of a spoken or written passage.

| TOEFL® iBT TARGET SKILLS |

- Identify and express main ideas
- Identify and express details
- Make inferences
- Skim to find the structure of a passage
- Take notes and complete an outline
- Organize information to compare
- Identify different kinds of rhetorical structure

 For extra practice of TOEFL iBT skills, go to pages 208–226.

1 Listening

CAMPUS CONVERSATION

PRE-LISTENING VOCABULARY

Read the sentences. Guess the meaning of the boldfaced words and phrases. Then match each word or phrase with a definition or synonym from the list below. Work with a partner and compare your answers.

_____ 1. Jenny, **what's on your mind**? You seem upset about something.

_____ 2. My teacher wants me to stand up in front of the class and give an **oral presentation** about the U.S. Civil War.

_____ 3. A 50-page term paper is one of the **requirements** of my psychology course.

_____ 4. After Barbara learned a few test-taking **strategies**, her grades began to go up.

_____ 5. Bob's friendliness is one of his best **traits**.

_____ 6. Vanessa seemed so **sophisticated** after she returned home from her semester in Paris.

_____ 7. When you are speaking in front of a lot of people, use **visuals** to help communicate your ideas.

_____ 8. People might not trust you if you refuse to **make eye contact** with them.

a. having knowledge about things such as art, literature, and music

b. look directly at someone while he or she is looking at you

c. "What is troubling you?"

d. part of a person's character or personality

e. a spoken report, not written

f. maps, pictures, or charts used to help someone learn

g. assignments that a student must complete

h. a plan or way of doing something

Culture Note: Course requirements at colleges and universities vary from school to school and from professor to professor. Some professors give written tests. Others assign papers or oral presentations. Some even require all three.

FIRST LISTENING

Read the questions. Listen to the conversation between a student and a professor. Take notes as you listen. Share your notes with a partner. Then use your notes to answer the questions.

1. What question does the student ask the professor? _____

_____

2. What does the professor answer? _____

_____

3. What advice does the professor give the student? _____

_____

SECOND LISTENING

Read the questions. Listen to the conversation again. Add details to your notes. Then use your notes to answer the questions. Work with a partner and compare your answers.

1. What is this conversation mainly about?
  (A) How to write a research paper
  (B) How to pass the course
  (C) How to give an oral presentation
  (D) How to maintain eye contact

2. Why does the student want to write a paper?
  (A) She received a low grade for her last oral presentation.
  (B) She feels too nervous when speaking in front of people.
  (C) She does not like speaking with her classmates.
  (D) She cannot attend class on the day of her presentation.

Listen again to part of the conversation. Then answer question 3.

3. Why does the professor ask, "So, what do you think you need to do to get a good grade?"?
   (A) To get her to think about possible strategies
   (B) To express doubt about her ability to give a presentation
   (C) To find out if she understands the course requirements
   (D) To ask for her opinion about grading in the course

Listen again to part of the conversation. Then answer question 4.

4. Why does the professor say, "Students will enjoy the story—some may already know it. And your presentation will make them understand it on a more sophisticated level."?
   (A) To question her choice of topic
   (B) To suggest a new strategy
   (C) To point out a problem
   (D) To encourage the student

5. Which of the following are strategies that the professor recommends? Choose TWO answers.
   (A) Using an outline while speaking
   (B) Reading the oral report to the class
   (C) Speaking in a sophisticated way
   (D) Using pictures and charts
   (E) Asking the audience questions

Listen again to part of the conversation. Then answer question 6.

6. What is the professor's attitude when he says, "I'm sure."?
   (A) Annoyed
   (B) Satisfied
   (C) Relieved
   (D) Optimistic

ACADEMIC LISTENING

FIRST LISTENING

Listen to the interview. Take notes using the outline to help you. Work with a partner to combine your notes.

Torrence's technique for learning a story: _____

The first time: _____

The second time: _____

The third time: _____

SECOND LISTENING

Read the questions. Listen to the interview again. Add details to your notes. Then use your notes to answer the questions. Work with a partner and compare your answers.

1. What is the main topic of the interview?
   (A) How to tell a story
   (B) How to enjoy reading
   (C) How to write a story
   (D) How to understand a story

2. According to Jackie Torrence, how many times should a person read a story before telling it?
   (A) One
   (B) Three
   (C) Five
   (D) Six

3. What is the interviewer's attitude toward Jackie Torrence?
   (A) Worried
   (B) Interested
   (C) Doubtful
   (D) Amused

Listen again to part of the conversation. Then answer questions 4.

4. What is the speaker implying when she says this?
   (A) Tell stories that you enjoy.
   (B) Tell stories that you have told before.
   (C) Tell stories that don't take a lot of time.
   (D) Tell stories that the listeners will enjoy.

5. What can be inferred about Jackie Torrence?
   (A) She writes good stories.
   (B) She is a good storyteller.
   (C) She prefers to write stories.
   (D) She wants to learn new stories.

6. How does Torrence explain how to tell a story?
   (A) By naming good storytellers
   (B) By dividing the process into steps
   (C) By comparing good and bad strategies
   (D) By telling a story as an example

7. What is the next topic that Torrence will most likely present?
   (A) How to write a good story
   (B) The names of good storytellers
   (C) Why her five steps are important
   (D) The fourth step for learning to tell a story

ANALYSIS

It is helpful to know the purpose of a test item. There are three types of questions in the listening section.

1. Basic Comprehension

- main ideas

- details

- the meaning of specific sentences

2. Organization

- the way information is structured

- the way ideas are linked

3. Inference

- ideas are not directly stated

- speaker's intention, purpose, or attitude not explicitly stated

Go back to the listening questions and label each question with 1, 2, or 3. Then work with a partner to see if you agree. Check the Answer Key for the correct answers. Which questions did you get right? Which did you get wrong? What skills do you need to practice?

2 Reading

BEHIND THE STORY OF "THE METAMORPHOSIS"

PRE-READING

In the following text, you will read about "The Metamorphosis," a short story written by Franz Kafka. Read the title and the first sentence in each paragraph. Then, with a partner, answer the questions.

1. What kind of insect does Kafka write about? _____

   _____

2. How many different explanations does the passage give about why Kafka used this insect? _____

   _____

3. What are the different explanations? List them. _____

   _____

READING

Read the text and answer the questions. Then work with a partner and compare your answers. When you disagree, go back to the text to find helpful information.

Behind the Story of "The Metamorphosis"

1   "The Metamorphosis" is a short story about a man who turns into a cockroach. The story is both funny and sad at the same time. It is funny because of how Gregor must learn to move his new "cockroach" legs and body. On the other hand, it is sad because he loses the love of his family as a result of his becoming so disgusting.

(continued on next page)

2   Why did Kafka choose to tell a story about a man who turns into a cockroach? Certainly many people are afraid of cockroaches and other insects. They think cockroaches are ugly and disgusting. Why would Kafka choose something that most of us hate? What was his purpose? Many critics have written their ideas about Kafka's purpose.

3   One explanation comes from a word that Kafka used in his story. Kafka wrote his story in German, and he used the German word *Ungeziefer*, or vermin, which can be used to mean a person who is rough and disgusting. In English, we do the same thing. If we call a person a "cockroach," we mean that the person is weak and cowardly. Gregor, the man, is like a cockroach. He is weak and disgusting. Why? Because he doesn't want to be the supporter of his family. He hates his job and wishes he didn't have to do it in order to pay off the family debt. In addition, his family has been like a parasite to him. Gregor's family members have all enjoyed relaxing, not working, while he alone has had to work. When he becomes a cockroach, he becomes the parasite to the family. So Gregor's true self is metamorphosed into an insect because his true self wants to be like a child again, helpless and having no responsibility.

4   Another explanation comes from Kafka's relationship with his father. Kafka was a small, quiet man. He saw himself as weak and spineless compared to his father, who was physically large and had a powerful personality. It is the same with Gregor. He also sees himself as a failure. By turning himself into an insect, Gregor is able to rebel against his father and, at the same time, punish himself for rebelling. This punishment results in his being physically and emotionally separated from his family with no hope of joining them again, and finally he dies.

5   Kafka's choice of an insect makes this story work because many people feel insects are disgusting. Gregor becomes the vermin, the disgusting son that nobody cares about. His family rejects him because of his appearance, yet he continues to love them to the end.

1. What is the passage mainly about?
   (A) Why family members should help each other
   (B) Why people think cockroaches are disgusting
   (C) Why writers use the image of insects in their stories
   (D) Why Kafka wrote about a man who becomes a cockroach

2. In paragraph 1, it can be inferred that "The Metamorphosis" is
   (A) short.
   (B) complex.
   (C) annoying.
   (D) funny.

3. What is the author's purpose in asking the questions in paragraph 2?
   (A) To criticize Kafka's use of a cockroach
   (B) To question the quality of Kafka's story
   (C) To introduce the main idea of the passage
   (D) To ask why people are afraid of cockroaches

4. From the last line in paragraph 2, it can be inferred that
   (A) Kafka spoke with critics about why he wrote this story.
   (B) critics agree about why Kafka used a cockroach in this story.
   (C) critics disagree about why Kafka wrote about a cockroach.
   (D) Kafka's purpose for using a cockroach was clear.

5. Before turning into a cockroach, Gregor
   (A) lived happily with his family.
   (B) had a lot of responsibilities.
   (C) was a parasite to his family.
   (D) had a quiet and relaxing life.

6. In paragraph 3, who does *we* refer to in the sentence, "If we call a person a 'cockroach,' we mean that the person is weak and cowardly."?
   (A) People
   (B) Critics
   (C) Writers
   (D) Teachers

7. In paragraph 3, the word *parasite* is closest in meaning to
   (A) parent.
   (B) worker.
   (C) supporter.
   (D) dependent.

8. In paragraph 3, the expression *metamorphosed into* is closest in meaning to
   (A) understood as.
   (B) changed into.
   (C) turned from.
   (D) seen as.

9. What is the writer's purpose in paragraphs 3 and 4?
   (A) To contrast two views on Kafka's use of a cockroach
   (B) To criticize Kafka's use of a cockroach
   (C) To explain Kafka's use of the word *Ungeziefer*
   (D) To compare people and cockroaches

10. In the end, Gregor
    (A) hates his family.
    (B) loves his family.
    (C) rejects his family.
    (D) punishes his family.

11. Look at the four squares   that indicate where the following sentence could be added to the passage. Where would the sentence best fit? Circle the letter that shows the point where you would insert this sentence.

Furthermore, like Kafka, Gregor saw himself as not very strong.

[A] Another explanation comes from Kafka's relationship with his father. Kafka was a small, quiet man. [B] He saw himself as weak and spineless compared to his father, who was physically large and had a powerful personality. [C] It is the same with Gregor. He also sees himself as a failure. [D] By turning himself into an insect, Gregor is able to rebel against his father and, at the same time, punish himself for rebelling. This punishment results in his being physically and emotionally separated from his family with no hope of joining them again, and finally he dies.

12. Which of the following expresses the essential information in this sentence from the passage?

He saw himself as weak and spineless compared to his father, who was physically large and had a powerful personality.

(A) Compared to his father, Kafka was strong and courageous.
(B) Kafka lacked strength and courage compared to his father.
(C) Kafka wanted to become more like his father.
(D) Compared to his father, Kafka felt unhealthy.

13. Read the first sentence of a summary of the passage. Then complete the summary by circling the THREE answer choices that express the most important ideas of the passage. Some sentences do not belong in the summary because they express ideas that are not presented in the passage or are minor ideas in the passage.

In "The Metamorphosis," Kafka tells the story of a man who turns into a cockroach for several reasons.

(A) Kafka wanted to show that Gregor worked hard to pay off his family's debts.
(B) The author tried to say that Gregor was happier as a cockroach than as a man.
(C) The author wanted to depict Gregor as ugly and disgusting.
(D) Kafka tried to demonstrate how cowardly Gregor was.
(E) The cockroach represented Gregor's desire to become helpless like a child.
(F) In the end Gregor loved his family, but they still rejected him.

3 Writing

In this section, you will read a short excerpt and listen to an excerpt on the same topic. Then you will write about the relationship between the two.

READING

Read the excerpt. As you read, complete the outline.

Anthropomorphism [æn′ θrow pə mɔr′ fɪzəm]

Definition: _____

    Example 1 _____

    Example 2 _____

Anthropomorphism

1   Anthropomorphism is giving human abilities or traits to an animal or an object that is not human. The word *anthropomorphism* comes from the Greek word *anthrōpos*, which means "human," and from *morphē*, which means "shape" or "form." Therefore, together the words mean "human form."

2   Anthropomorphism is common in the literature of ancient Greece. The ancient Greeks explained natural events, emotions, and experiences through anthropomorphism. In Greek literature Aphrodite was the goddess of beauty and love. Literally, she was "love" and "beauty" in the *shape* of a *woman*.

    Anthropomorphism is not limited to literature, however. People in everyday life use anthropomorphism for a number of reasons. Imagine that you have a plant sitting near your window. Day after day you see it leaning toward the window. You think to yourself that it wants to see out the window. The plant cannot "sit," nor can it "look out the window;" however, in an attempt to explain why the plant was moving toward the window, we anthropomorphize the plant. We might say that it sits and looks out the window, reaching for the light. A scientist might tell us that plants grow in the direction of light. By using an anthropomorphic technique, someone who is not a scientist can make sense out of an interesting or confusing experience.

3   Anthropomorphism can certainly make a story more interesting. However, more importantly, it helps people to better understand events and experiences.

LISTENING

Listen to the excerpt. Use the outline to take notes as you listen.

MAIN IDEAS	DETAILS
Gregor's dream	*A bad dream* *He realized that he . . .*
Gregor's job	
Gregor's problems	

WRITING

Write on the following topic. Follow the steps below to prepare.

> Describe how Kafka, the author, uses anthropomorphism to describe the man, Gregor Samsa.

Step 1

Work with a partner. Skim the reading and your notes from the reading and the listening tasks on pages 61–62. Answer the following questions to help you organize your ideas:

1. What is anthropomorphism? _____

_____

2. How does Kafka use anthropomorphism in "The Metamorphosis"?

_____

3. Is the use of anthropomorphism successful in this story? Why or why not?

_____

Step 2

Write for 20 minutes. Leave the last 5 minutes to edit your work.

To evaluate a partner's writing, use the Writing Evaluation Form on page 179.

4 Speaking

INDEPENDENT TASK

Speak on the following topic. Follow the steps below to prepare.

> Tell a short story about yourself. What animal, plant, or other nonhuman thing would you be? Describe your abilities and traits. You may choose to speak about a person you know well, instead of yourself.

Step 1

Work with a partner. Make a list of different animals, plants, and other nonhuman things. Choose one you think you are similar to. Think about your personality, strengths and weaknesses, and the way you look. Complete this chart to help you organize your ideas.

	YOU	NONHUMAN THING
Similarities		
Differences		

Step 2

Work with a partner. Take turns practicing a one-minute oral response. Use the information in your chart to help you.

Step 3

Change partners. Take turns giving a one-minute response to the topic again.

To evaluate your partner's response, use the Speaking Evaluation Form on page 180.

5 Skill Focus

IDENTIFYING AND USING RHETORICAL STRUCTURE

EXAMINATION

Look at the following items from the unit. Work with a partner and answer these questions about the items:

- What steps did you take to find your answer to these items?

- What are these items asking about? Does the question ask about meaning? vocabulary? organization?

- In each case, what was the writer's or speaker's purpose?

Item 1 (Academic Listening, page 55)

How does Torrence explain how to tell a story?
(A) By naming good storytellers
(B) By dividing the process into steps
(C) By comparing good and bad strategies
(D) By telling a story as an example

Item 2 (Academic Listening, page 56)

What is the next topic that Torrence will most likely present?
(A) How to write a good story
(B) The names of good storytellers
(C) Why her five steps are important
(D) The fourth step for learning to tell a story

Item 3 (Reading, page 59)

What is the writer's purpose in paragraphs 3 and 4?
(A) To contrast two views on Kafka's use of a cockroach
(B) To criticize Kafka's use of a cockroach
(C) To explain Kafka's use of the word *ungeziefer*
(D) To compare people and cockroaches

Item 4 (Reading, page 60)

Look at the four squares on the next page ☐ that indicate where the following sentence could be added to the passage. Where would the sentence best fit? Circle the letter that shows the point where you would insert this sentence.

Furthermore, like Kafka, Gregor saw himself as not very strong.

⬛A Another explanation comes from Kafka's relationship with his father. Kafka was a small, quiet man. ⬛B He saw himself as weak and spineless compared to his father, who was physically large and had a powerful personality. ⬛C It is the same with Gregor. He also sees himself as a failure. ⬛D By turning himself into an insect, Gregor is able to rebel against his father and, at the same time, punish himself for rebelling. This punishment results in his being physically and emotionally separated from his family with no hope of joining them again, and finally he dies.

Item 5 (Reading, page 59)

What is the author's purpose in asking the questions in paragraph 2?
(A) To criticize Kafka's use of a cockroach
(B) To question the quality of Kafka's story
(C) To introduce the main idea of the passage
(D) To ask why people are afraid of cockroaches

Tips

To do well on the TOEFL, it is essential to learn how to identify the rhetorical structure of a passage. It is also important to know which type of rhetorical structure you need to use in speaking and writing tasks.

Rhetorical structure items focus on the general organization of the whole passage or part of the passage (a paragraph or a single statement).

- **Pay attention to the rhetorical structure of the whole reading or listening text.**

Types of Rhetorical Structures: Whole Text

Description (of a person, thing, or process)

Comparison and/or contrast (giving similarities and differences)

Narration (telling a story)

Definition (telling what something is or what something means)

Classification (describing types of things in a group)

Opinion (giving a point of view)

Persuasion (arguing for or against something)

Item 1 is a rhetorical structure item focusing on the whole text. In this passage, the speaker is **describing the steps in a process**. The speaker uses three transitional expressions: "the first time you read a story . . . ," "the second time you read a story," and "the third time you read a story . . . " By using these transitions, the speaker is dividing her ideas into steps.

(continued on next page)

Therefore, the answer is (B), by dividing the process into steps.

Item 2 also asks about the rhetorical structure of describing steps in a process. If you notice this rhetorical structure, you also see that the answer to **Item 2** is (D), the fourth step for learning to tell a story.

Item 3 is an example of a rhetorical structure item that focuses on **contrasting information**. In the reading on pages 57–58, paragraph 3 begins with the sentence "One explanation comes from a word that Kafka used in his story." Then the writer discusses Kafka's use of the word *Ungeziefer* to explain why Kafka told this story. In paragraph 4, the writer gives a second possible explanation. The reader knows this because the writer begins the paragraph with "Another explanation comes from . . .". By noticing the relationship between the paragraph and the clues *one explanation/another explanation*, you know that the correct answer is (A), to contrast two views on Kafka's use of a cockroach.

- **Pay attention to the rhetorical structure of part of the text, that is, a paragraph or a specific statement.**

Types of Rhetorical Structures: Part of a Text

Add information

Introduce a topic

Give an opinion

Restate a point

Item 4 is a rhetorical structure item focusing on **adding information**. In the reading on pages 57–58, the writer first presents information about Kafka. Then the writer focuses on Gregor. The word *furthermore* (in the sentence to be inserted) indicates that the writer is adding information about Gregor. The phrase *like Kafka* clarifies that the writer is expressing an idea about Gregor and *not* about Kafka. Therefore, the answer is (D). Other words and phrases that add information include: *also, moreover,* and *in addition.*

Item 5 is a rhetorical structure item that focuses on **introducing a topic**. In paragraph 2 of the reading passage, the writer asks, "Why did Kafka choose to tell a story about a man who turns into a cockroach?" In this case the writer is not looking for an answer. The reader understands that the writer asked the question to introduce the topic. Therefore, the answer is (C), to introduce the main idea of the passage.

- **When completing a TOEFL speaking or writing activity, analyze the prompt to choose which structure is most appropriate.**

The rhetorical structure you use will help communicate your *purpose*. Choose a rhetorical structure that matches the type of question you are answering.

PRACTICE

1 *Listen to the following passage. Then, use the strategies for identifying rhetorical structure to answer the questions.*

1. How does the speaker begin the main part of her oral presentation?
   (A) By introducing herself to her audience
   (B) By telling the story of the Peach Boy
   (C) By explaining the use of anthropomorphism
   (D) By summarizing what she plans to say

2. Why does the speaker tell the story of Momotaro?
   (A) To convince her listeners to help each other
   (B) To present an example of anthropomorphism
   (C) To teach a lesson to children about cooperation
   (D) To introduce a famous Japanese story to her listeners

Listen again to part of the presentation. Then answer question 3.

3. Why does the speaker ask the question, "Why are there animals in this story and not just people?"?
   (A) To introduce her main idea
   (B) To get an answer from her classmates
   (C) To question the use of anthropomorphism
   (D) To present an opposite argument

Listen again to part of the presentation. Then answer question 4.

4. Why does the speaker use the expression *I think* when she says this?
   (A) To contrast her idea with another idea
   (B) To show that she is unsure
   (C) To define a new word
   (D) To give her opinion

2 *Read the Integrated Task, Reading, on page 61 again. What is the main rhetorical structure of this passage? Refer to the list of rhetorical structures in the TIPS box.*

3 *Listen again to the Integrated Task, Listening, on page 62. What is the main rhetorical structure of this passage? Refer to the list of rhetorical structures in the TIPS box.*

4 *Look back at the question for the Integrated Task, Writing, on page 62. Compare the organization you used with the organization your partner used. Are there any other ways you could organize the information?*

Language

| TOEFL® iBT TARGET SKILLS | |

- Identify and express main ideas
- Identify and express details
- Make inferences
- Listen and take detailed notes
- Integrate definitions and examples
- Distinguish main ideas from details

 For extra practice of TOEFL iBT skills, go to pages 208–226.

1 Listening

PRE-LISTENING VOCABULARY

Read the sentences. Guess the meaning of the boldfaced words and phrases. Then match each word or phrase with a definition or synonym from the list below. Work with a partner and compare your answers.

_____ 1. Not all Asian students are good at mathematics. That's just a **stereotype**.

_____ 2. I didn't call you last night because I **assumed** you were studying for today's test. I didn't know you went out dancing.

_____ 3. Gloria couldn't **handle** taking five courses, so she decided to drop economics and take it next semester.

_____ 4. My first year at college I lived in a dormitory, but after that I lived in an apartment **off campus**.

_____ 5. Our flight is delayed, so we are going to have to wait for another two hours! What **a drag**!

_____ 6. The **pace** in a big city is much faster than the pace in a small town.

_____ 7. When I first started to learn Spanish, my Chilean friend used to **make fun of** me. But now he says I speak Spanish very well.

_____ 8. In my hometown everyone looks more or less the same. When I moved to Los Angeles, I was surprised by the **diversity**.

_____ 9. You have been working hard for almost four years. **Hang in there!** You're almost finished!

a. a variety of different people and things

b. an idea about a particular type of person which people have that is wrong or unfair

c. manage, be comfortable with

d. don't give up

e. laugh at, often in a negative way

f. not on the grounds or land of a school

g. something boring or troublesome

h. speed

i. thought something is true even though you did not have proof

Culture Note: College students often live in residence halls, or dormitories. Dormitories have resident assistants, or RAs, who are typically third- or fourth-year students. RAs support younger students and plan social programs.

FIRST LISTENING

Read the questions. Listen to the conversation between a student and a resident assistant. Take notes as you listen. Share your notes with a partner. Then use your notes to answer the questions.

1. What is the student's problem? _____

_____

2. What advice does the RA give him? _____

_____

SECOND LISTENING

Read the questions. Listen to the conversation again. Add details to your notes. Then use your notes to answer the questions. Work with a partner and compare your answers.

1. What is this conversation mainly about?
   (A) Living in a college dormitory
   (B) Understanding different accents
   (C) Moving at a fast speed
   (D) Getting used to living in a new place

2. What problem did the RA have when he moved to New York?
(A) He had trouble in his classes.
(B) People assumed he was Chinese.
(C) He had to get used to the fast pace.
(D) It was difficult to understand different accents.

3. According to the student, what is his main problem?
(A) People off campus do not understand him.
(B) People think that he is Chinese.
(C) People in the city move too fast.
(D) People make fun of his accent.

Listen again to part of the conversation. Then answer question 4.

4. Why does the RA ask, "Aren't you?"
(A) He wants to insult the student.
(B) He thought the student was Chinese.
(C) He wanted to make a joke.
(D) He misunderstood the student.

Listen again to part of the conversation. Then answer question 5.

5. What is the RA's attitude when he says, "That's a drag."?
(A) Critical
(B) Sympathetic
(C) Argumentative
(D) Encouraging

6. What do the two speakers have in common?
(A) They are both from the South.
(B) People notice their accents.
(C) They both enjoy the pace of the city.
(D) They always have to repeat themselves.

ACADEMIC LISTENING

FIRST LISTENING

Listen to the interview about how gender affects language. Complete the charts on the next page as you listen. Work with a partner and compare your answers.

Which words refer to men? Which words refer to women? Which words refer to both?

WORDS	REFER TO MEN	REFER TO WOMEN	REFER TO BOTH
doctor			✓
bachelorette			
policeman			
firefighter			
mail carrier			

Which words do men use? Which words do women use? Which words do both men and women use?

WORDS	USED BY MEN	USED BY WOMEN	USED BY BOTH
purple			
lavender			
periwinkle			
mauve			
lovely			
cute			
adorable			

SECOND LISTENING

Read the questions. Listen to the interview again. Take notes. Then use your notes to answer the questions. Work with a partner and compare your answers.

1. What is the main idea of the interview?
   (A) Dr. Speakwell wants women to get respect.
   (B) Men and women use language differently.
   (C) There are words women use that men do not.
   (D) Today men and women can do the same jobs.

Listen again to part of the interview. Then answer question 2.

2. What is the interviewer's tone when she says, "Maybe I should call you "Doctorette?"
   (A) Serious
   (B) Humorous
   (C) Respectful
   (D) Embarrassed

Listen again to part of the conversation. Then answer question 3.

3. What is Dr. Speakwell suggesting about the word *actress* when she says this?
   (A) It makes female actors sound less intelligent.
   (B) It makes female actors sound very old.
   (C) It makes female actors sound more serious.
   (D) It makes female actors sound too formal.

4. According to Dr. Speakwell, why has gender been removed from words related to occupation?
   (A) Because both men and women do these jobs
   (B) Because both women and men say these words
   (C) Because men sometimes speak like women
   (D) Because men want to be equal to women

Listen again to part of the conversation. Then answer question 5.

5. What is the interviewer's tone when she responds, "Do you really think so?"?
   (A) Anger
   (B) Surprise
   (C) Agreement
   (D) Disagreement

6. Why does Dr. Speakwell use the example of Japanese men and women?
   (A) To show how many countries she has studied in
   (B) To show that language and gender are related to culture
   (C) To show that Japanese women are as strong as men
   (D) To show how Japanese women use word endings typically used by men

Listen again to part of the conversation. Then answer question 7.

7. What is the interviewer's attitude when she says, "I suppose."?
   (A) Surprise
   (B) Agreement
   (C) Disappointment
   (D) Doubt

2 Reading

CODE SWITCHING

PRE-READING

Read the first and last sentences of each paragraph. Then, work with a partner and answer the questions.

1. What's the main idea of the reading? _____

_____

2. What are two or three details that support the main idea? _____

_____

READING

Read the magazine article and answer the questions. Then, work with a partner and compare your answers. When you disagree, go back to the text to find helpful information.

1　Code switching is when people switch, or change, from one language to another while speaking. They might begin a conversation in one language and then, later in the conversation, switch to another. They might also begin a sentence in one language but end it in another. Or they might insert a word or phrase from another language. *When* and *why* people code switch depends on the speakers and the situation.

2　One reason people code switch is to show social closeness. Imagine that two women meet at a party in New York. Gabriela is Brazilian, and Pamela is British. In their conversation, Pamela asks:

Pamela:　Where are you from?
Gabriela:　Rio.
Pamela:　Really? Uma cidade muito bonita [A beautiful city]. I was there last year.
Gabriela:　Oh, do you speak Portuguese?
Pamela:　Um pouco [only a little]. . . .

Here, Pamela uses a little Portuguese in order to show closeness or friendliness to Gabriela.

3　On the other hand, people also code switch to create social distance. Sometimes this happens in immigrant homes in the United States where the children can speak English, but the parents understand only the language of their native country. Children can code switch to keep their parents from understanding everything they say. Likewise, parents may code switch when they share a language that their children do not understand.

4　One final reason that people code switch is lack of knowledge about a language or lack of attention to one's language. Imagine a teenage girl living in a Latino community in Los Angeles. Talking with her friends, she says, "Espérate [Wait a minute]. What did you just say???" It is possible that the teenager was not trying to show social closeness or distance. Perhaps she didn't know how to express the second idea in Spanish. Most likely, she may simply have switched to English without paying much attention to which language she was using.

5   Code switching occurs between people who share more than one common language; however, it can also occur between people who share a language and a dialect, or variation, of that language. A person may use one dialect at home and then switch to another dialect at school or work. One example is the way teenagers use slang when talking to their friends. For instance, a teen might say to his friend, "Gotta bounce. Me 'n' the crew're goin' shoppin' for some mad phat gear." *Gotta bounce* means "I have to leave," *the crew* means "my friends," and *mad phat gear* means "nice clothes." Therefore, the teen is saying, "I'm going shopping with friends," but only speakers of both English and this teen dialect can understand. Teens use their dialect because it helps them to show that they fit in with their friends. It also shows that they are separate from their parents.

6   Regardless of the situation, there are two important rules for code switching. First, the speakers have to know both languages or dialects—at least well enough to follow the changes. More importantly, the switches have to be grammatical. For example, the sentence "Tengo que do my homework" follows the subject + verb + object grammar rules in both Spanish and English.

7   One day you may be riding on a train, listening to the people next to you having a conversation. If you can understand only 50 percent of what they are saying, perhaps they are code switching—to show each other closeness—or—perhaps to stop you from listening in on their conversation!

1. What is this passage mainly about?
   (A) Showing closeness between speakers
   (B) Hiding your ideas from other people
   (C) Learning a new or foreign language
   (D) Switching between languages

2. Why does the author use the example of Pamela speaking Portuguese?
   (A) To show code switching to create closeness between speakers
   (B) To show code switching to create social distance
   (C) To show code switching with a dialect of a language
   (D) To show code switching by an immigrant to the U.S.

3. The word *dialect* can best be defined as
   (**A**) a language used by teens.
   (**B**) a variation of a language.
   (**C**) a sentence in two languages.
   (**D**) a foreign language.

4. In paragraph 5, why does the author use the sentence, "Code switching occurs between people who share more than one common language; however, it can also occur between people who share a language and a dialect, or variation, of that language."?
   (**A**) To make a transition
   (**B**) To summarize an idea
   (**C**) To give an example
   (**D**) To start a conclusion

5. According to the passage, what is the function of slang among some teenagers?
   (**A**) To share a common language with their parents
   (**B**) To create social distance from one another
   (**C**) To express closeness with one another
   (**D**) To show closeness with their parents

6. What rules does a speaker have to follow when code switching? Choose TWO answers.
   (**A**) Show closeness to the other speaker
   (**B**) Speak directly to the other person
   (**C**) Use languages both speakers know
   (**D**) Follow the grammar of the two languages
   (**E**) Complete a sentence before code switching

7. In paragraph 6, the phrase *Regardless of the situation* is closest in meaning to
   (**A**) in all cases.
   (**B**) in some conversations.
   (**C**) in some locations.
   (**D**) in all languages.

8. What can the reader infer from paragraphs 5 and 6?
   (**A**) Young people code switch a lot.
   (**B**) Americans code switch a lot.
   (**C**) Multilingual people code switch a lot.
   (**D**) Parents code switch a lot.

9. What adjective best describes the author's tone in paragraph 7?
   (**A**) Hopeful
   (**B**) Disappointed
   (**C**) Angry
   (**D**) Humorous

10. Look at the four squares ☐ that indicate where the following sentence could be added to the passage. Where would the sentence best fit? Circle the letter that shows the point where you would insert this sentence.

> In this case they may code switch to English or a teen dialect of English.

> On the other hand, people also code switch to create social distance. **A** Sometimes this happens in immigrant homes in the United States where the children can speak English, but the parents understand only the language of their native country. **B** Children can code switch to keep their parents from understanding everything they say. **C** Likewise, parents may code switch when they share a language that their children do not understand. **D**

11. Which of the following expresses the essential information in this sentence from the passage?

> Code switching occurs between people who share more than one common language; however, it can also occur between people who share a language and a dialect, or variation, of that language.

(A) People can code switch between French and Spanish, but they cannot use a dialect, such as slang.
(B) Code switching can be done in two ways: either between two languages or between a language and a variation of it.
(C) Speakers who code switch are creating a dialect, or variation, of two different languages or types of language.
(D) Code switching happens when two languages or dialects of a language are used by a single speaker.

12. Read the first sentence of a summary of the passage. Then complete the summary by circling the THREE answer choices that express the most important ideas of the passage. Some sentences do not belong in the summary because they express ideas that are not presented in the passage or are minor ideas in the passage.

> There are several different reasons people code switch.

(A) A person might code switch due to lack of attention to or lack of knowledge about a language.
(B) People code switch to create distance between themselves and people who do not know both languages.
(C) Some speakers code switch before they finish a single sentence.
(D) Speakers may code switch to show affection or closeness to another speaker.
(E) Code switching can involve inserting words from another language into a sentence.
(F) The grammar rules of both languages can be changed when code switching.

ANALYSIS

It is helpful to know the purpose of a test item. There are four types of questions in the reading section.

1. Basic Comprehension

- main ideas

- details

- the meaning of specific sentences

2. Organization

- the way information is structured in the text

- the way ideas are linked between sentences or between paragraphs

3. Inference

- ideas are not directly stated in the text

- author's intention, purpose, or attitude not explicitly stated in the text

4. Vocabulary and Reference

- the meaning of words

- the meaning of reference words such as *his*, *them*, *this*, or *none*

Go back to the reading questions and label each question with 1, 2, 3, or 4. Then work with a partner to see if you agree. Check the Answer Key for the correct answers. Which questions did you get right? Which did you get wrong? What skills do you need to practice?

3 Speaking

INTEGRATED TASK: READ, LISTEN, SPEAK

In this section, you will read a short excerpt and listen to an excerpt on the same topic. Then you will speak about the relationship between the two.

READING

Read the excerpt. Then, with a partner, discuss the answer to the following question.

Who do we stereotype? What is wrong with stereotyping? Give specific examples.

Stereotyping

1   Americans are loud. Blondes are stupid. Politicians are dishonest. These statements are all stereotypes: simple, generalized views of groups of people based on limited information. In fact, there are many Americans who are quiet, many blonde-haired women who are intelligent, and many politicians who are honest. We stereotype other people in order to categorize and understand our world better. Unfortunately, stereotyping leads to misunderstanding and conflicts.

2   Stereotypes can be either positive or negative, but they are always wrong. How can a stereotype be positive? For instance, it is not bad to say "Asians are good at mathematics," but it is not true. Some Asians, many in fact, are not good at math. These people may have other skills that are equally as strong. Therefore, even a positive stereotype may seriously limit our view of someone as an individual.

3   However, stereotypes are much more often negative. In general, they reduce individuals to a single, over-simplified image. Stereotypes do not show people as complex individuals. They make people or groups of people look the same, when, in fact, they are very different. Stereotyping can lead to misunderstanding, conflict, and sometimes even war.

LISTENING

Listen to the excerpt. Use the outline to take notes as you listen.

How do people react to Joseph's accent?

(+) _____

(–) _____

How does Joseph feel about people's reaction to his accent?

- _____
- _____
- _____

SPEAKING

Speak on the following topic. Follow the steps on the next page to prepare.

Explain the concept of stereotyping, and discuss Joseph's experience as an example.

Step 1

Work with a partner. Skim the reading and your notes from the reading and the listening tasks on pages 79–80. Complete this outline to help you organize your ideas.

Definition of stereotyping: _____

_____

Joseph's experience: _____

_____

_____

Step 2

Work with a partner. Take turns practicing a one-minute oral response. Use the information in your outline to help you.

Step 3

Change partners. Take turns giving a one-minute response to the topic again.

To evaluate your partner's response, use the Speaking Evaluation Form on page 180.

4 Writing

INDEPENDENT TASK

Write on the following topic. Follow the steps below to prepare.

What do you think of when you hear a certain language, dialect, or accent from your country? What stereotype(s) do you have of the people who speak in this way? How do you react to these people? Choose one group to focus on.

Step 1

- Brainstorm a list of the different groups in your country that speak a certain language or dialect or who speak with a certain accent. For example, what do people in the east or west of your country sound like? Do people in rural areas speak differently from people in the city? Choose one group to focus on.

- Brainstorm a list of stereotypes you have *or* that you know other people have about this group. List some adjectives to describe this group.

- Work in groups. Take turns describing the group you chose and the stereotype of this group. Give your partners feedback. React to the feedback your partners give you. What can you add or change about your topic?

Step 2

Write for 20 minutes. Leave the last 5 minutes to edit your work.

To evaluate a partner's writing, use the Writing Evaluation Form on page 179.

5 Skill Focus

IDENTIFYING AND USING MAIN IDEAS AND DETAILS

EXAMINATION

Look at the following items from this unit. Work with a partner and answer these questions about the items.

- Is the question asking about a larger, more general idea?
- Is the question asking about a specific, supporting idea?

Item 1 (Academic Listening, page 73)

What is the main idea of the interview?
(A) Dr. Speakwell wants women to get respect.
(B) Men and women use language differently.
(C) There are words women use that men do not.
(D) Today men and women can do the same jobs.

Item 2 (Reading, page 77)

What rules does a speaker have to follow when code switching? Choose TWO answers.
(A) Show closeness to the other speaker
(B) Speak directly to the other person
(C) Use languages both speakers know
(D) Follow the grammar of the two languages
(E) Complete a sentence before code switching

Item 3 (Reading, page 78)

Read the first sentence of a summary of the passage. Then complete the summary by circling the THREE answer choices that express the most important ideas of the passage. Some sentences do not belong in the summary because they express ideas that are not presented in the passage or are minor ideas in the passage.

There are several different reasons people code switch.

(A) A person might code switch due to lack of attention to or lack of knowledge about a language.

(B) People code switch to create distance between themselves and people who do not know both languages.

(C) Some speakers code switch before they finish a single sentence.

(D) Speakers may code switch to show affection or closeness to another speaker.

(E) Code switching can involve inserting words from another language into a sentence.

(F) The grammar rules of both languages can be changed when code switching.

Tips

To do well on the TOEFL, it is essential to learn how to identify and use main ideas and details correctly.

A **main idea** is a large, broad idea. The main idea in a passage is the most important point the writer or speaker wants you to know.

On the TOEFL, the main idea refers *only* to the main idea *of the whole passage*. Usually in reading and writing, every paragraph has one main idea. However, the TOEFL is different in this way. The TOEFL will not ask about the main idea of a paragraph.

Main idea questions usually ask, *What is the text mainly about?* or *What is the main idea of this passage?* The answer to a main idea question is either directly stated in the text or paraphrased, that is, the same idea is stated in different words. (See Unit 6 for more on paraphrasing.)

To identify the main idea, ask yourself:

- What is the larger, most general idea in a passage? What is the main point the writer or speaker wants to communicate?

Item 1 asks about the main idea of the passage. To answer this item correctly, you have to consider the whole passage, which is about the connection between language and gender. Therefore, the best choice is (B).

A **detail** is a piece of something larger. Details are not as general as main ideas. They often support or give more information about the main idea.

To identify details, ask yourself:

- Is the idea a piece of a larger idea?

- Does the idea add to or support the main idea?

Item 2 asks about details in the reading passage. The answers to detail questions will usually be *paraphrased*, that is, not stated directly from the passage. That is, you will see the same ideas but *not* the same words. To answer Item 2 correctly, you have to identify "use language both speakers know" and "follow the grammar of the two languages" as rules for code switching. Therefore, the best choices are (C) and (D). However, if you look back at the reading on pages 75–76, you will see that the words in the text are not the same as the words in the correct answer choices.

ANSWER CHOICES	WORDS IN THE TEXT
(C) Use languages both speakers know	First, the speakers have to know both languages or dialects.
(D) Follow the grammar of the two languages	The sentence "Tengo que do my homework" follows the subject + verb + object grammar rules of both Spanish and English.

Item 3 asks you to summarize information. To answer this item correctly, you have to choose the three details most closely connected to the main idea in the question stem: reasons for code switching.

These sentences are the correct choices because they are reasons for code switching:

(A) A person might code switch due to lack of attention to or lack of knowledge about a language.
(B) People code switch to create distance between themselves and people who do not know both languages.
(D) Speakers may code switch to show affection or closeness to another speaker.

The other choices are not reasons for code switching or are not true at all.
    Remember that the summary questions in each unit present a main idea. You then have to identify three details from six choices. (See Unit 7 for more on summarizing.)

PRACTICE

1 *Read the following paragraph written by an American student. As you read, complete the outline. Then, use the strategies for identifying main ideas and details to answer the questions.*

Main idea: _____

Details for support: (1) _____

(2) _____

One Language Isn't Enough

Everyone says that English is a global language—it is used all over the world. Certainly, much of the world's international business and politics are conducted in English. However, as Americans, we should be embarrassed by our lack of knowledge of other languages. Students in elementary and secondary schools and in colleges and universities may take language classes, but they are not enough for a student to communicate well in the language—even as tourists. People in other countries will not respect us if we do not try to understand their languages and cultures. In the long run, we may have serious problems if the business world ever changes to another language such as Spanish or Chinese. American schools need to prepare students to face the world with more than just English. Even though the world seems to be learning English, we as native speakers of English have a responsibility to learn about the languages and cultures of our global neighbors.

1. What is the main idea of this essay?
   (A) English is an international language.
   (B) Americans need to learn foreign languages.
   (C) People around the world study English.
   (D) Tourists can use English when they travel.

2. Which are details the writer uses to support the main idea? Choose TWO answers.
   (A) English is becoming an international language.
   (B) American schools do not teach foreign languages well enough.
   (C) Students in the United States study foreign languages.
   (D) Americans should be helpful to people who do not speak English.
   (E) Americans will have problems if the world stops using English.

3. What strategies did you use to identify the main idea and details?

2 *Listen to the following passage. As you listen, take notes using the outline below. Then, use the strategies for identifying main ideas and details to answer the questions.*

Main idea: _____

　　Detail 1: _____

　　Detail 2: _____

　　Detail 3: _____

　　Detail 4: _____

　　Detail 5: _____

1. What is the main idea of this passage?
   (A) Difficulties with language
   (B) Using slang in the United States
   (C) Making people understand your accent
   (D) Understanding humor in the United States

2. What strategies did you use to identify the main idea in this passage?

3. Based on your outline, which of the following is NOT a detail mentioned by the speaker?
   (A) You may have trouble understanding the local accent.
   (B) People in the U.S. might not understand your accent right away.
   (C) Americans use slang expressions that you might not understand.
   (D) Using a language in the real world is easier than using it in the classroom.

4. What strategies did you use to identify the details in this passage?

3 *Speak and write on the following topic. Follow the steps to prepare.*

Would visitors to your country have major problems if they did not speak the native language of your country?

Step 1

Review your notes from the reading and the listening tasks on pages 79–80. Make a list of possible problems you might have if you do not speak the language of the place you are visiting.

Possible problems if you do not speak the language of the place you are visiting:

_____

_____

_____

_____

_____

_____

Step 2

Write an outline of what you will speak and write about.

Main idea: _____

   Details for support: _____

_____

_____

Step 3

Work with a partner.

• Take turns giving a one-minute oral response.

• As you listen to your partner, complete this outline:

My partner's main idea: _____

   Details used for support: _____

_____

_____

• Share this outline with your partner. Is it the same as the outline he or she wrote in Step 2?

Step 4

Write your answer in a paragraph. Use your outline. Begin with the main idea, and then add the details to support your view. Give your paragraph to your teacher.

Tourism

| LISTENING |

Campus Conversation — A student talks to a professor about missing a deadline for a project.

Academic Listening — Town Hall Meeting in Hyannis, Cape Cod

| READING |

Magazine Article — *Transforming a Tradition*

| WRITING |

Integrated Task: Read, Listen, Write — Summarize the points made in the lecture on the benefits of tourism to Antarctica and explain how they cast doubt on the points made in the listening excerpt on problems with tourism in Antarctica.

| SPEAKING |

Independent Task — Give your opinion on the topic of tourists visiting the long-necked women of the Padaung tribe.

| SKILL FOCUS |

Paraphrasing — Paraphrasing is the ability to restate ideas from other sources in your own words without changing the meaning.

| TOEFL® iBT TARGET SKILLS |

- Identify and express main ideas
- Identify and express details
- Make inferences
- Recognize and paraphrase speakers' opinions
- Paraphrase main ideas and details

 For extra practice of TOEFL iBT skills, go to pages 208–226.

1 Listening

CAMPUS CONVERSATION

PRE-LISTENING VOCABULARY

Read the sentences. Guess the meaning of the boldfaced words and phrases. Then match each word or phrase with a definition or synonym from the list below. Work with a partner and compare your answers.

_____ 1. The students felt that they did not have enough time to complete their final project, but the professor refused to give them an **extension**.

_____ 2. The **due date** for this paper is tomorrow, and I haven't even started! What am I going to do?

_____ 3. Betty decided not to take the class after she looked at the course **syllabus**. She knew that the class required too much work for her.

_____ 4. Julio loves to write poetry, but lately he has had **writer's block**. He hasn't been able to write anything in over three weeks.

_____ 5. Tourism can have a positive **impact** on the economy of a city. It brings the city money and creates jobs.

_____ 6. Mary wanted to go on a **cruise** of the Greek Islands, but, because her husband gets seasick, they decided to go to Egypt instead.

_____ 7. One word can have different meanings depending on the **context** in which it is used.

_____ 8. I don't want you to tell me the answer to the math problem. But could you give me a **hint**?

_____ 9. I just picked up this brochure for a vacation in Paris. **Check it out**, and let me know if you want to go with me.

a. a plan that states exactly what students will learn and do in a course

b. a clue; information that helps you find an answer

c. extra time to complete an assignment

d. a problem that a writer has of not being able to think of new ideas

e. a specific situation or environment

f. influence, effect

g. look at it

h. a vacation on a large ship

i. the day by which you must complete an assignment

Culture Note: Professors usually give students a syllabus at the beginning of the semester. The syllabus contains all of the assignments and the dates on which they are due. Students are expected to complete their assignments on time. If a student is going to miss a due date, he or she might ask the professor for an extension for more time.

FIRST LISTENING

Read the questions. Listen to the conversation between a student and a professor. Take notes as you listen. Share your notes with a partner. Then use your notes to answer the questions.

1. Why does the student go to see the professor? _____

_____

_____

2. How does the professor help the student? _____

_____

_____

SECOND LISTENING

Read the questions. Listen to the conversation again. Add details to your notes. Then use your notes to answer the questions. Work with a partner and compare your answers.

1. What is the conversation mostly about?
   (A) Taking a Caribbean cruise
   (B) Writing a paper about tourism
   (C) Choosing a place to go on vacation
   (D) Searching for information online

2. What will happen if the student misses the new due date?
   (A) She will get another extension.
   (B) She will receive an incomplete.
   (C) She will receive a failing grade for the course.
   (D) She will visit the professor during office hours.

3. What is one effect of tourism NOT mentioned in the conversation?
   (A) Economic
   (B) Environmental
   (C) Sociocultural
   (D) Political

Listen again to part of the conversation. Then answer question 4.

4. What is the professor implying?
   (A) The information the student needs can be found on the Internet.
   (B) The student has not looked for information in the right places.
   (C) The Internet is sometimes difficult for students to use.
   (D) The professor does not use the Internet for research.

Listen again to part of the conversation. Then answer question 5.

5. What is the professor's attitude when he says, "Vicky, the due date is today."?
   (A) Impatient
   (B) Sympathetic
   (C) Calm
   (D) Excited

Listen again to part of the conversation. Then answer question 6.

6. Why does the professor ask, "Have you ever taken a vacation?"?
   (A) He is interested in her personal life.
   (B) He wants her to think of a specific context.
   (C) He wants ideas for his next vacation.
   (D) He is trying to change the topic of conversation.

ACADEMIC LISTENING

FIRST LISTENING

Listen to the passage. The speakers are at a town meeting to discuss the problem of tourism in their town, Hyannis, Cape Cod, Massachusetts. Take notes using the chart below. Work with another student to combine your notes.

SPEAKERS	OPINION ABOUT TOURISM
Mrs. Green	
Mr. Horowitz	
Ms. Keller	

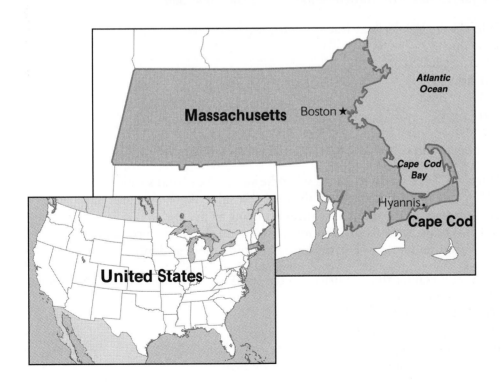

SECOND LISTENING

Read the questions. Listen to the town meeting again. Add details to your notes. Then use your notes to answer the questions. Work with a partner and compare your answers.

1. What is this passage mainly about?
   (A) How to attract more tourists to Cape Cod
   (B) The effects of tourism on a small town
   (C) Why tourists like to visit Hyannis
   (D) A decision made at a town meeting

2. According to the passage, when are tourists a problem?
   (A) In the summer
   (B) In the winter
   (C) All year round
   (D) On weekends

3. Which sentence best states Ms. Keller's opinion?
   (A) Tourists cause terrible traffic jams.
   (B) Tourists cause housing prices to go up.
   (C) Tourists bring the town needed money.
   (D) Tourists are going to other towns instead.

Listen again to part of the town meeting. Then answer question 4.

4. What is the speaker's attitude toward tourists when she says, "It's ridiculous."?
   (A) Sympathetic
   (B) Amused
   (C) Surprised
   (D) Angry

Listen again to part of the town meeting. Then answer question 5.

5. What did Mr. Horowitz mean when he said, "Now that's ridiculous."?
   (A) People in Hyannis make only a regular salary.
   (B) It is very funny that the waitress is living in her car.
   (C) The housing problem is more serious than the traffic problems.
   (D) Vacation homes in Hyannis are becoming more and more expensive.

6. What complaints about tourists do the speakers have? Choose TWO answers.
   (A) Traffic jams in the summer
   (B) Few tourists in the winter
   (C) Noisy streets at night
   (D) High housing prices
   (E) Weak economy

ANALYSIS

It is helpful to know the purpose of a test item. There are three types of questions in the listening section.

1. Basic Comprehension

- main ideas

- details

- the meaning of specific sentences

2. Organization

- the way information is structured

- the way ideas are linked

3. Inference

- ideas are not directly stated

- speaker's intention, purpose, or attitude not explicitly stated

Go back to the listening questions and label each question with 1, 2, or 3. Then work with a partner to see if you agree. Check the Answer Key for the correct answers. Which questions did you get right? Which did you get wrong? What skills do you need to practice?

2 Reading

TRANSFORMING A TRADITION

PRE-READING

Read the title of the passage and skim the first sentence of each paragraph. Then, look at the sentences below. Write the sentences in your own words. Do not change the meaning of the sentences.

1. At different times in her life, more rings are added until her neck carries up to 25 of them, weighing 5 to 10 kilos.

   _____

   _____

2. As long as there are tourists who will pay to see them, they will continue to wrap their daughters' necks.

   _____

   _____

READING

Read the passage and answer the questions. Then work with a partner and compare your answers. When you disagree, go back to the text to find helpful information.

Transforming a Tradition

1   Critics call it "a human zoo." Tour companies consider it a tourist attraction. Whichever is the case, the long-necked women of Padaung have become an important source of money for several small villages on the border of Thailand and Myanmar.

2   Each year around 10,000 tourists visit three small villages along the Thai/Myanmar border to see the famous long-necked women. The attraction is a tradition which requires women to stretch their necks by wearing brass coils, or rings. Originally from the Padaung tribe, the women and their families have been running from Myanmar to Thailand since the 1980s to escape poverty and war. Their new lives are very different from their lives as farmers in Myanmar. Now they spend their days talking with tourists, posing for pictures, and selling hand-made souvenirs.

3   When a Padaung girl turns 5, a thick coil of brass is wrapped around her neck. At different times in her life, more rings are added until her neck carries up to 25 of them, weighing 5 to 10 kilos. The rings push up her chin and press down her collarbone, making her neck longer.

4   Pa Peiy is a young woman with 20 neck coils. When asked to describe her early years of neck stretching, Pa Peiy said, "At first it was painful, but now it's OK. Now sleeping, eating, working . . . everything is OK. But I cannot take it off, so this is my life." Truly it is her life. Pa Peiy's neck is now so weak that if she takes off the coils, her head will fall forward and she will stop breathing.

5   Despite the discomfort, Padaung women in Thailand continue to wear the rings even though the tradition has almost disappeared in Myanmar. The simple reason for this fact is that there is money in it.

6   Ma Nang, a graceful woman with 24 neck rings, explains that in Myanmar she had worked hard growing food. Today, she sits while tourists take pictures of her. In one month she makes seventy to eighty dollars. Ma Nang added, "Sometimes I'm tired of tourists always looking at me, but it's easy work and good money for my family."

7   Each year, as the long-necked women become more and more popular, the controversy about them increases. In a hotel in Thailand, tourists discuss whether or not to visit Nai Soi. Sandra Miller, from Toronto, Ontario, feels that it's fine to visit Nai Soi. She explained, "I don't really see a problem. I mean, this is their tradition, and so, if I go,

it's like I'm helping them to preserve it. Spending my money is also helping them to feed their families and so on. They need the tourists."

8   Frederick Johnson, a visitor from Seattle, Washington, disagrees. "Actually I don't see that we're preserving tradition at all," Johnson explained. "This tradition has already died in Myanmar. These women are just harming their bodies to . . . to entertain us. It's degrading for these women. It's like paying to go see animals in a zoo."

9   For now, the future of the long-necked women is easy to predict. As long as there are tourists who will pay to see them, they will continue to wrap their daughters' necks. The controversy continues, with one side seeing the villages as examples of how tourism can save dying traditions, and others criticizing it as harmful and degrading to the Padaung women.

1. What is the main idea of this passage?
(**A**) Traveling to Thailand
(**B**) Women's fashion trends
(**C**) A controversy related to tourism
(**D**) The political conflict in Myanmar

2. In paragraph 2, the word *tribe* is closest in meaning to
(**A**) town.
(**B**) group.
(**C**) farm.
(**D**) village.

3. In these villages, what is the attraction for tourists?
(**A**) Learning about the history of Thailand
(**B**) Visiting the farms of the Padaung people
(**C**) Seeing women who stretch their necks with coils
(**D**) Buying coils for tourists to wear around their necks

4. In paragraph 2, all of the following reasons why the Padaung people moved to Thailand are mentioned EXCEPT
(**A**) to escape war.
(**B**) to make money.
(**C**) to start a new life.
(**D**) to work on farms.

5. According to the author, why do the women continue the neck-stretching tradition?
(**A**) To make money
(**B**) To remember the past
(**C**) To escape farming
(**D**) To create controversy

6. What is the best way of describing Nai Soi?
   (A) A tradition from Myanmar
   (B) A hotel for tourists in Thailand
   (C) A woman with coils on her neck
   (D) A village with long-necked women

7. What can be inferred about Sandra Miller?
   (A) She thinks that the tradition of wearing coils is dead.
   (B) She is going to visit a village of long-necked women.
   (C) She traveled to Thailand to help long-necked women.
   (D) She believes the coils are physically dangerous to the women.

8. In paragraph 8, which of the following is NOT an opinion expressed by Frederick Johnson?
   (A) The tradition of the long-necked women ended when they left Myanmar.
   (B) The long-necked women are hurting themselves physically.
   (C) Tourists are treating the long-necked women like animals.
   (D) The long-necked women are good entertainment for tourists.

9. In paragraph 8, the word *degrading* is closest in meaning to
   (A) entertaining.
   (B) disrespectful.
   (C) interesting.
   (D) disappointing.

10. How does the author present this topic?
    (A) By arguing one opinion on the issue
    (B) By comparing groups in Myanmar
    (C) By presenting both sides of the argument
    (D) By explaining the origins of the tradition

11. Look at the four squares ☐ that indicate where the following sentence could be added to the passage. Where would the sentence best fit? Circle the letter that shows the point where you would insert this sentence.

    According to tradition, these coils are a sign of wealth and beauty.

    Each year around 10,000 tourists visit three small villages along the Thai/Myanmar border to see the famous long-necked women. ☐A The attraction is a tradition which requires women to stretch their necks by wearing brass coils, or rings. ☐B Originally from the Padaung tribe, the women and their families have been running from Myanmar to Thailand since the 1980s to escape poverty and war. ☐C Their new lives are very different from their lives as farmers in Myanmar. Now they spend their days talking with tourists, posing for pictures, and selling handmade souvenirs. ☐D

12. Which of the following expresses the essential information in this sentence from the passage?

> "At first it was painful, but now it's OK. Now sleeping, eating, working … everything is OK. But I cannot take it off, so this is my life." (Pa Peiy)

(A) "The rings used to hurt a lot, but they are a normal part of my life now."
(B) "The coils used to be uncomfortable, but now they are comfortable."
(C) "Before, the coils were a problem, but now I enjoy wearing them."
(D) "I can do all of my daily tasks while wearing the coils around my neck."

13. Read the first sentence of a summary of the passage. Then complete the summary by circling the THREE answer choices that express the most important ideas of the passage. Some sentences do not belong in the summary because they express ideas that are not presented in the passage or are minor ideas in the passage.

> Tourists disagree about whether they should visit the long-necked women.

(A) Tourism is saving a dying cultural tradition.
(B) The women sometimes enjoy meeting the tourists.
(C) The women can remove the coils if they want to.
(D) Tourists treat Padaung women like animals in a zoo.
(E) The Padaung people were farmers when they were in Myanmar.
(F) Some Padaung women believe that it is an easy way to make money.

3 Writing

INTEGRATED TASK: READ, LISTEN, WRITE

In this section, you will read a short excerpt and listen to an excerpt on the same topic. Then you will write about the relationship between the two.

READING

Read the excerpt. Then, with a partner, discuss the answer to the following question:

According to the passage, what are the benefits of tourism in the Antarctic?

- _____
- _____
- _____

The Adventure of a Lifetime

We at the Antarctic Travel Society encourage you to consider an exciting guided tour of Antarctica for your next vacation.

The Antarctic Travel Society carefully plans and operates tours of the Antarctic by ship. There are three trips per day leaving from ports in South America and Australia. Each ship carries only about 100 passengers at a time. Tours run from November through March to the ice-free areas along the coast of Antarctica.

In addition to touring the coast, our ships stop for on-land visits, which generally last for about three hours. Activities include guided sightseeing, mountain climbing, camping, kayaking, and scuba diving. For a longer stay, camping trips can also be arranged.

Our tours will give you an opportunity to experience the richness of Antarctica, including its wildlife, history, active research stations, and, most of all, its natural beauty.

Tours are supervised by the ship's staff. The staff generally includes experts in animal and sea life and other Antarctica specialists. There is generally one staff member for every 10 to 20 passengers. These trained and responsible individuals will help to make your visit to Antarctica safe, educational, and unforgettable.

Lars-Eric Lindblad, who led the first tour of Antarctica in 1966, said, "You can't protect what you do not know." By conducting carefully planned, responsible tourist activity in Antarctica, the Antarctic Travel Society hopes to teach people what Antarctica is all about. We believe that, once the public sees its beauty, they will work even harder to protect it for future generations.

Contact the Antarctic Travel Society today for information to start planning your adventure of a lifetime!

LISTENING

Listen to the excerpt. Use the outline below to take notes as you listen. The main idea has been done for you.

Main Idea: _Antarctica is an important resource, but it is threatened_

by tourism. _____

What scientists study: _____

_____

_____

_____

_____

_____

_____

Effects of tourism: _____

_____

_____

WRITING

Write on the following topic. Follow the steps to prepare.

Summarize the points made in the lecture and explain how they cast doubt on the points made in the reading.

Step 1

- Review the reading and your outline on the listening task above.

- Fill in this chart to organize your ideas.

ARGUMENTS AGAINST TOURISM IN ANTARCTICA	ARGUMENTS FOR TOURISM IN ANTARCTICA

Step 2

Write for 20 minutes. Leave the last 5 minutes to edit your work.

> To evaluate a partner's writing, use the Writing Evaluation Form on page 179.

4 Speaking

INDEPENDENT TASK

Work in a group to debate the following topic. Follow the steps below to prepare.

| Do you think tourists should visit the long-necked women of the Padaung tribe?

Step 1

- Work in a group of three students. Each student takes one role:

  Student A will argue in favor of visiting the long-necked women.

  Student B will argue against visiting the long-necked women.

  Student C will act as moderator.

- Students A and B work individually to prepare a two-minute answer to the question.

Step 2

- Students A and B take turns presenting a one-minute oral argument.

- Student C presents a one-minute summary of each of the arguments, chooses the most convincing argument, and gives an explanation.

> To evaluate your partner's response, use the Speaking Evaluation Form on page 180.

5 Skill Focus

PARAPHRASING

EXAMINATION

Look at the following items from the unit. Work with a partner and answer these questions about the items:

- What key words or ideas in the text helped you to answer the question correctly?

- If you answered the question incorrectly, how was your choice different from the correct answer?

Item 1 (Academic Listening, page 94)

Which sentence best states Ms. Keller's opinion?
(A) Tourists cause terrible traffic jams.
(B) Tourists bring the town needed money.
(C) Tourists cause housing prices to go up.
(D) Tourists are going to other towns instead.

Item 2 (Reading, page 98)

In paragraph 8, which of the following is NOT an opinion expressed by Frederick Johnson?
(A) The tradition of the long-necked women ended when they left Myanmar.
(B) The long-necked women are hurting themselves physically.
(C) Tourists are treating the long-necked women like animals.
(D) The long-necked women are good entertainment for tourists.

Item 3 (Reading, page 99)

Which of the following expresses the essential information in this sentence from the passage?

> "At first it was painful, but now it's OK. Now sleeping, eating, working … everything is OK. But I cannot take it off, so this is my life." (Pa Peiy)

(A) "The rings used to hurt a lot, but they are a normal part of my life now."
(B) "The coils used to be uncomfortable, but now they are comfortable."
(C) "Before, the coils were a problem, but now I enjoy wearing them."
(D) "I can do all of my daily tasks while wearing the coils around my neck."

Tips

To do well on the TOEFL, it is essential to recognize paraphrases and to be able to paraphrase information. When you paraphrase, you present ideas in your own words *without changing the writer's or speaker's meaning.*

To recognize paraphrases, notice that

- A paraphrase contains the same ideas as the original text but the words are different.

- A paraphrase often has a different sentence structure compared to the original.

- A paraphrase identifies the original text and the author or speaker.

- In writing, a paraphrase does not have quotation marks *except* for any specific words or phrases that are picked up from the original text.

To paraphrase

- Read or listen to the text carefully.

- Circle or note key words and ideas.

- Write or say the key ideas in your own words. Use expressions such as *in other words*, *what the author/speaker meant was . . .*

- Vary the sentence structure.

- In writing, use quotation marks if you use specific words or phrases exactly from the original text.

- Mention the original text, author, or speaker. Use expressions such as *according to* or *in [title] the author suggests.*

- Reread and edit your paraphrase several times, making sure you have included all of the key words and ideas.

In **Item 1**, if you listened carefully to Ms. Keller, you noted that *tourists*, *essential*, and *economy* were the key ideas in the passage. The answer (B), *Tourists bring the town needed money*, does not repeat Ms. Keller's exact words. However, the answer does include the speaker's idea.

In **Item 2**, three of the choices are paraphrases of Mr. Johnson's ideas.

MR. JOHNSON'S EXACT WORDS	ITEM CHOICES
"This tradition has already died in Myanmar."	(A) The tradition of the long-necked women ended when they left Myanmar.
"These women are just harming their bodies."	(B) The long-necked women are hurting themselves physically.
"It's degrading for these women. It's like paying to go see animals in the zoo."	(C) Tourists are treating the long-necked women like animals.

Even though choice (C) repeats the word *animal*, it is not a big problem because *animal* is a common word and it would be difficult to find another word to represent Mr. Johnson's words accurately. Only choice (D), *The long-necked women are good entertainment for tourists*, is not one of Mr. Johnson's ideas.

In **Item 3,** it was important to understand the key pieces of Pa Peiy's idea:

- At first the coils hurt.

- Now they do not hurt as much (or at all).

- She can't take them off.

- She sees them as part of her daily life.

Choice (A) contains all of these ideas. Therefore, it is the best choice. (B) is not correct because Pa Peiy does not say that the coils are comfortable. She says they are "OK," but it is not clear what she means. Similarly, (C) is not correct because the woman does not suggest that she enjoys wearing the coils. (D) is not correct because it does not contain the idea that the coils used to be painful.

PRACTICE

1 *Read each quotation. Choose the response that is the best paraphrase of the quotation. Use the strategies for recognizing paraphrases to help you. Then, work with a partner and discuss your answers.*

1. "Travel is 90 percent anticipation and 10 percent recollection."
   —Edward Streeter
   (A) The best part of traveling is the time after you return home.
   (B) The best part of traveling is the time before your trip.
   (C) The best part of traveling is when you are in a new country.
   (D) The best part of traveling is telling your friends about your trip.

2. "No man should travel until he has learned the language of the country he visits. Otherwise he voluntarily makes himself a great baby—so helpless and so ridiculous."—Ralph Waldo Emerson
   (A) Young children can learn a new language more quickly than adults can.
   (B) Before traveling, learn the language, or you will look foolish because you will need help.
   (C) Traveling is for babies and ridiculous people, not for responsible adults.
   (D) People will laugh at you if you cannot speak the language of the country you visit.

3. "The traveler sees what he sees, the tourist sees what he has come to see."
   —G. K. Chesterton
   (A) Travelers often plan their sightseeing, and so do tourists.
   (B) Travelers enjoy their own culture, but tourists enjoy the culture of the places they visit.
   (C) Travelers carefully plan their trips, but tourists go to a country to discover new things.
   (D) Travelers travel with an open mind, but tourists travel with expectations.

2 *Paraphrase each of the following quotations. Use the strategies for paraphrasing. Then work with a partner and discuss your answers. Edit your paraphrases and give them to your teacher.*

1. "If you look like your passport picture, you're too ill to travel."
   —Will Kommen

   _____

   _____

2. "Most travel is best of all in the anticipation or the remembering; the reality has more to do with losing your luggage." —Regina Nadelson

   _____

   _____

Humor

LISTENING	
Campus Conversation	A student talks to a professor about a teaching assistant's responsibilities.
Academic Listening	Lecture: *The Story of* I Love Lucy

READING	
Magazine Article	*Cosby: A Different Kind of Family Show*

SPEAKING	
Integrated Task: **Read, Listen, Speak**	Explain why the joke in the listening excerpt was funny according to the theories presented in the reading excerpt.

WRITING	
Independent Task	Write about a funny TV show or movie that you enjoyed and why you thought it was funny.

SKILL FOCUS	
Summarizing	Summarizing means finding the essential information from a written or spoken text, and leaving out less important details, then using this information in writing or speaking.

TOEFL® iBT TARGET SKILLS

- Identify and express main ideas
- Identify and express details
- Make inferences
- Categorize information
- Skim a reading and summarize it
- Summarize a listening and relate it to a reading
- Make an outline to prepare a summary

 For extra practice of TOEFL iBT skills, go to pages 208–226.

1 Listening

CAMPUS CONVERSATION

PRE-LISTENING VOCABULARY

Read the sentences. Guess the meaning of the boldfaced words and phrases. Then match each word or phrase with a definition or synonym from the list below. Work with a partner and compare your answers.

_____ 1. After the chemistry lecture, we all went to the **lab** to try the experiment the professor had demonstrated.

_____ 2. Rachel was studying for her chemistry test last night. She had to stay up all night to **get through** all of her notes.

_____ 3. My aunt Agnes likes to **gossip** about the people in our family, so I never tell her anything about myself.

_____ 4. My father was an English literature **major** in college, and now he's a high school English teacher.

_____ 5. Getting my first job was a real **learning experience**. I discovered things about business that I never could have learned in school.

_____ 6. I tried to do the chemistry lab experiment **on my own**; however, it was too difficult. I had to ask a classmate for help.

_____ 7. The chapters in the textbook **correspond** with the chapters in the workbook. If we study a chapter in the text, we need to complete the same chapter in the workbook.

_____ 8. Most of the students did badly on the exam, so the professor offered a **make-up test** the following week.

_____ 9. Sofia missed all of her classes last week when her parents were visiting. Now she has to work twice as hard to **catch up** in all of her classes.

a. a student's main subject at college or university

b. an opportunity to do something for the first time and learn new things

c. a classroom in which students do research experiments

d. match, agree

e. talk about someone's personal life

f. get to the end of something, complete

g. a second chance at an exam

h. independently

i. to come from behind someone or something and get to the same place

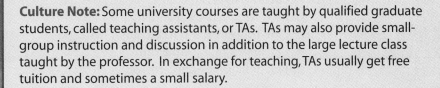

Culture Note: Some university courses are taught by qualified graduate students, called teaching assistants, or TAs. TAs may also provide small-group instruction and discussion in addition to the large lecture class taught by the professor. In exchange for teaching, TAs usually get free tuition and sometimes a small salary.

FIRST LISTENING

Read the questions. Listen to the conversation between a student and a professor. Take notes as you listen. Share your notes with a partner. Then use your notes to answer the questions.

1. What is the student's problem?

_____

2. What is the professor going to do?

_____

SECOND LISTENING

Read the questions. Listen to the conversation again. Add details to your notes. Then use your notes to answer the questions. Work with a partner and compare your answers.

1. What is this conversation mainly about?
   (**A**) College courses
   (**B**) Make-up exams
   (**C**) Teaching assistants
   (**D**) Lab experiments

2. According to the passage, what does Sam's TA do in the lab?
   (A) He conducts experiments.
   (B) He follows the text closely.
   (C) He gives make-up exams.
   (D) He tells jokes and stories.

3. According to the conversation, why did Sam and his classmates do poorly on the exam?
   (A) They studied only one chapter in the lab.
   (B) The exam was too difficult.
   (C) They wanted to take a make-up test.
   (D) The TA doesn't know much about chemistry.

4. Which task is NOT mentioned as a job that TAs do?
   (A) Teaching a class by themselves
   (B) Leading discussion groups
   (C) Preparing lectures for professors
   (D) Grading exams and papers
   (E) Answering students' questions

 Listen again to part of the conversation. Then answer question 5.

5. What is the student's attitude when he says, "You won't tell him I said anything, will you?"?
   (A) Angry
   (B) Worried
   (C) Happy
   (D) Relieved

 Listen again to part of the conversation. Then answer question 6.

6. What can be inferred when the professor says, "What?"?
   (A) She is surprised by what the student said.
   (B) She did not hear what the student said.
   (C) She thinks the student is telling a lie.
   (D) She believes the student is joking with her.

ACADEMIC LISTENING

FIRST LISTENING

 Listen to a lecture. Take notes using the chart on the next page to help you. Fill in the missing information. Work with a partner to combine your notes.

IN REAL LIFE	ON TELEVISION
Lucille Ball	**Lucy Ricardo**
a successful movie actress	
Desi Arnaz	**Ricky Ricardo**

SECOND LISTENING

Read the questions. Listen to the lecture again. Add details to your notes. Then use your notes to answer the questions. Work with a partner and compare your answers.

1. What is the lecture mainly about?
   (A) A radio program in the 1940s
   (B) How to become a TV star
   (C) The creation of a TV show
   (D) Two famous movie stars

2. What is the speaker's attitude toward the topic?
   (A) Sympathetic
   (B) Enthusiastic
   (C) Bored
   (D) Critical

Listen again to part of the lecture. Then answer question 3.

3. Why does the speaker say, "Remember that this was all before people had televisions in their homes."?
   (A) To give historical context
   (B) To compare movies and television
   (C) To question the show's popularity
   (D) To present his main idea

4. According to the speaker, what was *I Love Lucy* about?
   (A) A bandleader
   (B) A movie star
   (C) A funny couple
   (D) A housewife

5. Why were Lucille and Desi worried about making a TV show?
   (A) They had only been married for a short time.
   (B) Desi wanted to make all the decisions.
   (C) They had never worked together before.
   (D) TV was something new at the time.

Listen again to part of the lecture. Then answer question 6.

6. Why does the speaker say, "People in the audience could understand Lucy—because, really, who doesn't want to be a star."?
   (A) To show why everyone likes Lucy
   (B) To find out who in the audience wants to be famous
   (C) To present why he wants to be famous
   (D) To question the popularity of *I Love Lucy*

2 Reading

COSBY: A DIFFERENT KIND OF FAMILY SHOW

PRE-READING

In the following text, skim the title and the first and last sentences of each paragraph. Then answer the following question.

What is **The Cosby Show** about? _____

READING

Read the magazine article and answer the questions. Then work with a partner and compare your answers. When you disagree, go back to the text to find helpful information.

Cosby: A Different Kind of Family Show

1   Heathcliff Huxtable is the name of Bill Cosby's TV character on *The Cosby Show*. Actually, his family and friends just call him "Cliff." To the rest of the world he is "Dr. Huxtable," a kind and friendly obstetrician[1] married to a successful lawyer, named Clair.

2   Cliff and Clair Huxtable are the loving African-American parents of five children: four girls and a boy. They live in a nice big house in Manhattan filled with pretty furniture. They are well dressed, and their children, ranging in age from preschool to high school, are bright and charming. Grandma and Grandpa are part of the fun, too. What's so funny about that? No pies are thrown; no funny costumes are worn. Instead, Dr. Huxtable relaxes at home in a sweater and does simple fatherly things. The children often bicker and make up, and sometimes there is tension between husband and wife. In the end Cliff and Clair look at each other, and we know what they are thinking: You're a pain in the neck, but I still love you.

3   Again, what's so funny about that? It's quite simple. Cliff and Clair show us family life in America not as it is, but as it could be. In a perfect world, both husband and wife have satisfying, high-paid careers. They still have time and energy to love their kids, and when pressures build up, they are able to laugh. Bill Cosby is the master of the chuckle. He is able to do amazingly funny things with his face. When he raises his eyebrows, smiles, and chuckles, we know that everything is going to be all right—and this is comforting to all of us in the real world. Dr. Huxtable is here to show us that yes, life is a little frustrating at times, but if we chuckle our way through our problems and if we love the people around us, things are going to be OK.

4   In one show, Cliff has a cold but doesn't want to admit it to himself or anyone else. Every time someone asks him if he's sick, he denies it crossly. Finally, at the end of the show, he admits it, and, like a child, asks his wife to take care of him: "I'm sick. Will you take care of me?" As Clair helps him climb the stairs she responds, "Yes." Cliff continues with a series of questions like "Will you put me in the bed? Will you take my temperature? Will you make soup for me?" Clair says "Yes"

---

[1] *obstetrician:* A doctor who deals with the birth of children

each time. Finally, like a child who tries to use the situation to his advantage, Cliff asks, "Will you buy me a pony[2]?" We identify with Cliff's imperfections and are comforted to see that someone loves him anyway.

5   This is good medicine for America. What America needs to see right now is a happy family. Henry Louis Gates Jr., a professor of African-American studies at Harvard, tells us that Bill Cosby is a very smart man. Instead of focusing on the very real problems of race and money, he shows us "a black family dealing with all the things black people deal with, the same as all other people." For example, Theo, the teenage son, has been borrowing money from all his sisters. They finally tell him he needs to pay them back. NOW! But Theo has a problem. He doesn't have any money to pay them back with. So he asks his father for an advance on his allowance. Cliff says, "Son, you're already backed up to your 50th birthday. No." This is a familiar problem for many American families, but Cliff uses the humor of exaggeration to get his point across.

6   *The Cosby Show* is sure to please many people. I predict that the Huxtables will be in our lives for several years to come.

_____
[2] *pony:* A very small horse

1. What is the passage mainly about?
   (A) Typical family life in the United States
   (B) Growing up in an American city
   (C) A television show about a family
   (D) The problems of African-American families

2. In paragraph 2, all of the following are true of Cliff and Clair Huxtable EXCEPT
   (A) They have four children.
   (B) They wear nice clothes.
   (C) They have a large home.
   (D) They have nice furniture.

3. In paragraph 2, the expression *a pain in the neck* is closest in meaning to
   (A) an annoying person
   (B) a physical problem
   (C) an angry person
   (D) a good husband

4. Why is it funny when Cliff asks his wife if he can have a pony?
   (A) Cliff knows that people in the city usually do not have ponies.
   (B) He is a grown man asking for something a child usually wants.
   (C) He is asking his wife for something he can buy for himself.
   (D) Cliff knows that his wife will buy him a pony if he asks for one.

5. In paragraph 5, what is the author implying when he says, "This is good medicine for America. What America needs to see right now is a happy family."?
   (A) Family life in the United States is in trouble.
   (B) People in America take a lot of bad medicine.
   (C) The United States has many unhealthy people.
   (D) Americans need TV shows that make them laugh.

6. In paragraph 5, what is Theo's problem?
   (A) He fights too much with his four sisters.
   (B) He borrowed a lot of money from his family.
   (C) He is too old to still be living with his parents.
   (D) He is upset about being the only son in the family.

7. In paragraph 5, what does the word *This* refer to in the sentence, "This is a familiar problem for many American families, but Cliff uses the humor of exaggeration to get his point across."?
   (A) Using humor to make a point
   (B) Paying back borrowed money
   (C) Celebrating important birthdays
   (D) Giving money to family members

8. Why does the author make the comment, "No pies are thrown; no funny costumes are worn."?
   (A) To show that the family is funny
   (B) To show that the family is boring
   (C) To show that the family is polite
   (D) To show that the family is normal

9. In paragraphs 2 and 3, why does the author repeat the question "What's so funny about that?"?
   (A) To emphasize that the Huxtables are like a regular family
   (B) To compare a black family with a white family
   (C) To question if *The Cosby Show* is really funny
   (D) To ask for more information about the show

10. Look at the four squares ☐ that indicate where the following sentence could be added to the passage. Where would the sentence best fit? Circle the letter that shows the point where you would insert this sentence.

   He thinks doing this will make him look weak.

   In one show, Cliff has a cold but doesn't want to admit it to himself or anyone else. [A] Every time someone asks him if he's sick, he denies it crossly. [B] Finally, at the end of the show, he admits it, and, like a child, asks his wife to take care of him: "I'm sick. Will you take care of me?" [C] As Clair helps him climb the stairs she responds, "Yes." Cliff continues with a series of questions like "Will you put me in the bed? Will you take my temperature? Will you make soup for me?" [D] Clair says "Yes" each time. Finally, like a child who tries to use the situation to his advantage, Cliff asks, "Will you buy me a pony?" We identify with Cliff's imperfections and are comforted to see that someone loves him anyway.

11. Which of the following expresses the essential information in this sentence from the passage?

   Life is a little frustrating at times, but if we chuckle our way through our problems and if we love the people around us, things are going to be OK.

   (A) Life is sometimes difficult, but we should just forget about our problems.
   (B) If we keep laughing, our problems will disappear and we will have happy lives.
   (C) If we have people in our lives who love us, we can handle our serious problems.
   (D) Life will be fine if we have a positive attitude and have friends and family around us.

12. Read the first sentence of a summary of the passage. Then complete the summary by circling the THREE answer choices that express the most important ideas of the passage. Some sentences do not belong in the summary because they express ideas that are not presented in the passage or are minor ideas in the passage.

   The Cosby Show is a very popular American TV program.

   (A) *Cosby* offers an example of a happy American family.
   (B) Dr. Huxtable's friends and family call him "Cliff."
   (C) Grandma and Grandpa Huxtable live with Cliff, Clair, and the children.
   (D) Members of the Huxtable family often fight with each other.
   (E) The show is about a black family with the same problems as everyone else.
   (F) Viewers see that they can survive difficult times with laughter.

ANALYSIS

It is helpful to know the purpose of a test item. There are four types of questions in the reading section.

1. Basic Comprehension

- main ideas
- details
- the meaning of specific sentences

2. Organization

- the way information is structured in the text
- the way ideas are linked between sentences or between paragraphs

3. Inference

- ideas are not directly stated in the text
- author's intention, purpose, or attitude not explicitly stated in the text

4. Vocabulary and Reference

- the meaning of words
- the meaning of reference words such as *his, them, this,* or *none*

Go back to the reading questions and label each question with 1, 2, 3, or 4. Then work with a partner to see if you agree. Check the Answer Key for the correct answers. Which questions did you get right? Which did you get wrong? What skills do you need to practice?

3 Speaking

INTEGRATED TASK: READ, LISTEN, SPEAK

In this section, you will read a short excerpt and listen to an excerpt on the same topic. Then you will speak about the relationship between the two.

READING

Read the excerpt on the next page. Then, with a partner, discuss the answer to the following question.

What are two reasons that people find jokes or situations funny?

1. _____

2. _____

What's So Funny?

1   It is extremely difficult to explain why something is funny. No one knows for sure why we laugh at certain ideas and situations. However, research is beginning to tell us more about how and why humor affects us.

2   Some psychologists say that people laugh because of the element of surprise in humor. When the audience hears the funny part at the end of a joke, the "punch line," they experience a familiar idea in a new, humorous way. These psychologists say that a joke or a situation is funny because two ideas do not match. This is called incongruity. There can be a mismatch, or incongruity, between characters in a joke or story. There might also be a mismatch between what happens in a funny situation and what usually happen in "real life." On some level, when ideas that don't match are put together, this surprises us and causes us to laugh.

3   According to other researchers, humor can make people feel that they are better than other people. If we see ourselves as superior, we will feel better. This kind of humor is good if it doesn't hurt another person. Jokes about certain jobs or certain types of people can make a person feel superior.

4   Ultimately, scientists cannot yet explain why something is funny because it comes from deep inside of us. One thing they are sure of is that laughter is essential for keeping us healthy. As one wise old woman once said, "A good laugh a day keeps the doctor away."

LISTENING

Listen to the excerpt. Answer the following questions as you listen.

1. Who is the caller? _____

2. What kind of joke does she tell? _____

3. What is the "punch line" (the part of the joke that makes people laugh)?

_____

4. What is the funny message in the joke? _____

SPEAKING

Speak on the following topic. Follow the steps on the next page to prepare.

Explain why the caller's joke was funny according to the theories presented in the reading.

Step 1

Work with a partner. Skim the reading and your notes from the reading and the listening tasks on pages 117–118. Complete this outline to help you organize your ideas.

Reasons That a Joke is Funny

-
-

Details of the Caller's Joke

- Type of joke:
- Topic:
- Punch line:

Step 2

Work with a partner. Take turns practicing a one-minute oral response. Use the information in your outline to help you.

Step 3

Change partners. Take turns giving a one-minute response to the topic again.

> To evaluate your partner's response, use the Speaking Evaluation Form on page 180.

4 Writing

INDEPENDENT TASK

Write on the following topic. Follow the steps below to prepare.

Write about a funny TV show or movie. Why did you think it was funny?

Step 1

Think of a funny TV show or a movie that you enjoyed. Use the questions below to help you. Take notes after each question.

1. Who were the people or characters? _____

2. What was the TV show or movie about? _____

3. Was there any incongruity in the humor? _____

4. Did the humor make other characters or the audience feel superior in any way?

   _____

5. Why else was it funny? _____

Step 2

Work in groups. Take turns describing the show or movie to the members of your group and why you think it is funny.

Step 3

Write for 20 minutes. Leave the last 5 minutes to edit your work.

To evaluate a partner's writing, use the Writing Evaluation Form on page 179.

5 Skill Focus

SUMMARIZING

EXAMINATION

Look at the following items from the unit. Work with a partner and answer this question about the items.

What aspect of the text or passage does each question focus on?

- Main idea?

- Large details?

- Small details?

- Your personal opinions?

Item 1 (Academic Listening, p. 111)

What is the lecture mainly about?
(A) A radio program in the 1940s
(B) How to become a TV star
(C) The creation of a TV show
(D) Two famous movie stars

Item 2 (Reading, p. 114)

What is the passage mainly about?
(A) Typical family life in the United States
(B) Growing up in an American city
(C) A television show about a family
(D) The problems of African-American families

Item 3 (Reading, p. 116)

Read the first sentence of a summary of the passage. Then complete the summary by circling the THREE answer choices that express the most important ideas of the passage. Some sentences do not belong in the summary because they express ideas that are not presented in the passage or are minor ideas in the passage.

> *The Cosby Show* is a very popular American TV program.

(A) *Cosby* offers an example of a happy American family.

(B) Dr. Huxtable's friends and family call him "Cliff."

(C) Grandma and Grandpa Huxtable live with Cliff, Clair, and the children.

(D) Members of the Huxtable family often fight with each other.

(E) The show is about a black family with the same problems as everyone else.

(F) Viewers see that they can survive difficult times with laughter.

Tips

To do well on the TOEFL, you need to be able to **summarize** information. A **summary** is a shorter version of a text. A summary gives the essential, or most important, parts of a written or spoken text and leaves out the less important details. The Listening and Reading sections on the TOEFL have questions that ask you to recognize summaries. In many of the Integrated and Independent Tasks, you often have to summarize information.

Summarizing is different from **paraphrasing**. When you summarize, you give the main idea of the *whole* text and include the most important details. Paraphrasing usually focuses on a *part* of the text. When you paraphrase, you give the meaning of the piece of text in your own words. (See Unit 6, Skill Focus, Paraphrasing.)

When summarizing in speaking or writing:

- Give the general, main idea of the text.

- Give only important details, not minor ones.

- Do not give your opinion or analysis.

To answer **Item 1** correctly, you had to choose the statement that gave the more general, main idea of the lecture. In the lecture you hear about (A) "A radio program in the 1940s" but this is not an important part of the lecture. You also hear about TV stars and movie stars. However, the lecture does not specifically say (B) "How to become a TV star," and it does not give information about (D) "Two famous movie stars." We hear only about one movie star, Lucille Ball. The lecture was mainly about how *I Love Lucy* began. Therefore, the best choice is (C) "The creation of a TV show."

(continued on next page)

Item 2 is similar. To answer this item correctly, you need to identify the main idea of the text. The ideas in choices (A), (B), and (D) are all in the passage, but they are minor details or ideas that are simply not true in the context of the reading. Therefore, (C) "A television show about a family" is the best choice because it summarizes the main idea of the passage. It tells us what the passage is mainly about.

If you answered **Item 3** correctly, you notice that three statements helped to summarize the reason why *The Cosby Show* is popular:

(A) *Cosby* offers an example of a happy American family.
(E) The show is about a black family with the same problems as everyone else.
(F) Viewers see that they can survive difficult times with laughter.

The other three statements were less important details in the text. They should not be included in your summary.

To complete the Integrated and Independent Tasks, you also had to summarize. In the Integrated Task you had to summarize the information in the reading before you answered the speaking question. In the Independent Task you had to summarize important parts of the TV show or movie you chose to write about.

PRACTICE

Read the passage. Then follow the steps below.

"I think a sense of humor is important in this world because it gives a person a sense of hope and it breaks up the repetition of everyday life. Jokes are structured humor. They help people who don't have confidence in their sense of humor. Jokes give them confidence to make other people laugh. I think that everyone has the potential to be funny and that everyone has the potential to tell a really good joke. Anyone can make people laugh, and everyone has a sense of humor. It's up to you how much you want to develop that."

—Terry Moore, a stand-up comic

Step 1

Work with a partner. Together, outline a summary of Terry Moore's comments.

• Her main idea: _____

• The important details: _____

_____

Step 2

Work with another partner. Compare and edit your outlines.

Step 3

Write a summary of Terry Moore's comments. Use the Tips on page 121.

Summary

_____

_____

_____

Step 4

Exchange summaries with a partner. Evaluate each other's writing. Use the Writing Evaluation Form on page 179. Discuss what strategies you used to help you write your summary.

Fashion

| LISTENING |

Campus Conversation   A student talks to a career advisor about how to dress for job interviews.

Academic Listening   Interview: *Fashion in the Workplace*

| READING |

Essay   *Traditional Fashion for Today's Woman*

| WRITING |

Integrated Task: Read, Listen, Write   Write about the potential risks and benefits of cosmetic surgery.

| SPEAKING |

Independent Task   Give your opinion on the topic of schools having a dress code or uniform policy. Include details and examples in your explanation.

| SKILL FOCUS |

Comparing and Contrasting   Comparing and contrasting means recognizing relationships, analyzing similarities and differences, and distinguishing two points of view.

| TOEFL® iBT TARGET SKILLS |

- Identify and express main ideas
- Identify and express details
- Make inferences
- Categorize information
- Analyze opinions in a reading
- Discuss a position using examples

 For extra practice of TOEFL iBT skills, go to pages 208–226.

1 Listening

CAMPUS CONVERSATION

PRE-LISTENING VOCABULARY

Read the sentences. Guess the meaning of the boldfaced words and phrases. Then match each word or phrase with a synonym from the list below. Work with a partner and compare your answers.

_____ 1. Professor, I have an idea for a research paper topic. Can I **run it by you?**

_____ 2. After graduating from law school, Kathryn joined her father's law **firm** in Chicago.

_____ 3. According to her **résumé**, Kathryn has a bachelor's degree from the University of Nebraska and a master's degree from Boston University.

_____ 4. While he was in college, Larry did an **internship** at a bank. The bank managers liked him so much that they hired him after graduation.

_____ 5. Bob bought a new **dress shirt** and tie to wear to his sister's wedding.

_____ 6. My father is pretty **conservative**. He does not want his children to begin dating until they graduate from college.

_____ 7. You said you had a question for me. **Shoot!**

_____ 8. My boss wants the report now, but I'm not finished. He's **furious!**

_____ 9. On a hot summer day I prefer to wear a shirt with short **sleeves**, but my boss insists that I wear a long-sleeved shirt with a tie.

_____ 10. When you start a new job, you should try to **put your best foot forward.** Don't complain or ask for too much.

a. a job a student does for little or no pay to get experience

b. Ask me.

c. a shirt with a collar, often worn with a tie

d. a business or company

e. extremely angry

f. tell you about it to get your opinion from the beginning

g. a list of your education and job experience

h. try to make a good impression

i. traditional, unchanging

j. part of clothing that covers the arms

Culture Note: Most students in their last year of college or university begin to interview for jobs. Colleges and universities typically have a career services office which can help students find information about jobs, write a résumé, and prepare for job interviews.

FIRST LISTENING

Read the questions. Listen to the conversation between a student and a career advisor. Take notes as you listen. Share your notes with a partner. Then use your notes to answer the questions.

1. Why does the student go to see Mr. Greenwood?

_____

_____

2. What is Mr. Greenwood's advice?

_____

_____

SECOND LISTENING

Read the questions on the next page. Listen to the conversation again. Add details to your notes. Then use your notes to answer the questions. Work with a partner and compare your answers.

1. What is this conversation mainly about?
   (A) How to find a new job
   (B) How to write a résumé
   (C) How to choose a career
   (D) How to dress for an interview

2. What jobs is the student interviewing for? Choose TWO answers.
   (A) Elementary school teacher
   (B) University professor
   (C) Software designer
   (D) Career counselor
   (E) Tattoo artist

3. What advice does Mr. Greenwood give the student regarding his earring?
   (A) He should not wear it to the interview.
   (B) He should decide for himself whether or not to wear it.
   (C) He should find out if earrings are appropriate at the two places.
   (D) He should wear it to the interview at the firm but not at the school.

 Listen again to part of the conversation. Then answer question 4.

4. What does Mr. Greenwood mean when he says, "not a dark suit, like bankers wear—that would be too much."?
   (A) A dark suit would be too warm.
   (B) A dark suit would be too formal.
   (C) A dark suit would be too expensive.
   (D) A dark suit would be too much trouble.

 Listen again to part of the conversation. Then answer question 5.

5. What is David's attitude when he says, "I know I have the skills for both jobs."?
   (A) Embarrassed
   (B) Nervous
   (C) Insecure
   (D) Confident

 Listen again to part of the conversation. Then answer question 6.

6. What can be inferred when Mr. Greenwood says, "Both places should be happy to have you."?
   (A) He has a high opinion of David.
   (B) He fears David will not get either job.
   (C) He thinks David will be happy to get these jobs.
   (D) He suspects David is not ready for his interviews.

ACADEMIC LISTENING

FIRST LISTENING

Listen to an interview about fashion in offices. Take notes using the chart below. Work with another student to combine your notes.

NEW TREND IN FASHION: EMPLOYEES CAN DRESS DOWN AT WORK	
Benefits of This Change	**Drawbacks of This Change**

SECOND LISTENING

Read the questions. Listen to the interview again. Add details to your notes. Then use your notes to answer the questions. Work with a partner and compare your answers.

1. What is the main idea of the interview?
   (**A**) There is a trend toward dressing down in the workplace.
   (**B**) Casual clothes are less expensive than clothes for business.
   (**C**) Employees work longer hours if they are dressed comfortably.
   (**D**) Fashion designers introduce new trends at fashion shows.

2. What is Marco Bellini's profession?
   (**A**) Office worker
   (**B**) News reporter
   (**C**) Event organizer
   (**D**) Fashion designer

3. Why do most employees like the fact that supervisors also dress down?
   (A) People in the workplace dress better than they used to.
   (B) The supervisors can save more money than they used to.
   (C) People in the office feel more equal than they used to.
   (D) Employees work longer hours than they used to.

4. How does the speaker demonstrate that business has improved?
   (A) By comparing casual and business styles
   (B) By explaining how the changes affect the employees
   (C) By describing the difference in the workday
   (D) By discussing how much money the company makes

5. According to Bellini, why do some people complain about this new trend in workplace fashion?
   (A) It is difficult to know who is a worker and who is a supervisor.
   (B) Employees have to work longer hours for the same salary.
   (C) Supervisors want to dress differently from the regular workers.
   (D) Workers have to spend more money buying clothes for work.

 Listen again to part of the interview. Then answer question 6.

6. What does Marco Bellini mean when he says, "My pleasure!"?
   (A) He enjoys his work as a designer.
   (B) He likes the reporter.
   (C) He likes attending fashion shows.
   (D) He is happy to do the interview.

 Listen again to part of the interview. Then answer question 7.

7. What is his tone when Marco Bellini says, "Actually, business has improved."?
   (A) Surprise
   (B) Confusion
   (C) Disappointment
   (D) Doubt

ANALYSIS

It is helpful to know the purpose of a test item. There are three types of questions in the listening section.

1. Basic Comprehension

- main ideas

- details

- the meaning of specific sentences

2. Organization

- the way information is structured
- the way ideas are linked

3. Inference

- ideas are not directly stated
- speaker's intention, purpose, or attitude not explicitly stated

Go back to the listening questions and label each question with 1, 2, or 3. Then work with a partner to see if you agree. Check the Answer Key for the correct answers. Which questions did you get right? Which did you get wrong? What skills do you need to practice?

2 Reading

TRADITIONAL FASHION FOR TODAY'S WOMAN

PRE-READING

Read the title of the passage and the first and last sentences of each paragraph on the next page. Then, with a partner, make predictions about the opinions of young women in Sri Lanka.

YOUNG WOMEN IN SRI LANKA
Reasons they wear saris
Reasons they do not like to wear saris

READING

Read the passage and answer the questions. Then work with a partner and compare your answers. When you disagree, go back to the text to find helpful information.

Traditional Fashion for Today's Woman

by Shanika DaSilva

1   Even though I live in Los Angeles (or "the United States") today, I am very proud of the traditional clothing of my native country, Sri Lanka. I still love the rich cultural traditions there. However, when I go back home to visit, I can see that attitudes toward traditional fashions are changing, especially for women.

2   Traditionally, women in Sri Lanka wear saris. A sari is a long piece of cloth worn like a dress. The sari is wrapped around a woman's waist and then is draped over her shoulder. Under the sari, women wear a matching blouse. Most older women wear saris every day. Younger women, on the other hand, tend to wear dresses or pants rather than saris. Some of them think saris are too old-fashioned. Others simply think that saris are not practical for their everyday life. On hot days they can be very warm, and it can be difficult to walk in them because they are so long. In general, if young women are hanging out with friends, they want to wear something more modern.

3   This is not to say that all young Sri Lankan women want to be more modern. In some cases it depends on their family history. There are two main groups of people in Sri Lanka—the Sinhalese and the Tamils. There are also some other ethnic groups, like the Sri Lankans, who are part European. The women who are part European tend to wear Western clothing because they had relatives who also wore Western clothing. But the women who are Sinhalese or Tamil tend to be more traditional. Therefore, today in Sri Lanka a woman's background can still influence the type of clothing she chooses to wear.

4   Even though fashion in Sri Lanka is heavily influenced by the West, Sri Lankans have not given up their traditional way of dressing. In fact, as Sri Lankans become more aware of fashion, they are becoming more daring and adventurous about wear-

ing saris. Babi Darmasena, a 25-year-old woman, says, "A sari looks nicer and more elegant than a dress." She is happy with the variety of designs now available in stores. Darmasena admits that she feels pressured into wearing a sari on formal occasions, especially weddings. She adds, "My parents would never hear of me wearing a Western-style dress."

5   There seems to be an unwritten rule for women to wear saris for formal events. However, rather than feel limited by this, women take advantage of it. Punya Premadasa, who owns a sari shop in the capital, Colombo, says that there are a number of possible ways to wear a sari. Among the many choices is to drape it over one arm like a shawl instead of draping it over the shoulder. Or, if the blouse is finely decorated, then it does not need to be covered at all by the sari.

6   I am not upset about these changes. The world changes, and we have to expect our traditions to change a little, too. As I see it, the sari is just changing with the times.

1. What is the main idea of the passage?
   (A) Women in Sri Lanka prefer Western styles to traditional styles.
   (B) Women in Sri Lanka wear a sari on formal occasions.
   (C) Attitudes about wearing saris are changing in Sri Lanka.
   (D) Tamil and Sinhalese women in Sri Lanka still usually wear saris.

2. How does the author know that fashion trends are changing in Sri Lanka?
   (A) She sees the changes when she visits her country.
   (B) Her family tells her about the changes.
   (C) She reads about the changes in magazines.
   (D) She hears about the changes on TV.

3. In paragraph 2, why does the author use the phrase *on the other hand* in the sentence, "Younger women, on the other hand, tend to wear dresses or pants rather than saris."?
   (A) To present a similar idea about older women
   (B) To contrast what older and younger women do
   (C) To express doubt about the choices of younger women
   (D) To emphasize her point about older women in Sri Lanka

4. In paragraph 2, younger women prefer Western clothes to saris for all of the following reasons EXCEPT
   (A) Saris are old-fashioned.
   (B) Saris are hot on warm days.
   (C) Saris are difficult to walk in.
   (D) Saris are practical for everyday life.

5. In paragraph 3, why does the author mention the Tamils and the Sinhalese?
   (A) To compare two large groups who have long histories in Sri Lanka
   (B) To give examples of groups who typically wear dresses and pants
   (C) To contrast them with other Sri Lankans who are more Western
   (D) To question recent trends in Sri Lankan fashion

6. In paragraph 4, what can be inferred about Babi Darmasena?
   (A) She prefers to wear Western-style dresses and pants.
   (B) She wishes she were more adventurous with fashion.
   (C) She disagrees with her parents' view of saris.
   (D) She wears a sari on formal occasions.

7. In paragraph 4, what does Babi Darmasena mean when she says, "My parents would never hear of me wearing a Western-style dress."?
   (A) Her parents agree with her opinions about fashion.
   (B) Her parents insist that she wear a sari to formal events.
   (C) Her parents want her to wear dresses to weddings.
   (D) Her parents feel pressure to dress formally at weddings.

8. In paragraph 5, what does the word *this* refer to in the sentence, "However, rather than feel limited by this, women take advantage of it."?
   (A) An everyday occasion
   (B) An unwritten rule
   (C) A traditional sari
   (D) A formal event

9. Look at the four squares ☐ that indicate where the following sentence could be added to the passage. Where would the sentence best fit? Circle the letter that shows the point where you would insert this sentence.

   In this way, women can show a modern sense of style while still following tradition.

   ☐A There seems to be an unwritten rule for women to wear saris at formal events. However, rather than feel limited by this, women take advantage of it. ☐B Punya Premadasa, who owns a sari shop in the capital, Colombo, says that there are a number of possible ways to wear a sari. ☐C Among the many choices is to drape it over one arm like a shawl instead of draping it over the shoulder. Or, if the blouse is finely decorated, then it does not need to be covered by the sari at all. ☐D

10. Which of the following expresses the essential information in this sentence from the passage?

    This is not to say that all young Sri Lankan women want to be more modern.

    (A) Most young Sri Lankan women want to be more modern.
    (B) Some young Sri Lankan women enjoy being more traditional.
    (C) Few young Sri Lankan women follow Western fashion trends.
    (D) Young Sri Lankan women are more fashionable than older women.

11. Read the first sentence of a summary of the passage. Then complete the summary by circling the THREE answer choices that express the most important ideas of the passage. Some sentences do not belong in the summary because they express ideas that are not presented in the passage or are minor ideas in the passage.

Women in Sri Lanka have differing opinions about wearing saris.

(A) A sari is a long piece of cloth worn like a dress by women in parts of Asia.

(B) Many women in Sri Lanka want to dress in more modern or Western clothes.

(C) Most women in Sri Lanka agree that dresses are appropriate for formal occasions.

(D) Women from more traditional groups in Sri Lanka often wear saris.

(E) Some women in Sri Lanka are beginning to wear saris in new ways.

(F) Women in Sri Lanka can find many beautiful designs available in sari shops.

3 Writing

INTEGRATED TASK: READ, LISTEN, WRITE

In this section, you will read a short excerpt and listen to an excerpt on the same topic. Then you will write about the relationship between the two.

READING

Read this passage. Then, with a partner, discuss the answer to the following question.

| What reasons does the author give for *not* having cosmetic surgery?

Beauty? At What Price?

1   Cosmetic surgery, also called plastic surgery, is becoming more popular every year. Almost every day we hear about famous people and even our neighbors changing the shape of their nose, having wrinkles and lines removed from their face, having fat removed with a procedure called liposuction, and many other, medically unnecessary, procedures. People have cosmetic surgery to look better and feel better about themselves. But at what price?

2   Recently there has been more discussion about the risks of plastic surgery. Stories about accidents and surgeries that went terribly wrong are in the news more and more. The fact is: Mistakes happen, patients suffer, and sometimes they even die.

3   One of the most serious problems with cosmetic surgery is related to anesthesia, the drug that stops people from feeling pain during surgery.

(continued on next page)

If patients receive too little or too much anesthesia, they can die or suffer permanent damage.

4   Having plastic surgery at a private clinic is another big risk. Even patients in good physical condition can have complications. Without proper care, patients can have a heart attack or stop breathing. If a patient has serious medical problems during a cosmetic procedure, there might not be enough time to get to a hospital for help. The result can cost patients their lives.

5   Studies have reported other problems with plastic surgery clinics:
  • Encouraging unnecessary surgery
  • Giving inaccurate information
  • Letting unqualified staff members counsel patients
  • Not collecting enough information about the patients' medical history
  • Offering lower prices to patients having more than one procedure
In fact, any surgical procedure should be done at a qualified hospital where patients can get help in case of an emergency.

6   With all of these dangers, it is difficult to understand why people choose to have cosmetic surgery. People should be happy with themselves. We should change our definition of beauty—not our bodies. The personal cost of cosmetic surgery seems too high.

LISTENING

Listen to the excerpt. Then answer the questions.

1. According to the speaker, what have people done in the past to change their appearance? _____

2. According to the speaker, what do people do today to change their appearance? _____

3. What reasons does the speaker give for people to have plastic surgery?

_____

WRITING

Write on the following topic. Follow the steps below to prepare.

❚ **What are the potential risks and benefits of cosmetic surgery?**

Step 1

Review the reading on pages 135 and 136, and your notes from the listening task above. Work with a partner and fill in the chart on the next page.

BENEFITS OF COSMETIC SURGERY	RISKS OF COSMETIC SURGERY

Step 2

Write for 20 minutes. Leave the last 5 minutes to edit your work.

To evaluate a partner's writing, use the Writing Evaluation Form on page 179.

4 Speaking

INDEPENDENT TASK

Speak on the following topic. Follow the steps below to prepare.

Some schools, usually elementary through high school, have dress codes or require students to wear uniforms. (This is not very common in colleges and universities, except at military schools.) What do you think of elementary schools or high schools having a dress code or uniform policy? Include details and examples in your explanation.

Step 1

Work with a partner. Answer the questions.

1. Why do you think some schools require students to wear uniforms?

   _____

2. What do you think students' attitudes are about wearing uniforms?

   _____

3. What do you think parents' attitudes are about uniform policies?

   _____

Step 2

Work with a partner. Complete the chart on the next page. Consider the benefits (pros) and drawbacks (cons) of having a dress code. Consider the point of view of the students, parents, and teachers/administrators.

	PROS	CONS
Students		
Parents		
Teachers / School Administrators		

Step 3

Work with a partner. Take turns practicing a one-minute oral response. Use the information from the questions in Step 1 and the chart in Step 2 to help you.

Step 4

Change partners. Take turns giving a one-minute response to the topic again.

To evaluate your partner's response, use the Speaking Evaluation Form on page 180.

5 Skill Focus

COMPARING AND CONTRASTING

EXAMINATION

Look at the items on the next page from the unit. Work with a partner and answer the questions about the items.

- How many different people, things, or ideas are being discussed in each item?

- What key words or phrases helped you to answer the question in Item 1 or complete the task in Item 2?

- Do the items focus on similarities, differences, or both?

Item 1 (Reading, p. 133)

In paragraph 2, why does the author use the phrase *on the other hand* in the sentence "Younger women, on the other hand, tend to wear dresses or pants rather than saris."?
(A) To present a similar idea about older women
(B) To contrast what older and younger women do
(C) To express doubt about the choices of younger women
(D) To emphasize her point about older women in Sri Lanka

Item 2 (Integrated Task, Writing, p. 136)

Write on the following topic. Follow the steps below to prepare.

1 **What are the potential risks and benefits of cosmetic surgery?**

Tips

To do well on the TOEFL, it is essential to learn how to recognize relationships and see similarities and differences, and to express ideas by **comparing** and **contrasting**. To do this you need to categorize ideas into different parts.

When comparing and contrasting:

- Use block or point-by-point organization.

- Use comparative forms.

- Use transition words.

Organization

There are two ways to categorize or organize your ideas when comparing and contrasting. You do this in writing, but you can also follow these rules when you speak.

In **block organization**, all of the similarities are discussed, and then the differences are discussed separately. For example, if you are writing about attitudes toward saris in Sri Lanka, you can write first about the ways in which older and younger women mostly agree. Then you can write about the difference in attitude between the older and younger women.

In **point-by-point organization**, ideas are discussed one at a time. Again, if you are comparing and contrasting the attitudes of older and younger women, you can first discuss their opinions about wearing saris on formal occasions. Then you can write about their opinions about wearing saris as everyday fashion.

(continued on next page)

Comparative Forms

To compare and contrast, use comparative forms such as *-er* (big → bigger, pretty → prettier) and *more/less than* (confident → more confident, attractive → less attractive).

Transition Words and Phrases

Transitions such as *but, on the other hand, however,* and *unlike* show contrast. *Similarly, and, also,* and *likewise* are words used in comparisons to show similarities.

To answer **Item 1** correctly, you need to notice that the phrase "*on the other hand*" was pointing to a difference between older and younger women's attitudes about wearing saris. Before, the text noted that older women preferred saris. "*On the other hand*" shows a contrasting idea is coming: that younger women wear dresses or pants more often than saris. Therefore, the answer is (B) "To contrast what older and younger women do."

To complete the **Integrated Writing Task**, you need to think about the potential risks and benefits of cosmetic surgery. To do this, you need to compare and contrast the two sides. If you used block organization, you might have put all of the risks in one paragraph and all of the benefits in another paragraph. If you used point-by-point organization, you might have written about one procedure at a time. For example, in one paragraph you might have written about the benefits and risks of liposuction. With both kinds of organization, you needed to use comparative forms (*more/less dangerous than, prettier/less pretty, more expensive than, cheaper than,* etc.). You also should have used transition words or phrases such as *on the other hand* and *similarly.*

PRACTICE

1 *Listen to the two ads. Then follow the steps below.*

Step 1

Take notes using the chart to help you. Share your notes with a partner.

	DR. CLAUDIA CRAWFORD'S TOTAL MAKEOVER CLINIC	SUNNYVALE COMMUNITY HOSPITAL
What services do they offer?		
What other information do you learn about these two places?		

Step 2

Work with a partner. Discuss your answers to the following questions. Then ask your partner one more question.

1. Which place provides more services? Explain your answer.

   _____

2. Which place seems more expensive? Explain your answer.

   _____

3. _____

Step 3

Write a short essay comparing and contrasting the two places. End your essay by stating whether or not you would ever go to either place for cosmetic surgery. Use these questions to help you organize your ideas.

1. In what ways are the clinic and the hospital similar?

   _____

2. In what ways are they different?

   _____

3. If you wanted to get cosmetic surgery, which would you go to? Why?

   _____

2 *Look at the passage you wrote for the Integrated Writing Task on page 136. Check to see if you used block or point-by-point organization, comparative forms, and transition words and phrases. Edit your writing. Then give your passage to your teacher.*

Punishment

| LISTENING |

Campus Conversation
A professor talks to a student about plagiarism and academic dishonesty.

Academic Listening
Panel Discussion: *Expert Opinions on Spanking*

| READING |

Newspaper Article
To Spank or Not to Spank?

| SPEAKING |

Integrated Task: Read, Listen, Speak
Debate the arguments for and against the death penalty.

| WRITING |

Independent Task
Write about the proper punishment for a serious crime, such as murder.

| SKILL FOCUS |

Using Detailed Examples
Using detailed examples shows your ability to illustrate an idea and to support general statements with concrete examples.

| TOEFL® iBT TARGET SKILLS |

- Identify and express main ideas
- Identify and express details
- Make inferences
- Recognize a speaker's attitude
- Categorize opinions
- Analyze arguments
- Express an opinion using detailed examples

 For extra practice of TOEFL iBT skills, go to pages 208–226.

1 Listening

PRE-LISTENING VOCABULARY

Read the sentences. Guess the meaning of the boldfaced words and phrases. Then match each word or phrase with a definition or synonym from the list below. Work with a partner and compare your answers.

_____ 1. When I try to translate **word-for-word** from my language into English, the meaning is never quite right.

_____ 2. According to the **syllabus** for the history course, we have to read three books and write four papers.

_____ 3. A reporter from the *Boston Daily News* was found guilty of **plagiarism**. Instead of doing his research, he just copied from other articles.

_____ 4. The news reported that the **source** of the information was the president, but the president denies saying it.

_____ 5. If you take information from a text, you have to **cite** the title and author of the text in the reference section of your research paper.

_____ 6. After getting out of jail, Robert Johnson was put on **probation** for six months. If his behavior is good, he will not have to go back to jail.

_____ 7. Sheila was **expelled** from the university for cheating on an exam. Now she will have to find another university to go to.

_____ 8. I still **keep in touch** with my favorite high school teacher. I visit him when I go back to my hometown.

_____ 9. Sonia is a very **bright** young woman. Her grades are always very high.

a. intelligent

b. a list of readings and assignments for a course

c. using someone else's words as your own

d. a person, book, or document that gives you information

e. a period of time when your performance is being closely watched

f. asked officially to leave school

g. identify where information comes from

h. exactly the same words

i. stay in contact

> **Culture Note:** In academic writing and speaking, a student should *never* use the ideas of another person or information from a specific source without clearly stating where the ideas or information come from. Failure to cite one's sources is considered "academic dishonesty." Academic papers and speeches should focus on the student's point of view; however, students should include ideas and information from other sources as support for or against their own ideas.

FIRST LISTENING

Read the questions. Listen to the conversation between a student and a professor. Take notes as you listen. Share your notes with a partner. Then use your notes to answer the questions.

1. What does the professor want to speak with the student about?

_____

_____

2. What did the student do wrong?

_____

_____

SECOND LISTENING

Read the questions on the next page. Listen to the conversation again. Add details to your notes. Then use your notes to answer the questions. Work with a partner and compare your answers.

1. What is this conversation mainly about?
   (A) A student complains about plagiarism.
   (B) A student gets caught for plagiarism.
   (C) A student apologizes for plagiarism.
   (D) A student gets expelled for plagiarism.

2. Where did the student find the information on page 3?
   (A) From an Internet search
   (B) From her own ideas and analysis
   (C) From a textbook on the syllabus
   (D) From a paper written for another class

3. What is the next step for this student?
   (A) Graduating from college
   (B) Being expelled from school
   (C) Going on academic probation
   (D) Attending a meeting of the ARB

4. What does the professor expect the student's punishment to be?
   (A) Being expelled from the university
   (B) Attending a meeting of the ARB
   (C) Being put on academic probation
   (D) Rewriting the paper

Listen again to part of the conversation. Then answer question 5.

5. What is the student's attitude when she says, "Expelled."?
   (A) Angry
   (B) Relieved
   (C) Amused
   (D) Surprised

Listen again to part of the conversation. Then answer question 6.

6. Why did the professor say, "All right then. See you in class."?
   (A) To end their meeting
   (B) To make the student feel guilty
   (C) To disagree with the student
   (D) To anger the student

Listen again to part of the conversation. Then answer question 7.

7. What does the professor mean when she says, "You should know better."?
   (A) The student should know plagiarism is wrong.
   (B) The student should apologize for her actions.
   (C) The student should rewrite the paper.
   (D) The student should study harder.

ACADEMIC LISTENING

FIRST LISTENING

 Listen to the discussion. Take notes using this chart to help you. Work with a partner to combine your notes.

EXPERT	OPINION OF SPANKING	REASONS
Donald Sterling		
Phyllis Jones		
Lois Goldin		

SECOND LISTENING

 Read the questions. Listen to the panel discussion again. Add details to your notes. Then use your notes to answer the questions. Work with a partner and compare your answers.

1. What is this passage mainly about?
   (A) Raising young children
   (B) Violence in today's society
   (C) Effects of spanking on adults
   (D) Views on corporal punishment

2. According to Sterling, what impact does spanking have on children?
   (A) It teaches children to stay out of trouble.
   (B) It leads to future abuse and crime.
   (C) It results in more divorce and unhappy families.
   (D) It gives parents more control over their children.

3. According to the passage, which speaker would be most likely to spank his or her child?
   (A) The announcer
   (B) Donald Sterling
   (C) Phyllis Jones
   (D) Lois Goldin

4. Which of the following statements best describes the opinion of Dr. Jones?
(A) Spanking increases the crime rate.
(B) Spanking is a choice for parents to discipline their kids.
(C) Children need discipline, but spanking does not work.
(D) Parents need to spank young children.

5. How do the three speakers present their opinions?
(A) By telling personal stories
(B) By using specific examples
(C) By offering supporting facts
(D) By asking interesting questions

Listen again to part of the discussion. Then answer question 6.

6. What is the speaker's attitude when he says, "And then their children grow up to be violent, and the cycle continues."?
(A) Optimistic
(B) Concerned
(C) Apologetic
(D) Angry

Listen again to part of the discussion. Then answer question 7.

7. Why does Goldin say "But look at the statistics."?
(A) She wants people to see their error in thinking.
(B) She wants to show that spanking makes society less violent.
(C) She wants people to do more research on the topic.
(D) She wants to emphasize that parents spank their kids less than before.

2 Reading

TO SPANK OR NOT TO SPANK?

PRE-READING

Read the title of the passage and the first sentence of each paragraph on the next page. Work with a partner. Answer these questions.

1. What is the writer's main idea? _____

2. What happened to Dale Clover? _____

_____

_____

_____

READING

Read the newspaper report and answer the questions. Then work with a partner and compare your answers. When you disagree, go back to the text to find helpful information.

To Spank or Not to Spank?

1 UP—Minneapolis, MN—A father was recently arrested by the police for spanking his child, starting a debate among the American public about spanking. Is spanking, or other types of corporal punishment, an acceptable form of discipline for children? Or is it a form of child abuse?

2 The case that has everyone talking is the arrest of Dale Clover, a thirty-six-year-old father of three, at a shopping mall in St. Louis, Missouri. He was arrested after an employee at the mall saw him spanking his five-year-old son, Donny, and called the police. The father was arrested for child abuse. Mr. Clover admits that he hit his son but says that it wasn't child abuse. He says it was discipline.

3 Across the country, parents disagree on this issue: What is the difference between loving discipline and child abuse? Some parents like Rhonda Moore see a clear difference between spanking and child abuse. Rhonda Moore believes a little bit of pain is necessary to teach a child what is right and wrong. "It's like burning your hand when you touch a hot stove. Pain is nature's way of teaching us." Moore believes that spanking is done out of love, but child abuse is done out of anger, when the parent loses control. "When I spank my children, I always talk to them before and afterward, and explain why they are being spanked. I explain what they did wrong, and they remember not to do it again." Moore says that her children respect her as a parent and understand that she is spanking them for their own good.

4 In contrast, Taylor Robinson, father of four, feels that parents should never hit their children for any reason. Robinson wants his children to learn right and wrong, but not because they are afraid of being hit. "Spanking teaches children to fear their parents, not respect them. When a parent spanks a child, what the child learns is that problems should be solved with violence." Robinson believes that children learn that it is acceptable for parents to hurt their children. "None of these are lessons that I want to teach my children. I want my children to learn to talk about their problems

(continued on next page)

and solve them without violence, but spanking doesn't teach that."

5   Parents are split about corporal punishment, and doctors also disagree about the issue. Dr. John Oparah thinks our child abuse laws sometimes go too far; that is, they make it difficult for parents to discipline their children. Oparah says that today many children do not respect their parents. "Children need strong, loving discipline. Sometimes spanking is the best way to get a child's attention, to make sure the child listens to the parent." Oparah says that he knows loving parents who have had police officers come to their home because their children have reported being spanked. Oparah believes parents should not be treated like criminals. "As a society, we complain all the time that our young people are getting into more and more trouble, committing crimes—yet when parents try to control their children, they're punished.

Some parents are afraid to discipline their children because their neighbors might call the police."

6   Most doctors, however, say that there are many harmful effects of spanking. Dr. Beverly Lau is opposed to spanking. Lau argues that spanking can lead to more violent behavior in children. She points to research that shows that children who are spanked are more violent when they grow up. "A child may stop misbehaving for the moment, but over time, children who are spanked actually misbehave more than children who are not spanked." Lau adds that research shows that, if you want a peaceful family, parents should not spank their children.

7   The issue of spanking and corporal punishment will continue to be debated among parents and in the courts. In the meantime, if he is convicted of child abuse, Dale Clover could get up to five years in prison.

1. What is the main idea of this passage?
   (A) Doctors believe that spanking is harmful to children.
   (B) Parents and doctors disagree about the benefits of spanking children.
   (C) Spanking teaches children the difference between right and wrong.
   (D) Child abuse laws make it difficult for parents to discipline their kids.

2. In paragraph 2, who called the police in the Dale Clover case?
   (A) His five-year-old son
   (B) A mall employee
   (C) Dale Clover himself
   (D) Clover's wife

3. In paragraph 3, why does Rhonda Moore give the example of touching a hot stove?
   (A) To argue that parents need to control their children
   (B) To demonstrate that spanking is wrong
   (C) To question the laws about child abuse
   (D) To show the benefits of spanking

4. Why does the author include Rhonda Moore and Taylor Robinson in this article?
   (A) To give examples of parents who spank their children
   (B) To compare the views of a parent and a doctor
   (C) To contrast the opinions of two parents
   (D) To argue against spanking one's children

5. In paragraph 4, all of the following are lessons Taylor Robinson believes children learn from spanking EXCEPT
   (A) children should fear their parents
   (B) problems can be resolved with violence
   (C) it is acceptable for parents to hurt their kids
   (D) people should talk about problems, without violence

6. In paragraph 5, in the sentence "Dr. John Oparah thinks our child abuse laws sometimes go too far," the phrase *go too far* is closest in meaning to
   (A) are too hard on children
   (B) take control away from parents
   (C) are not strong enough to stop abuse
   (D) teach children respect for their parents

7. In paragraph 6, why does the author use the word *however* in the sentence, "Most doctors, however, say that there are many harmful effects of spanking."?
   (A) To contrast Oparah's view from other doctors'
   (B) To question the views of most doctors
   (C) To support Oparah's opinions
   (D) To introduce a similar opinion

8. In paragraph 6, what is the author's primary purpose?
   (A) To question Beverly Lau's opinions about spanking
   (B) To explain why parents should spank their kids
   (C) To compare two different views on spanking
   (D) To show the harmful effects of spanking

9. In paragraph 7, what can be inferred about Dale Clover's case?
   (A) Dale Clover is guilty of child abuse.
   (B) Dale Clover's case has not ended yet.
   (C) It is likely that Clover will be convicted.
   (D) Clover might be in jail longer than five years.

10. Why does the author use the example of Dale Clover?
(A) To support the idea that spanking makes a family stronger
(B) To support the idea that spanking is a controversial subject
(C) To support the idea that spanking is necessary for disciplining children
(D) To support the idea that spanking teaches children to know right from wrong

11. Look at the four squares ☐ that indicate where the following sentence could be added to the passage. Where would the sentence best fit? Circle the letter that shows the point where you would insert this sentence.

> He added that he wanted to teach his son that it was wrong to take candy from a store without paying, which is what the boy had done.

The case that has everyone talking is the arrest of Dale Clover, a thirty-six-year-old father of three, at a shopping mall in St. Louis, Missouri. [A] He was arrested after an employee at the mall saw him spanking his five-year-old son, Donny, and called the police. [B] The father was arrested for child abuse. [C] Mr. Clover admits that he hit his son but says that it wasn't child abuse. He says it was discipline. [D]

12. Which of the following expresses the essential information in this sentence from the article?

> "A child may stop misbehaving for the moment, but over time, children who are spanked actually misbehave more than children who are not spanked."

(A) If you want children to learn the difference between right and wrong, spanking offers long-term results.
(B) Children who are spanked actually misbehave more because they want the attention from their parents.
(C) Spanking does not improve children's behavior in the long run; in fact, they behave badly more often than other children.
(D) Children who are spanked eventually begin to behave better than children who are not spanked.

13. Select the appropriate phrases from the answer choices and match them to the two arguments on the next page: in favor of or against spanking. TWO of the choices will NOT be used.
(A) Spanking teaches the difference between right and wrong.
(B) Child abuse is when a parent hits a child because of anger.
(C) Spanking teaches fear rather than respect.
(D) Problems should be solved without violence.
(E) Many children don't respect their parents.
(F) Spanking makes children listen.
(G) Spanking leads to more violent behavior.
(H) Children who are spanked, spank their own kids later in life.
(I) Other forms of discipline are more effective.
(J) Spanking can be effective when done in a loving home.

ARGUMENTS IN FAVOR OF SPANKING	ARGUMENTS AGAINST SPANKING

ANALYSIS

It is helpful to know the purpose of a test item. There are four types of questions in the reading section.

1. Basic Comprehension

- main ideas
- details
- the meaning of specific sentences

2. Organization

- the way information is structured in the text
- the way ideas are linked between sentences or between paragraphs

3. Inference

- ideas are not directly stated in the text
- author's intention, purpose, or attitude not explicitly stated in the text

4. Vocabulary and Reference

- the meaning of words
- the meaning of reference words such as *his, them, this,* or *none*

Go back to the reading questions and label each question with 1, 2, 3, or 4. Then work with a partner to see if you agree. Check the Answer Key for the correct answers. Which questions did you get right? Which did you get wrong? What skills do you need to practice?

3 Speaking

INTEGRATED TASK: READ, LISTEN, SPEAK

In this section, you will read a short excerpt and listen to an excerpt on the same topic. Then you will speak about the relationship between the two.

READING

Read the excerpt. Then, with a partner, discuss the answer to the following question.

▌ **Why does the author believe the death penalty is wrong?**

THE DEATH PENALTY IS *Dead* WRONG

1   If you look at the statistics, you will see that the United States is using the death penalty less and less as a punishment for serious crimes. America should celebrate this fact because every execution only means the loss of *another* human life.

2   We need to stop executing criminals because it is just another type of murder. What message are we sending to our children? We teach them that one human being must not kill another, and then we use execution as a form of punishment. It just doesn't make sense.

Financially it doesn't make sense either. Various sources report that it costs about $1.5 million more to execute a person than it does to keep him or her in prison for 40 years.

3   Granted, there are dangerous people in our society who need to be taken off the streets for our safety—if not their own safety. But killing them is not the answer. We need to be more creative and caring when trying to solve our problems. We need to try to stop crime before it happens through proper education, social support, and heath care.

4   For people who still believe that "life in prison" is not enough punishment for dangerous criminals, consider this: From 1973 to 1994, 117 people were released from "death row," where prisoners wait to be executed. New methods of investigating crimes, especially DNA testing, are providing new evidence. This evidence frees or exonerates[1] men and women who had been given death sentences by the courts.

[1] *exonerate:* officially say that someone who was blamed for a crime is not guilty

5   Clearly our system is a human one. But humans make mistakes. If we execute someone—and later find out that the person was not guilty—we are in a tragic situation. Isn't this another kind of murder?

Death Penalty Statistics*	1999	2003	2004
Executions	98	65	59
People on Death Row (as of Oct. 1)	3625	3504	3471
Death Sentences	252	144	130**
Percentage of Executions by Area:			
South:	75%	89%	85%
Midwest:	12%	11%	12%
West:	12%	0%	3%
Northeast:	0%	0%	0%

Other Death Penalty Statistics	Since 1973
Total Executions:	944
Exonerated or Freed from Death Row:	117

* As of December 15, 2004 with no more executions scheduled for the year
** Based on ¾ of the year
Source: *The Death Penalty in 2004: Year End Report*, Death Penalty Information Center, December 2004

LISTENING

Listen to the excerpt. Use the outline to take notes as you listen. The main idea has been done for you.

Main Idea: _Execution is proper punishment for murderers._

Detailed example for support: _____

Who was involved? _____

What happened? _____

Why did the speaker give this example? _____

SPEAKING

Debate the following topic. Follow the steps on the next page to prepare.

❙ **What are the arguments for and against the death penalty?**

Step 1

Work in a group of three students. Each student takes one role:

Student A will argue in favor of the death penalty.

Student B will argue against the death penalty.

Student C will act as moderator.

Step 2

Students A and B work individually to prepare a one-minute response to the question. Use the chart to help you organize your ideas.

FOR	AGAINST

Step 3

- Students A and B take turns presenting a one-minute oral argument.
- Student C presents a one-minute summary of each of the arguments, chooses the most convincing argument, and gives an explanation.

> To evaluate your partner's response, use the Speaking Evaluation Form on page 180.

4 Writing

INDEPENDENT TASK

Write on the following topic. Follow the steps on the next page to prepare.

If a person is convicted of a serious crime such as murder, how do you think the person should be punished?

Step 1

- Review your notes from the reading, listening, and speaking tasks on pages 154–156.

- Work in groups of three or four students. Brainstorm other forms of punishment besides the death penalty. Take notes using the chart to help you organize your ideas.

GROUP MEMBERS	FORMS OF PUNISHMENT	OPINION

Step 2

Write for 20 minutes. Leave the last 5 minutes to edit your work.

> To evaluate a partner's writing, use the Writing Evaluation Form on page 179.

5 Skill Focus

USING DETAILED EXAMPLES

EXAMINATION

Look at the following items from the unit. Work with a partner and answer the questions below each item.

Item 1 (Reading, p. 151)

In paragraph 3, why does Rhonda Moore give the example of touching a hot stove?
(A) To argue that parents need to control their children
(B) To demonstrate that spanking is violent
(C) To question the laws about child abuse
(D) To show the benefits of spanking

- Go back to the Reading on page 149 and reread paragraph 3. What is the main point of the paragraph? How does the example of touching a hot stove explain the main point?

Item 2 (Reading, p. 152)

Why does the author use the example of Dale Clover?
(A) To support the idea that spanking makes a family stronger.
(B) To support the idea that spanking is a controversial subject
(C) To support the idea that spanking is necessary for disciplining children
(D) To support the idea that spanking teaches children to know right from wrong

- What is the main point of the article? How does the example of Dale Clover support the main point?

Item 3 (Integrated Task, Listening, p. 155)

Listen to the excerpt. Use the outline to take notes as you listen. The main idea has been done for you.

Main Idea: _Execution is proper punishment for murderers._

Detailed example for support: _____

Who was involved? _____

What happened? _____

Why did the speaker give this example? _____

- What is the main point of the listening? What examples and details does the speaker use to support his main idea? What technique does the speaker use to convey his opinion?

Tips

To do well on the TOEFL, it is important to learn how to identify and use **detailed examples**. Detailed examples help you understand a speaker's or writer's ideas and opinions. In academic speaking and writing, you need to be able to provide concrete examples and specific information to illustrate your ideas. Support your general statements with detailed examples about time, place, persons, and events.

In Listening and Reading

- Pay attention to a speaker's or writer's examples.

- Ask yourself, "What are his or her main points? What examples help explain the points?"

In Speaking and Writing

- Choose a detailed example that will help support your idea. Detailed examples can be a short story or a description.

- Include only information that helps to support your idea. Don't include extra, unimportant information. Extra information might also confuse your listener or reader. Only use details in your example that *directly* support your ideas.

- Be sure the connection between your idea and your detailed example is clear. Sometime you may need to explain the connection, especially if your detailed example is long. Use signal words to show that you are introducing an example: *for example, for instance, such as, including.*

To answer **Item 1** correctly, you should notice the parent's main point is that children can learn important lessons from painful experiences. She gives the example of the hot stove to support her idea. She connects her example to her opinion when she says "Pain is nature's way of teaching us." She does not give extra information. Therefore, the best choice is (D), "To show the benefits of spanking."

To answer **Item 2** correctly you should notice that the author uses Dale Clover's story as a detailed example to support his main idea or purpose. The writer does not give his own opinion about spanking. Choices (A), (C), and (D) are not correct. (A) is not stated in the passage. (C) and (D) express opinions in the reading, but they are not the author's opinions. At the end of the article, the author returns to Dale Clover's story to remind the reader that this controversy continues. Therefore, (B), "To support the idea that spanking is a controversial subject" is the best choice.

Item 3 asks you to outline the speaker's detailed examples.

Main Idea: *Execution is proper punishment for murderers.*

Detailed example for support: *The story of Tammy Thompson and Gloria Jean Gibson*

Who was involved? *Tammy Thompson and Gloria Jean Gibson.*

What happened? *Gibson shot and killed Thompson when they were arguing over some money.*

Why did the speaker give this example? *To show that it is not fair for a murderer to continue living.*

To support his opinion, the speaker gives detailed examples and uses the technique of telling a story about the murder of Tammy Thompson. He further describes the conflict between two women.

PRACTICE

1 *Work with a partner to debate the following topic. Follow the steps below to prepare.*

| **All students cheat on exams. Do you agree or disagree?**

Step 1

Work with a partner. Each student takes one role:

Student A will agree with the statement.

Student B will disagree with the statement.

Step 2

Students A and B brainstorm arguments. Use the chart to help you organize your ideas.

AGREE	DISAGREE

Step 3

Students work individually. Use the outline to help you organize your ideas.

Main Idea: _____

Detailed example for support: _____

Step 4

Students take turns presenting a one-minute oral argument. Be sure to include your main point and at least one detailed example.

> To evaluate your partner's response, use the Speaking Evaluation Form on page 180.

2 *Write your response to the statement in Exercise 1. Choose the opposite argument. For example, if you agreed with the statement in Exercise 1, now disagree with it*

Write for 20 minutes. Leave the last 5 minutes to edit your work. Begin with your main idea. Then give a detailed example for support.

> To evaluate a partner's writing, use the Writing Evaluation Form on page 179.

Marriage

| LISTENING |

Campus Conversation
A student talks to a librarian about researching a report on marriage.

Academic Listening
Lecture: *Finding a Spouse*

| READING |

Letter to the Editor
What's Wrong with Tradition?

| WRITING |

Integrated Task: Read, Listen, Write
Summarize the points made in the reading excerpt about polygamy, society, and religion, giving support with examples from the listening excerpt about Mormons and marriage.

| SPEAKING |

Independent Task
Compare and contrast your views on marriage with the views of a partner. Highlight some of the similarities and differences.

| SKILL FOCUS |

Identifying and Using Cohesive Devices
Cohesive devices are words and phrases that connect parts of a written or spoken text and signal how ideas are related and organized.

| TOEFL® iBT TARGET SKILLS |

- Identify and express main ideas
- Identify and express details
- Make inferences
- Categorize and compare information
- Analyze opinions
- Express an opinion

 For extra practice of TOEFL iBT skills, go to pages 208–226.

1 Listening

CAMPUS CONVERSATION

PRE-LISTENING VOCABULARY

Read the sentences. Guess the meaning of the boldfaced words and phrases. Then match each word or phrase with a synonym or definition from the list below. Work with a partner and compare your answers.

_____ 1. I found a lot of the information for my political science paper on the library **databases**. They are a much more reliable source of information than the Internet is.

_____ 2. Prash decided to write his research paper about Indian families. After speaking with his professor, he decided to **narrow** his topic to the role of fathers in Indian families.

_____ 3. The topic "Indian Families" is too **broad** for a short five-page paper.

_____ 4. For my sociology research, I want to do a **cross-cultural** study of how children are educated in Korea and Mexico.

_____ 5. That newspaper article about the divorce rate really **got me thinking** about how challenging it is to have a happy marriage.

_____ 6. I found an interesting quotation by Mao Tse-Tung, so I'm going to try to **incorporate** it into my paper about China in the 1960s.

_____ 7. I like many things about this university, **in particular**, its libraries.

_____ 8. Whenever you do an Internet search, you need to enter specific **search criteria** so that you will find what you are looking for.

_____ 9. Last year my grade point average was a 2.0. But my **current** GPA is a 3.5. I'm doing a lot better in all of my classes.

_____ 10. At first, my grandmother thought using e-mail would be too difficult for her, but after a few days, she **got the hang of it**.

_____ 11. OK, I have my books, my laptop, and my class notes. I'm **all set** to go to the library.

a. caused me to think

b. include or contain

c. learned how to do something

d. ready to do something

e. limit, make more specific

f. an organized collection of information that can be searched by computer

g. related to now, these days

h. specifically

i. comparing two or more different cultures

j. words and phrases used to do research by computer

k. wide, large

Culture Note: Students should seek help with research assignments from librarians. They can lead students to appropriate Internet sites, databases, and other sources. This can save time and frustration.

FIRST LISTENING

Read the questions. Listen to the conversation between a student and a librarian. Take notes as you listen. Share your notes with a partner. Then use your notes to answer the questions.

1. Why does the student go to the library?

_____

_____

2. How does the librarian help the student?

_____

_____

SECOND LISTENING

 Read the questions. Listen to the conversation again. Add details to your notes. Then use your notes to answer the questions. Work with a partner and compare your answers.

1. What is this conversation mainly about?
   (A) How to write a research paper
   (B) How to find a spouse
   (C) How to find information in a library
   (D) How to plan a wedding

2. What was wrong with the student's first topic?
   (A) It was too boring.
   (B) It was too narrow.
   (C) It was too childish.
   (D) It was too large.

3. What topic is the student going to research?
   (A) Why people decide to get married
   (B) How to plan a wedding
   (C) Marriage between cultures
   (D) Marriage customs in Brazil

 Listen again to part of the conversation. Then answer question 4.

4. What is the student's attitude when she says, "Um—Marriage."?
   (A) Amused
   (B) Excited
   (C) Confused
   (D) Disappointed

 Listen again to part of the conversation. Then answer question 5.

5. What is the student's attitude when she says, "Still about 130,000!"?
   (A) Excited
   (B) Angry
   (C) Frustrated
   (D) Relieved

ACADEMIC LISTENING

FIRST LISTENING

 Listen to the lecture. Take notes using the chart below. Work with a partner to combine your notes.

MARRIAGE CUSTOMS	
In China in the first half of the 1900s	**In Traditional Hopi Culture**

SECOND LISTENING

 Read the questions. Listen to the lecture again. Add details to your notes. Then use your notes to answer the questions. Work with a partner and compare your answers.

1. What is this passage mainly about?
   (A) Finding a marriage partner
   (B) Chinese marriage traditions
   (C) Having babies
   (D) Hopi marriage customs

2. According to the Chinese culture of the first half of the 1900s, who chooses a marriage partner?
   (A) The individual
   (B) The parents
   (C) The matchmaker
   (D) The society

3. According to the speaker, what is a *kiva*?
   (A) A native people
   (B) A home for boys
   (C) A secret visit
   (D) An American custom

Listen again to part of the conversation. Then answer question 4.

4. Why does the speaker use the expression *in contrast*?
   (A) To introduce a question
   (B) To conclude his talk
   (C) To add an opposite idea
   (D) To add a similar point

5. How does the professor present his ideas?
   (A) By comparing and contrasting traditions
   (B) By arguing one view over another
   (C) By telling a story
   (D) By presenting opinions

Listen again to part of the conversation. Then answer question 6.

6. What can be inferred from this statement?
   (A) Most girls have more than one child.
   (B) Boys only visit one girl in their village.
   (C) The boys made secret visits for a few months.
   (D) After the girl got pregnant, the couple got married.

ANALYSIS

It is helpful to know the purpose of a test item. There are three types of questions in the listening section.

1. Basic Comprehension

- main ideas
- details
- the meaning of specific sentences

2. Organization

- the way information is structured
- the way ideas are linked

3. Inference

- ideas are not directly stated
- speaker's intention, purpose, or attitude not explicitly stated

Go back to the listening questions and label each question with 1, 2, or 3. Then work with a partner to see if you agree. Check the Answer Key for the correct answers. Which questions did you get right? Which did you get wrong? What skills do you need to practice?

2 Reading

WHAT'S WRONG WITH TRADITION?

PRE-READING

Read the title and skim the first and last line of each paragraph. Work with a partner and predict the answers to the following questions.

1. What is the man writing about? _____

2. How are his opinions different from those of his classmates?

- His opinion: _____

- His classmates' opinion: _____

READING

Read the passage and answer the questions. Then work with a partner and compare your answers. When you disagree, go back to the text to find helpful information.

What's Wrong with Tradition?

Dear Editor:

1   I am a 27-year-old student from Vietnam. My purpose in coming here is to get a business degree. I am very grateful to have the chance to get an education in a country famous for business leadership. However, I am tired of the questions that people ask me about my personal life. American students seem to think that their way of dating, that is, dating romantically before marriage, is the only way but I disagree.

2   My parents are a perfect example of my point. They have been married for thirty-five years. Their marriage has all the characteristics of a happy one: deep friendship, love, and trust. They have six children, and I am the second son. Because of their help, I am able to study in the United States. They have always worked hard to raise their children in the right way. When I finish my degree, I will go back to my country and help them.

(continued on next page)

3   American people are always surprised when I tell them that my parents met for the first time on their wedding day. In addition, Americans can't believe that such a marriage could be happy, but I have seen my parents with my own eyes. They love each other faithfully, and they are proud of the children that their marriage has produced. They learned to love each other slowly, as time passed. However, I believe they share a true and everlasting love.

4   When people ask, "Are you looking for a girlfriend?" I tell them no. For me, studying comes first. When I go back to my country and start working, my parents will help me find a good wife. She will be someone with a good family background, someone I can trust. Good apples come from good trees. If I marry a good apple, we can make a beautiful, growing tree together. No divorce. No AIDS. No broken heart.

5   I want a peaceful, happy life just like my parents have. Why can't Americans understand this?

Tran (Paul) Nguyen

1. What is the main idea of Mr. Nguyen's letter to the editor?
 (A) He has trouble finding someone to date.
 (B) His parents have a very happy marriage.
 (C) He prefers the American dating custom.
 (D) He likes Vietnam's tradition of arranged marriage.

2. In paragraph 1, what does the word *here* refer to in the sentence, "My purpose in coming here is to get a business degree."?
 (A) The newspaper
 (B) The United States
 (C) Vietnam
 (D) A wedding

3. How does the writer feel when Americans ask him about his personal life?
 (A) He is annoyed.
 (B) He is happy.
 (C) He is confused.
 (D) He is disappointed.

4. In paragraph 1, why does the writer use the word *but* in the sentence, "American students seem to think that their way of dating, that is, dating romantically before marriage, is the only way, but, I disagree."?
 (A) To present a contrasting idea
 (B) To present a similar idea
 (C) To present a conclusion
 (D) To add more information

5. In paragraph 2, the writer gives all of the following as characteristics of a happy marriage EXCEPT
   (**A**) friendship
   (**B**) love
   (**C**) trust
   (**D**) education

6. In paragraph 3, why does the writer use the expression *in addition* in the sentence, "In addition, Americans can't believe that such a marriage could be happy, but I have seen my parents with my own eyes."?
   (**A**) To express contrast
   (**B**) To add information
   (**C**) To offer an example
   (**D**) To give a summary

7. In paragraph 4, what does Mr. Nguyen mean by, "Good apples come from good trees."?
   (**A**) The fruit in Vietnam is very good.
   (**B**) Romantic dating leads to good marriages.
   (**C**) Good families produce good children.
   (**D**) It is important to take care of good fruit trees.

8. In paragraph 4, what is the writer implying when he comments, "No divorce. No AIDS. No broken heart."?
   (**A**) People who choose their partners may have these problems.
   (**B**) People who get married may have these problems.
   (**C**) People who are single may have these problems.
   (**D**) People who have arranged marriages may have these problems.

9. What is the writer's purpose in writing this letter?
   (**A**) To question American business practices
   (**B**) To argue for arranged marriages
   (**C**) To explain the idea of romantic dating
   (**D**) To discuss marriage traditions around the world

10. Look at the four squares ☐ that indicate where the following sentence could be added to the passage. Where would the sentence best fit? Circle the letter that shows the point where you would insert this sentence.

    I admit that it was probably very challenging for them to live together at first.

    American people are always surprised when I tell them that my parents met for the first time on their wedding day. **A** In addition, Americans can't believe that such a marriage could be happy, but I have seen my parents with my own eyes. **B** They love each other faithfully, and they are proud of the children that their marriage has produced. **C** They learned to love each other slowly, as time passed. **D** However, I believe they share a true and everlasting love.

11. Which of the following expresses the essential information in this sentence from the passage?

> Americans can't believe that such a marriage could be happy, but I have seen my parents with my own eyes.

(A) People in the U.S. think arranged marriages are unhappy, and I have seen this in my parents' marriage.

(B) Unlike what Americans think, my parents' marriage shows that arranged marriages can work.

(C) People in the U.S. doubt that arranged marriages can be happy, but my parents disagree.

(D) My parents look like they have a happy marriage; however, as Americans say, they are not really happy.

12. Select the appropriate phrases from the answer choices and match them to the views described in the passage. TWO of the choices will NOT be used.

(A) Arranged marriage is part of the traditional culture.

(B) Couples may face serious problems like divorce.

(C) Individuals look for their own partners.

(D) Nguyen's parents love each other faithfully.

(E) Parents find a spouse for their children.

(F) People are often surprised to hear about arranged marriages.

(G) The couple meets on their wedding day.

(H) They believe in romantic dating.

(I) Vietnamese people disagree about arranged marriage.

MARRIAGE IN VIETNAM	MARRIAGE IN THE UNITED STATES

3 Writing

INTEGRATED TASK: READ, LISTEN, WRITE

In this section, you will read a short excerpt and listen to an excerpt on the same topic. Then you will write about the relationship between the two.

READING

Read the excerpt. Then, with a partner, discuss the answers to the following questions.

1. What is polygamy? _____

2. How is polygamy viewed by each of the following religions?

- Christianity: _____
- Judaism: _____
- Islam: _____

Polygamy, Society, and Religion

1   Many people around the world believe that marriage is a union between one man and one woman. In most societies, polygamy—when a man has more than one wife at one time—is not practiced. In fact, it is illegal in most societies, including the United States.

2   Christianity, Judaism, and Islam, three of the world's major religions, do not encourage polygamy. In fact, Christianity and Judaism strictly prohibit polygamy. It is not acceptable according to their religious teachings.

3   Islam, on the other hand, does not *encourage* polygamy, but it does not completely *prohibit* it either. In some countries where the government is run according to Islamic law, polygamy is sometimes possible. Islam recognizes that there are cases in life when polygamy might be the best choice. For example, if a man dies, leaving his wife and children alone, another man who is married might marry this woman in order to give her the social support of a husband and family.

LISTENING

Listen to the excerpt. Use the chart to take notes as you listen.

MORMONS AND MARRIAGE	
In the Past	**Today**

WRITING

Write on the following topic. Follow the steps below to prepare.

Summarize the points made in the reading, giving support with examples from the listening.

Step 1

Work with a partner. Skim the reading and your notes from the reading and the listening tasks on pages 171–172. Answer the following questions to help you organize your ideas.

1. What are the Christian, Jewish, and Islamic views of polygamy?

_____

2. What is the view of polygamy in the United States?

_____

3. What was the Mormon view of polygamy in the past?

_____

4. What is the Mormon view of polygamy today?

_____

Step 2

Write for 20 minutes. Leave the last 5 minutes to edit your work.

To evaluate a partner's writing, use the Writing Evaluation Form on page 179.

4 Speaking

INDEPENDENT TASK

Speak on the following topic. Follow the steps below to prepare.

Compare and contrast your views on marriage with the views of a partner. Highlight some of the similarities and differences.

Step 1

- Think about your views on marriage. Fill in the chart under the heading *Your Views of Marriage*.

- Ask your partner the questions in the chart. Complete the chart with his/her answers.

QUESTIONS	YOUR VIEWS OF MARRIAGE	YOUR PARTNER'S VIEWS OF MARRIAGE
Should all people get married? Why or why not?		
What kinds of things should people look for in a marriage partner?		
When should a person get married? (At what age or point in life?)		
Why should two people get married? Explain briefly.		
Your own question: _____ _____ _____		

Step 2

Work with a partner. Take turns practicing a one-minute oral response. Use the information in your chart to help you.

Step 3

Change partners. Take turns giving a one-minute response to the topic again.

To evaluate your partner's response, use the Speaking Evaluation Form on page 180.

5 Skill Focus

IDENTIFYING AND USING COHESIVE DEVICES

EXAMINATION

Look at the following items from the unit. Work with a partner and answer this question about the items.

- What words or phrases in the text helped you to answer these questions?

Item 1 (Academic Listening, p. 166)

Why does the speaker use the expression *in contrast*?
(A) To introduce a question
(B) To conclude his talk
(C) To add an opposite idea
(D) To add a similar point

Item 2 (Reading, p. 169)

In paragraph 3, why does the writer use the expression *in addition* in the sentence, "In addition, Americans can't believe that such a marriage could be happy, but I have seen my parents with my own eyes."?
(A) To express contrast
(B) To add information
(C) To offer an example
(D) To give a summary

Item 3 (Independent Task, Speaking, p. 173)

Speak on the following topic. Follow the steps below to prepare.

Compare and contrast your views on marriage with the views of a partner. Highlight some of the similarities and differences.

Tips

To do well on the TOEFL, it is important to learn how to identify and use **cohesive devices.**

Cohesive devices are words and phrases that connect ideas. Some cohesive devices signal or show the steps in a process (*first*, *second*, and *next*), cause and effect (*because* and *since*), or examples (*for example*). Below are some other common cohesive devices. They signal the addition of a new idea, contrast, or an expected result.

- **To add a new idea, use:**
  and, in addition, furthermore, similar to (something or someone), similarly

- **To show contrast, use:**
  but, in contrast, however, nevertheless

- **To present an expected result, use:**
  as a result, therefore

Unit 8 presented other cohesive devices, called transition expressions, used to express comparison and contrast. Review these words and expressions on page 140.

To answer **Item 1** correctly, you should notice that *in contrast* connects two different ideas: traditions in which *parents* choose the marriage partner and traditions in which the *children* choose. The expression *in contrast* introduces this change in idea. Therefore, the best choice is (C) "To add an opposite idea."

To answer **Item 2** correctly, again, you need to notice the relationship between the ideas before and after the phrase *in addition*. The writer states, "American people are always surprised when I tell them that my parents met for the first time on their wedding day." Then he adds more, related information with the expression *in addition*: "In addition, Americans can't believe that such a marriage could be happy, but I have seen my parents with my own eyes." Therefore, the best choice is (B) "To add information."

To prepare for **Item 3**, you needed to complete a chart with your views of marriage and your partner's views. Then you needed to speak for one minute comparing and contrasting your views. In comparing and contrasting, you should have used cohesive devices that signaled contrast such as *but, in contrast, however,* and *nevertheless*.

PRACTICE

1 *Read the passages. Circle the word or phrase in each pair that best completes the sentences. Then work with a partner. Discuss why you chose your answers. Use the Tips in the previous section to help you.*

Passage 1

The Hopi allowed boys to go out alone at night and secretly visit young girls. After a few months, most girls became pregnant. The Hopi culture is not the only one that allowed young people to visit each other at night. Some Bavarian people of southern Germany once had a "windowing" custom that took place when young women left their windows open at night so that young men could enter their bedrooms. (**1. In contrast to / Similar to**) the Hopi tradition, when a woman became pregnant, the couple usually got married. (**2. However / Similarly**), women who did not get pregnant after windowing were often unable to find a husband. This was because fertility was a very important requirement for women in this culture, (**3. and / but**) the windowing custom allowed them to prove their fertility to others in the community. Some people are surprised when they learn of this unique custom because they expect the people of southern Germany to follow the rules of the Catholic religion, which teach that it is wrong for unmarried women to become pregnant. (**4. As a result / Nevertheless**), the windowing custom is only one example of the surprising marriage customs that are found around the world, even among people whose religious beliefs require more common marriage practices.

Passage 2

One view of marriage that surprises most of us today was held by John Noyes, a religious man who started the Oneida Community in the state of New York in 1831. He began it as an experiment of a different way of living. Noyes decided that group marriage was the best way for men and women to live together. In this form of marriage, men and women changed partners frequently. They were expected to love all members of the community equally. (**1. In addition / However**), children belonged to all members of the community, (**2. and / but**) all the adults worked hard to support themselves and shared everything they had. Members of the Oneida Community lived this lifestyle for many years without any serious problems; (**3. however / therefore**), John Noyes eventually left the community in 1876. (**4. Nevertheless / As a result**), without his leadership, members of the community quickly returned to the traditional marriage of one woman and one man.

2 *Speak on ONE of the following topics. Follow the steps below to prepare.*

1. Would you want to have an arranged marriage?

2. Would you want to arrange a marriage for your child?

Step 1

Use this outline to organize your ideas. When you express your opinion, use some of the words and phrases in the Tips on page 175 to add cohesive structure.

Main Idea: _____

_____

_____

Choose to use one of the following:

- A contrasting idea: _____
- An additional idea: _____
- A comparison: _____
- A result: _____

Step 2

Work with a partner. Take turns practicing a one-minute oral response. Use the information in your outline to help you. As you speak, try to use two or three cohesive devices to connect your ideas.

Step 3

Change partners. Take turns giving a one-minute response to the topic again.

3 *Write a paragraph as a response to your topic in Exercise 2. Use cohesive devices to connect your ideas. Give your paragraph to your teacher.*

Evaluation Forms for Integrated and Independent Tasks

Exchange papers with a partner. Evaluate each other's writing using the grid below. Discuss strengths and weaknesses. Use the evaluation to revise and edit your writing. Write a second draft and give it to your teacher.

4 = always   **3** = most of the time   **2** = some of the time   **1** = rarely or never

UNIT	1	2	3	4	5	6	7	8	9	10
CONTENT										
The response . . .										
addresses the topic.										
is organized.										
shows connections between ideas.										
LANGUAGE										
The writing incorporates . . .										
effective vocabulary.										
correct grammar.										
correct spelling and punctuation.										
TOTAL:										

SPEAKING

As you and your partner respond to the topic, evaluate each other's speaking using the grid below. Discuss strengths and weaknesses. Use the evaluation to improve your presentation.

4 = always   **3** = most of the time   **2** = some of the time   **1** = rarely or never

UNIT	1	2	3	4	5	6	7	8	9	10
CONTENT										
The response . . .										
addresses the topic.										
covers the main points.										
contains good examples.										
has ideas that connect well.										
LANGUAGE										
The response . . .										
is free of hesitations.										
exhibits clear pronunciation.										
incorporates effective vocabulary.										
incorporates correct grammar.										
TOTAL:										

Audioscript

Unit 1: Advertising

CAMPUS CONVERSATION

PAGE 3, FIRST LISTENING

Ad 1

Student: Hi, Professor Burton. I was wondering if I could talk to you for a minute—I wanted to bring up a point you made in yesterday's lecture.

Professor: Sure, Eric. I do actually have to run in a minute though—I have an appointment at 10:30. But come in. Have a seat.

S: OK—thanks, Well, I'll make it quick. You know—how you were talking about infomercials? Well, I know that infomercials try to be more informative than other regular commercials, and you mentioned that the information is true, but can we really trust everything they say?

P: Well, as far as I know, companies can't make false claims about their products or they could be held liable for false advertising and then of course get sued.

S: Well, that may be so, but in my experience, the product isn't always what it appears to be. Like, just last semester, my friend bought an ab machine after hearing about it on TV. The claim was that after using it for only 10 minutes a day for 6 weeks, you could lose two inches of fat!

P: So, your friend didn't get any results?

S: Well, she said she felt a little different, but come on, the company exaggerated the claim. It would take a lot more exercise than using this ab machine for 10 minutes a day to lose two inches of fat. Do you think she can return it and get her money back?

P: Remember what we discussed in class, "caveat emptor"—let the buyer beware. Did your friend read the fine print in the owner's manual? I would guess it probably says that results can vary.

PAGE 4, SECOND LISTENING

4. *Listen again to part of the conversation. Then answer question 4.*

Student: You know how you were talking about infomercials? Well, I know that infomercials try to be more informative than other regular commercials, and you mentioned that the information is true, but can we really trust everything they say?

Professor: Well, as far as I know, companies can't make false claims about their products or they could be held liable for false advertising and then of course get sued.

What does the professor mean when he says, "Well, as far as I know, companies can't make false claims about their products"?

5. *Listen again to part of the conversation. Then answer question 5.*

Student: Well that may be so, but in my experience, the product isn't always what it appears to be. Like, just last semester, my friend bought an ab machine after hearing about it on TV.

What is the student's attitude when he says, "Well that may be so, but in my experience, the product isn't always what it appears to be"?

ACADEMIC LISTENING

PAGE 5, FIRST LISTENING

Ad 1

Announcer: You park your car, and your worst nightmare happens! When you come back . . . it's gone! It can happen anywhere . . . and chances are, one day, it will happen to you!

That's why you need the incredible Thief Buster security system. It's easy to use and 100 percent effective. If someone so much as touches your car, an alarm will ring. And if that doesn't stop the thief, the engine will turn off when he tries to start the car. So why put your car at risk any longer? Get a Thief Buster security system today! Thief Buster . . . protection for your peace of mind!

Ad 2

Brad: Hello?

Lisa: Hi, Brad! It's Lisa. How was your job interview?

B: It was terrible! I was wearing that dark blue jacket . . . you know . . . the one with the gold buttons . . .

L: Uh-huh?

B: Well, I noticed that the boss kept looking at my shoulders. I couldn't figure it out, so I took a quick look and saw all these white, powdery flakes.

L: From your head?

B: Yeah, it was dandruff! You could really see it too . . . because of the jacket. It was so embarrassing . . . and it totally threw me off. I just couldn't concentrate on the questions.

Announcer: Dandruff can be a small problem with big consequences. Luckily there's Rinse Away dandruff shampoo to take care of even your toughest dandruff. Don't let the embarrassment of an itchy, flaky scalp slow you down. Just Rinse Away and feel the confidence. Rinse Away—your sure cure for dandruff!

PAGE 5, SECOND LISTENING

4. *Listen again to part of the conversation. Then answer question 4.*

Announcer: So why put your car at risk any longer? Get a Thief Buster Security System today! Thief Buster . . . protection for your piece of mind.

In the first ad, why does the announcer say, "So why put your car at risk any longer? Get a Thief Buster Security System today"?

5. *Listen again to part of the conversation. Then answer question 5.*

In the second ad, what is the speaker's attitude toward his problem when he says this?

B: Well, I noticed that the boss kept looking at my shoulders. I couldn't figure it out. So I took a quick look and saw all these white, powdery flakes.

INTEGRATED TASK

PAGE 12, LISTENING

Professor: Good morning, everyone!

Good morning. As you remember, last week we talked about the history of radio advertising. And so today we're going to continue by talking about techniques that advertisers use to get us to buy the products they're selling. In other words . . . the methods they use to persuade us to buy. One of the most effective techniques is to manipulate, or control, our emotions. Advertisers call this an emotional appeal. Today I'm going to talk about several emotional appeals. And to show you . . . to show you what I'm talking about, I'm going to play some real radio ads. Is everyone with me at this point? O.K., then. Let's get started.

One of the most popular emotional appeals is the appeal to humor. If something is funny, it's likely to grab us . . . our attention I mean. So, funny ads are often easy to remember. They also give us a good feeling . . . which is another reason why humor is popular. Here's an example of a humorous ad:

Speaker: It's flea season again! Fleas! Those pesky bugs jump into your dog's hair, bite his skin, make him itch. Unfortunately, most flea treatments involve bathing with harsh chemicals. Not fun for me—or my dog. That's why I'm getting the Doggie's Friend flea collar. It goes around your dog's neck and makes a noise that drives fleas crazy . . . so off they jump!

Announcer: Don't delay. Get a Doggie's Friend today.

Unit 2: Extreme Sports

CAMPUS CONVERSATION

PAGE 19, FIRST LISTENING

Professor: OK, Who's next?

Susan: I am, Professor.

P: OK, Susan. Come on in and have a seat. What can I do for you?

S: Um—I guess I need your advice. I don't know what to do. I'm under so much pressure I can't sleep.

P: Sounds serious. Why don't you tell me about it?

S: My parents are obsessed with the idea of my going to medical school. That's all they talk about!

P: I'm not sure I get it. What's the problem exactly?

S: I don't want to be a doctor! Why can't they see that? All *I* think about is becoming an Olympic runner. All I want to do is run longer and faster. I need to practice. My plan is to become famous all over the world and make a lot of money.

P: Perhaps your parents aren't the only ones with an obsession.

S: Yeah, but it's what I really want to do!

P: Susan, how are you doing in your other classes this semester? You know in my class you are barely getting a C+.

S: Um, well, actually, my grades are suffering a little. And I know it's because I spend so much time training. But I'm

planning to transfer to a school in Boston. It's known for its sports program, and they offered me a full scholarship!

P: Wow! Have you told your parents about this?

S: No, they'll just get angry. I'm so sick of hearing about med school, med school, med school!

P: Perhaps they don't understand how serious you are about a career in sports. If you tell them about your scholarship, they may forget their obsession with your becoming a doctor.

S: Well . . . I'll give it a shot, but they're not going to like it.

P: Give them a chance. They might surprise you. In the meantime keep your grades up. You don't want to fail out of school.

S: OK, but if they get angry, I'm going to tell them to speak to you.

P: Fair enough. Now, go get some rest, and work harder in your courses.

S: OK. Thanks, Professor. Bye.

P: Bye now.

PAGE 19, SECOND LISTENING

4. *Listen again to part of the conversation. Then answer question 4.*

S: All I want to do is run longer and faster. I need to practice. My plan is to become famous all over the world and make a lot of money.

P: Perhaps your parents aren't the only ones with an obsession.

What does the professor imply when she says, "Perhaps your parents aren't the only ones with an obsession"?

5. *Listen again to part of the conversation. Then answer question 5.*

P: Perhaps they don't understand how serious you are about a career in sports. If you tell them about your scholarship, they may forget their obsession with your becoming a doctor.

S: Well . . . I'll give it a shot, but they're not going to like it.

What is Susan's attitude when she says, "Well, I'll give it a shot, but they're not going to like it"?

6. *Listen again to part of the conversation. Then answer question 6.*

P: Give them a chance. They might surprise you. In the meantime keep your grades up. You don't want to fail out of school.

What does the professor mean when she says, "Give them a chance. They might surprise you"?

ACADEMIC LISTENING

PAGE 20, FIRST LISTENING

Professor: So, we've already talked a bit about the growth of extreme sports—things like mountain climbing and parachuting. As psychologists, we need to ask ourselves, why is this person doing this? Why do people take these risks and put themselves in danger when they don't have to?

One common trait among risk takers is that they enjoy strong feelings or sensations. We call this trait "sensation seeking." A "sensation seeker" is someone who's always looking for new sensations. What else do we know about sensation seekers?

Well, as I said, sensation seekers like strong emotion. You can see this trait in many parts of a person's life, not just in extreme sports. For example, many sensation seekers enjoy hard rock music. They like the loud sound and strong emotion of the songs. Similarly, sensation seekers enjoy frightening horror movies. They like the feeling of being scared and horrified while watching the movie. This feeling is even stronger for extreme sports, where the person faces real danger. Sensation seekers feel that danger is very exciting.

In addition, sensation seekers like new experiences that force them to push their personal limits. For them, repeating the same things every day is boring. Many sensation seekers choose jobs that include risk, such as starting a new business, or being an emergency room doctor. These jobs are different every day, so they never know what will happen. That's why many sensation seekers also like extreme sports. When you climb a mountain or jump out of an airplane, you never know what will happen. The activity is always new and different.

PAGE 21, SECOND LISTENING

4. *Listen again to part of the conversation. Then answer question 4.*

As psychologists, we need to ask ourselves, why is this person doing this? Why do people take these risks and put themselves in danger when they don't have to?

Why does the speaker ask, "As psychologists, we need to ask ourselves, why is this person doing this?"

INTEGRATED TASK

PAGE 27, LISTENING

Wheels on Fire (WOF): Let's start with the high point of your career. Can you pick one out to share with us?

Tony Hawk (TH): Oh yes, definitely. For me, the high point came when I was traveling to France and I had to fill out a tourist information card. You know, the thing you fill out when you're entering a new country? Well, I got to write down "skateboarder" as my occupation. How cool!

WOF: You mean that was better than what you accomplished at the 1999 Summer X Games?

TH: You mean landing the 900? That was awesome, too. But that was pure obsession—story of my life. Nothing new for me there.

WOF: How was landing that trick an obsession for you?

TH: Well, like everything else I do on a skateboard, I have to get it right. It took me 13 years of practice to perfect the 900, and on that day, I think it took me something like 12 times before I made it.

WOF: Did you really work on one trick for 13 years? That does seem like an obsession!

TH: Yeah, but you know, it's a good obsession—if you can say that obsession is good. It's like this—I was this weird, skinny kid at school. Once I got into skateboarding and started wearing baggy skater clothes, it got worse. I was a freak. All the jocks picked on me. And I didn't have a chance with the girls—forget it. But skating—that was my escape. Every day after school I escaped to the skate park, and the focus on skating, this really intense focus that took all my concentration— I guess that was one way I could block out all the pain of growing up.

SKILL FOCUS

PAGE 30, PRACTICE, Exercise 1

Interviewer: Did your parents support your obsession with skating?

Tony Hawk: Yeah, they were great. Mom took me and some friends down to the Oasis Skate Park when we were about 10 years old. They had this flat beginners' area where you could practice before you were ready to skate in the empty swimming pools. I was so skinny that the skate equipment didn't even fit me right. But once I got hooked, nothing else mattered. I drew pictures of skating all day, and I even skated in the house.

Interviewer: Your parents let you skate in the house?

TH: Yeah. They were pretty cool. Mom and Dad were older when they had me, so I guess you can say they were relaxed enough to let me do what I needed to do.

Interviewer: How about your schoolwork? Were you able to get by in school?

TH: Yeah, that was fine. I don't mean to brag or anything, but I was a gifted student. So I was able to get my schoolwork done with decent grades. My only problem was being able to sit still in class. I had so much physical energy. But school was basically OK for me until some of the teachers started taking my skateboard away. They started lecturing me about the dangers of the sport.

Interviewer: That couldn't stop you from skating!

TH: No way. The cool thing was that my parents worked it out for me to go to a different high school. The principal there was awesome. He let us design our own PE (physical education) classes, so take a wild guess. What class did I create?

Interviewer: Skateboarding.

TH: You got it. That was my PE class. . . .

2. *Listen again to part of the interview. Then answer question 2.*

TH: But once I got hooked, nothing else mattered. I drew pictures of skating all day, and I even skated in the house.

Interviewer: Your parents let you skate in the house?

Why does the interviewer ask, "Your parents let you skate in the house?"

3. *Listen again to part of the interview. Then answer question 3.*

TH: But school was basically OK for me until some of the teachers started taking my skateboard away. They started lecturing me about the dangers of the sport.

Interviewer: That couldn't stop you from skating!

What is the interviewer's attitude when she says, "That couldn't stop you from skating!"?

4. *Listen again to part of the interview. Then answer question 4.*

TH: The cool thing was that my parents worked it out for me to go to a different high school. The principal there was awesome. He let us design our own PE (physical education) classes, so take a wild guess. What class did I create?

Why does Tony ask, "What class did I create?"

Unit 3: Fraud

CAMPUS CONVERSATION

PAGE 35, FIRST LISTENING

Student: Hi.

Financial Aid Advisor: Hello. Welcome to Student Financial Services. How can I help you?

S: Hi. I'd like to get information about scholarships. I think I'm going to need some help paying my tuition next year.

FA: OK, let's see what we can do. Have a seat here at one of the computers.

S: Thanks.

FA: All . . . right. Now, here . . . Click on "find a scholarship" and you'll see a list of organizations that give scholarships.

S: Wow. All these???

FA: They're divided into categories: sports scholarships, scholarships for students interested in music, scholarships from religious organizations. There are several for minorities . . .

S: There's so much information here!

FA: Just take your time.

S: You know, on the web I saw ads for "scholarship search agencies," companies that can find scholarships for students. They even promise to find scholarships or you get your money back. Do you know anything about them?

FA: Well, just be careful. There are some search services you can trust, but keep in mind that there are also a lot of scams out there.

S: Scams?

FA: Yeah, it's a type of fraud: they promise to help, but in the end they just take your money.

S: Well, how do you know if the service is reputable or just a scam?

FA: Well, the first thing you can do is to get information about the company. Find out if any of your friends have used the company and if they recommend it.

S: OK.

FA: Also, be suspicious if a service asks you for money up front or if they promise to get you a scholarship. Scholarship services can never make such a promise because they don't control the organizations that give the scholarships.

S: Man, I can't believe they would do that to students! We need money, and they are taking it from us.

FA: Isn't it terrible? So, you're better off looking for a scholarship directly from this office.

S: Yeah. How late are you open? This is going to take a while.

FA: Well, it's almost 5 o'clock. We're open 9–5, Monday through Friday.

S: OK, I'll come back tomorrow after my class.

FA: Good idea.

S: Thanks a lot. See you tomorrow.

PAGE 36, SECOND LISTENING

5. Listen again to part of the conversation. Then answer question 5.

FA: All . . . right. Now, here . . . Click on "find a scholarship" and you'll see a list of organizations that give scholarships.

S: Wow. All these???

After he looks at the computer screen, what is the student's attitude when he says, "Wow. All these???"

6. Listen again to part of the conversation. Then answer question 6.

FA: Well, it's almost 5 o'clock. We're open 9–5, Monday through Friday.

S: OK, I'll come back tomorrow after my class.

Why does the student say, "OK, I'll come back tomorrow after my class."?

ACADEMIC LISTENING

PAGE 37, FIRST LISTENING

Narrator: Today we are going to hear from four people who were victims of a scam.

Listen to Joe: I really don't know why I sent him the money. My daughter's always telling me not to give out my credit card number over the phone, but this guy Frank was so nice and friendly that I believed him. I guess I'm pretty gullible. If someone tells me something, I usually believe them. That's OK most of the time, but sometimes it gets me into trouble.

Listen to Rosa: Frank seemed like such a nice young man, and so concerned about me. You see, I lost my husband a year ago, and I don't have many friends. I don't get many phone calls and I sometimes get very lonely, so I really enjoyed talking to him. I really thought I could trust him.

Listen to Peter: I've heard about telephone fraud like this, and I always thought I was very careful. But while I was talking to Frank, I kept thinking about how much my wife would like going to Hawaii. I lost my job recently, so I don't have any extra money. I guess I got too excited about the free vacation and didn't think carefully.

Listen to Beth: Well, Frank put so much pressure on me! He kept saying that he wanted to help me, and how I had to decide right away. He said that if I didn't send the money, he would give the prize to someone else. I wasn't sure I could trust him, but he made me decide so quickly; I just didn't have time to think!

PAGE 37, SECOND LISTENING

2. Listen again to part of the conversation. Then answer question 2.

Joe: My daughter's always telling me not to give out my credit card number over the phone, but this guy Frank was so nice and friendly that I believed him. I guess I'm pretty gullible. If someone tells me something, I usually believe them. That's OK most of the time, but sometimes it gets me into trouble."

What is Joe's purpose when he says, "I guess I'm pretty gullible"?

4. Listen again to part of the conversation. Then answer question 4.

Peter: I lost my job recently, so I don't have any extra money. I guess I got too excited about the free vacation and didn't think carefully.

What is Peter's attitude when he says, "I guess I got too excited about the free vacation and didn't think carefully"?

INTEGRATED TASK

PAGE 43, LISTENING

More and more people are turning away from their doctors and, instead, going to individuals who have no medical training and who sell unproven treatments. They go to quacks to get everything from treatments for colds to cures for cancer. And they are putting themselves in dangerous situations.

One year ago, Matt Bloomfield was told he had cancer. His doctors decided to treat his cancer immediately. A few months after the treatments, however, Matt found out that the cancer was still growing. He became sick and depressed. Because he always had pain, the doctors gave him more medicine, but it didn't help. Finally, the doctors told him that they were unable to do anything more; he had only six months to live. Matt would do anything to save his life. He went to see a doctor who turned out to be a complete quack.

Unit 4: Storytelling

CAMPUS CONVERSATION

PAGE 53, FIRST LISTENING

Student: Excuse me Professor Everett, can I talk to you?

Professor: Sure what's on your mind?

S: Well, I was wondering if I could write a research paper instead of doing the oral presentation you assigned in class.

P: Sorry, Sheila. That's really not possible. It's one of the course requirements and 20% of your final grade.

S: But I *really* don't like talking in front of people. I get too nervous.

P: Oh, come on, you'll do fine. There's nothing to worry about. It'll just be me and your classmates.

S: I know that. But if I don't do well, it will affect my grade, and I'm doing really well so far this semester.

P: Well, this is a challenge you'll have to face if you want to pass the course. But we can talk about strategies you could use to do better.

S: Um, yeah, OK.

P: So, what's your topic?

S: I wanted to talk about how, in literature, writers give animals human traits.

P: OK. Great. So, what do you think you need to do to get a good grade?

S: Uh . . . , speak clearly?

P: Yeah, that's part of it, but what about the content of your presentation?

S: I guess I should really be prepared.

P: Right, and an important part of being prepared is organization. A good way to get organized is to use an outline to structure your presentation.

S: Uh-huh.

P: Have you thought about how to structure your presentation?

S: I want to talk about the Japanese story "Momotaro," "Peach Boy"—how the animals in the story have human traits. There's a dog, a monkey and a bird, and they become friends with the boy and help him fight against evil.

P: Uh-huh.

S: I could talk about why the story has animals.

P: That sounds interesting. Students will enjoy the story—some may already know it. And your presentation will make them understand it on a more sophisticated level.

S: Any other advice?

P: Well, another good strategy is to use visuals—pictures and charts—so that your audience will *see* your ideas as they listen to you. And don't forget to make eye contact. If you look people in the eye, they'll pay more attention. You might also notice if you are not being clear enough.

S: Uh-uh.

P: And I think rehearsing is important.

S: Rehearsing?

P: Yeah. Practice your presentation.

S: OK . . . so, you're sure I can't just do a research paper instead . . .

P: I'm sure.

S: OK, thanks.

P: See you in class. Let me know if you have any questions.

S: OK, bye.

PAGE 53, SECOND LISTENING

3. *Listen again to part of the conversation. Then answer question 3.*

P: So, what's your topic?

S: I wanted to talk about how, in literature, writers give animals human traits.

P: OK. Great. So, what do you think you need to do to get a good grade?

S: Uh . . . , speak clearly?

Why does the professor ask, "So, what do you think you need to do to get a good grade"?

4. *Listen again to part of the conversation. Then answer question 4.*

S: I could talk about why the story has animals.

P: That sounds interesting. Students will enjoy the story—some may already know it. And your presentation will make them understand it on a more sophisticated level.

S: Any other advice?

Why does the professor say, "Students will enjoy the story—some may already know it. And your presentation will make them understand it on a more sophisticated level"?

6. *Listen again to part of the conversation. Then answer question 6.*

P: And I think rehearsing is important.

S: Rehearsing?

P: Yeah. Practice your presentation.

S: OK . . . so, you're sure I can't just do a research paper instead . . .

P: I'm sure.

S: OK, thanks.

What is the professor's attitude when he says, "I'm sure"?

ACADEMIC LISTENING

PAGE 54, FIRST LISTENING

Interviewer: You have an interesting technique that you recommend for storytelling, for learning a story. And that is to read it five times before you tell it. Why is that?

Torrence: Yes. Well, the first time you tell a story, you see that you like it. And I always say don't ever tell a story you don't like, 'cause you've wasted your time and the time of your listener.

Then, the second time you read, read it for the pictures. Read it for the pictures that you're going to create. As you read about the character, you read a personality into those characters. You give those characters a look, you see them as familiar individuals. They may look like your husband, your wife, your daughter, your son.

The third time you read it, read it for the words. Now this is a very important part of the story because words make that story. You can make it or break it by saying the right or wrong words.

PAGE 55, SECOND LISTENING

4. Listen again to part of the conversation. Then answer question 4.

What is the speaker implying when she says this?

"Well, the first time you tell a story, you see that you like it. And I always say don't ever tell a story you don't like, 'cause you've wasted your time and the time of your listener."

INTEGRATED TASK

PAGE 62, LISTENING

One morning, Gregor Samsa woke up from a bad dream and realized he was some kind of terrible insect. He was a cockroach, and he was as large as a man! Lying on his back, he could see his large brown belly and thin legs. He tried to turn over onto his side, but every time he tried, he would roll onto his back again.

He began to think about his job as a traveling salesman. He hated his job, but he had to do it to support his father, mother, and sister because his father no longer worked. He looked at the clock and realized he had overslept—it was 6:30! He was late. The next train left at 7:00. He would have to hurry to make it. A few minutes later his mother yelled to him: "It's 6:45. You're late. Get up!" When he answered her, he was surprised to hear his voice; it sounded so high. "Yes, mother. I'm getting up now." His sister now whispered through the door, "Gregor, are you all right? Do you need anything?"

Well, it was time to get up. Surely, as soon as he got out of bed, he would realize this had all been a bad dream. He tried to move his back part out first, but it moved so slowly, and he had a hard time. His thin little legs seemed useless, just moving and moving in the air, not helping him at all. Then he tried the front part. This worked better, but he still couldn't move enough to get out of bed. He began rocking back and forth, stronger and

stronger, and finally threw himself onto the floor, hitting his head as he fell.

SKILL FOCUS

PAGE 67, PRACTICE, Exercise 1

Um—Good morning. Can you hear me OK? Yeah? OK. Yeah—I'm a little nervous.

Ah—today I would like to talk to you about a Japanese folk tale called-ah- "Momotaro." I'm going to tell you part of the story and discuss the anthropomorphism in the—ah—story. Ah—anthropomorphism is giving human qualities or traits to non-human characters, like animals.

Um—In "Momotaro," an elderly, childless couple finds a boy in a giant peach that is floating down the river. They call the boy Momotaro, the Peach Boy.

When Momotaro grows up, he decides to fight against evil. One day, he hears about evil ogres, called *oni*. The oni are threatening people in a place called Onigashima. So, he goes off to fight them—with the help of three animals: a dog, a bird, and a monkey. Together the four friends fight against and defeat the *oni*.

Now, um—the question is, why are there animals in this story and not just people? I think one reason is that this story is for children. Children like animals and can learn the lesson of the story from them.

So—in this story each character has unique talents and abilities. The dog can run fast and has a loud voice. The monkey is energetic and good at jumping and climbing. The bird can fly high in the sky and act as a guide. All of the animals were good at fighting against evil together. They were a good team.

In "Momotaro" part of the lesson is cooperation, working together. Momotaro gets the three animals—who naturally might fight against each other—to cooperate with him in order to fight the dangerous enemy. The four friends had to work together in order for everyone to be safe. So, this is what kids learn from the story.

3. Listen again to part of the presentation. Then answer question 3.

Now, um—the question is, why are there animals in this story and not just people?

Why does the speaker ask the question, "Why are there animals in this story and not just people?"

4. Listen again to part of the presentation. Then answer question 4.

Why does the speaker use the expression I think when she says this? "I think one reason is that this story is for children"?

Unit 5: Language

CAMPUS CONVERSATION

PAGE 71, FIRST LISTENING

Resident Assistant: Hey, Bo Hyun. How's your first semester going?

Student: Oh, yeah—it's OK.

RA: Just OK?

S: Yeah. Getting used to being in college is *one thing* . . . but getting used to living in a new country—and in a big city like New York—*is another.*

RA: Whaddaya mean?

S: Well, first of all, everyone thinks I'm Chinese!

RA: Aren't you?

S: No!!! You *know* I'm Korean!

RA: I know—I know. That's just a stereotype. Some people just don't think—they just assume you're Chinese.

S: Well, yeah, I guess I can handle that. But my real problem is English.

RA: But your English is great!

S: Well, I appreciate that coming from a native speaker. But people on the street—in stores and restaurants—don't understand my English!

RA: Really? I always understand you!

S: Well, maybe you are just used to my accent. But when I talk to people off campus, I always have to repeat myself over and over.

RA: That's a drag.

S: But, you know, I have a hard time understanding the New York accent! And people here speak so fast!

RA: You know, when I came here three years ago, it was the same for me. I'm from Augusta, Georgia, you know—in the south. I *really* had a hard time getting used to the pace up here.

S: Oh, yeah. That's another thing.

RA: Yeah, in Augusta, people move at a more relaxed pace. Here everyone seems to be running from place to place—and now I do it, too.

S: Yeah. Me too! My feet are always tired!

RA: Yeah, and talk about accents! Have you *heard* the way I speak?

S: Yeah, I like it! It's slow and musical—I can understand everything you say.

RA: You know, people here always make fun of my accent. They don't mean anything by it. They think it's charming.

S: Yes, it is!

RA: Yeah, but after a while it gets kind of annoying—you know what I mean?

S: Yeah.

RA: But I don't want to focus on the negative 'cause I'm really glad I came to New York. The city has a lot to offer—and diversity is part it. You take the good with the bad, right?

S: Yeah.

RA: So, you'll get used to it here. Hang in there.

S: Yeah. OK. I will.

RA: And always feel free to stop by my room if you want to talk. That's what I'm here for.

S: OK, thanks a lot.

PAGE 71, SECOND LISTENING

4. *Listen again to part of the conversation. Then answer question 4.*

S: Well, first of all, everyone thinks I'm Chinese!

RA: Aren't you?

Why does the RA ask, "Aren't you"?

5. *Listen again to part of the conversation. Then answer question 5.*

S: Well, maybe you are just used to my accent. But when I talk to people off campus, I always have to repeat myself over and over.

RA: That's a drag.

What is the RA's attitude when he says, "That's a drag"?

ACADEMIC LISTENING

PAGE 72, FIRST LISTENING

Gigi Jones: I know you've written a lot about gender and language, Dr. Speakwell.

Dr. Speakwell: Yes, I have. I find it very interesting. For example, you just called me "Doctor." That used to always suggest a man, not a woman.

GJ: Maybe I should call you "Doctorette."

DS: Actually, I prefer to be called "Doctor."

GJ: Why is that?

DS: Well, you know, English has several feminine words that people sometimes use when they're referring to women. You probably know them, right? Poetess, songstress, bachelorette? Now these words aren't used too often, but they exist in the language. However, some women don't like such words because they feel as if these words make women less important than men.

GJ: What do you mean by that?

DS: For instance, if you say the word actress, people don't always think of a serious artist. They might think of some silly, beautiful female who's more worried about her makeup than she is about Shakespeare. But when you say actor—that's not silly at all. That's a serious word, a respectable word.

GJ: I see.

DS: That's why I would never call myself a doctorette. Or a professoress—never!

GJ: OK, Fine. I'll call you doctor.

DS: And I'll call you Ms. Jones. That's a very good example of how the language has changed in recent years, partly as a result of the women's movement.

GJ: You mean the title of Ms.?

DS: Not just that. We've changed dozens of words related to occupations. Think of all the words that used to end in -man. Policeman, fireman, mailman, . . .

GJ: I guess they've all changed. Now we say police officer, firefighter, . . . but what about mailman?

DS: Mail carrier. And do you know why? We've removed gender from these words because, after all, both men and women can do these jobs well.

GJ: I suppose. But not everyone would agree with you.

DS: Maybe not. But you know, even though I believe men and women are equal in their abilities, I do think there are differences in the way they speak.

GJ: Do you really think so?

DS: Absolutely. Look at all the color words that women know! If a man and woman go shopping together, the man will look at a shirt and say, I like the purple one. But a woman will look at the same shirt and might call it purple too or lavender . . . or periwinkle. . . .

GJ: Or mauve?

DS: Right! Women use more words for color. They also use some adjectives that men don't use . . . such as lovely, cute, adorable.

GJ: I guess you're right. Most men don't seem to use those words.

DS: Most of them don't. But you know, language and gender are both so closely related to culture. In fact, I've studied seventeen countries, and I found out that in Japan, for example, men and women use different word endings. So if a man doesn't want to sound bossy, he'll use the feminine word ending, -no, instead of -ka. Ka sounds more masculine, more direct.

GJ: So a man will talk like a woman in certain situations. That's fascinating. Thank you. Thank you very much, Dr. Speakwell.

DS: My pleasure.

PAGE 73, SECOND LISTENING

2. Listen again to part of the interview. Then answer question 2.

Gigi Jones: I know you've written a lot about gender and language, Dr. Speakwell.

Dr. Speakwell: Yes, I have. I find it very interesting. For example, you just called me "Doctor." That used to always suggest a man, not a woman.

GJ: Maybe I should call you "Doctorette."

What is the interviewer's tone when she says, "Maybe I should call you Doctorette"?

3. Listen again to part of the conversation. Then answer question 3.

What is Dr. Speakwell suggesting about the word actress when she says this?

DS: For instance, if you say the word actress, people don't always think of a serious artist. They might think of some silly, beautiful female who's more worried about her makeup than she is about Shakespeare. But when you say actor—that's not silly at all. That's a serious word, a respectable word.

5. Listen again to part of the conversation. Then answer question 5.

DS: But you know, even though I believe men and women are equal in their abilities, I do think there are differences in the way they speak.

GJ: Do you really think so?

DS: Absolutely. . . .

What is the interviewer's tone when she responds, "Do you really think so?"?

7. Listen again to part of the conversation. Then answer question 7.

GJ: I guess they've all changed. Now we say police officer, firefighter, . . . but what about "mailman"?

DS: Mail carrier. And do you know why? We've removed gender from these words because, after all, both men and women can do these jobs well.

GJ: I suppose. But not everyone would agree with you.

What is the interviewer's attitude when she says, "I suppose"?

INTEGRATED TASK

PAGE 80, LISTENING

Lisa: Hi. This is Lisa. I'm doing a project on accents for my sociolinguistics course, so I'm interviewing some of my friends from grad school. . . . This is my friend Joseph. Joseph, can you give me a little background on where you grew up?

Jospeh: Kingston, Jamaica is what I call home. And I've lived in the States, here in North Carolina, for six years.

L: So do you feel that you have an accent?

J: Well, I wasn't aware of my accent until I came here. Obviously, growing up in Kingston, no one told me I had an accent because we all spoke the same way.

L: So how did you feel about your accent when you came here?

J: Well, when I came here, many people commented on my accent. So I started to be aware of it. I still get comments all the time. I mean they always say things, things . . .

L: Like?

J: Oh, just, I mean, people say, "Oh, I love your accent. It's so musical."

L: So they like your accent.

J: Yes, but I also remember—when I first came—I felt that I spoke so slowly, everyone else spoke so much faster . . . Some people stereotyped me because of that. I could tell that they were thinking, "He's not very bright. You know, a slow mouth has a slow brain . . . he speaks slowly so he must be thinking slowly too." So that made me feel pretty self-conscious. Also, whenever I opened my mouth I could see people thinking "I wonder where he's from . . . " and that would be the first question. "Where are you from?" And then I'd have to go into this long explanation about my background. I guess I got tired of it.

L: But wasn't that a good way to meet people?

J: Hmm. Maybe . . . But there's a difference between meeting people and making friends. I mean . . . here I was, a first-year student, meeting lots of people, but I always felt that the other students didn't really understand who I was. It made me feel like um... like I didn't fit in.

SKILL FOCUS

PAGE 86, PRACTICE

Exercise 2

Speaking a foreign language in a classroom is one thing, but living in a society where you have to use this language on a daily basis is completely different. So here are some language problems you may encounter while in the United States:

- You might not understand the local accent right away. Regional accents vary greatly. In a group of people from all over the U.S., Americans can usually pick out who is from Boston, New York, the Midwest, or the South, just by the way they speak. Give yourself some time to get used to the local accent, and in time, you will probably find yourself speaking in the same way.

- Americans might not understand you right away. You will also have your own accent and you might use a different vocabulary. Try to speak slowly at first to make sure you are understood. Don't be shy. Ask others to speak slowly if you have trouble understanding them.

- Americans use a lot of slang in their speech. Their language is very colorful and full of imagery and it might take some time to completely understand it.

- Humor is also an important part of American English. Some international students have a little trouble adapting to this informal style of conversation, and they also have trouble understanding whether the person they are speaking with is being serious or not. This, however, should be interpreted as a sign of friendliness rather than a show of disrespect.

- You might not know all of the abbreviations and technical terms used in your study program or workplace. Terms such as "poli sci" for political science, "dorms" for dormitories, or "TA" for teaching assistant, are just a few examples of campus slang you will encounter. The abbreviation is often the first syllable of the word or, if two or more words are together, their initials. If you don't understand a word or an abbreviation, simply ask the meaning.

You should give yourself time to adapt to the language and don't hesitate to ask people to repeat what they have said, to speak slowly, or to explain what they mean. It would be wise to carry a small dictionary with you in case of an emergency. Most importantly, don't be afraid to make mistakes. This will all be part of your learning experience.

Unit 6: Tourism

CAMPUS CONVERSATION

PAGE 91, FIRST LISTENING

Student: Hi Professor.

Professor: Hi Vicky. What's up?

S: I was wondering if I could get an extension for my final paper.

P: Vicky, the due date is today! It's right on the syllabus with all of the other assignments. I made it very clear in the first class that I don't give extensions, unless, of course, there are special circumstances.

S: I know, and I'm really sorry. I was trying to make the due date, but I just didn't know what to write about. It's like I have writer's block or something.

P: Are you clear about what the assignment is?

S: Um–yeah—write about the impact of tourism in a specific context—like a specific place where tourists go.

P: OK, so, what seems to be the trouble?

S: It's just that . . . I can't really see any big problems with tourism. People enjoy traveling—the tourists help the local economy. Everybody wins!

P: Vicky, there's a little more to it than that. In fact, there's lot out there on the topic. . . . OK, let's focus in on a context. Have you ever taken a vacation?

S: Sure. I went on a cruise to the Caribbean with my family when I was in high school. It was great. Yeah, so last week I thought I'd write about the impact that cruises have, but I couldn't come up with anything.

P: Well, what about the environmental effects or the socio-cultural effects, you know, how tourism impacts the people and culture of a particular place?

S: But how would I go about finding out about things like that? I searched the Internet for hours, but the websites that came up were mostly ones that sell luxury cruise vacations!

P: Look—as I say—a lot has been written on this topic. You just need to look for it. The Internet isn't always your best bet.

S: Could I have a hint where I could find more information on this?

P: OK, yeah, start with the publications by the UNEP, the United Nations Environmental Programme. They have done a lot of research on this topic.

S: The UNEP. Got it. OK, I'll check it out. Thanks a lot.

P: So, I'll give you an extra week. Does that sound reasonable?

S: Yeah, I think so.

P: Otherwise, you will get an "incomplete" as a grade for the class, and that will stay on your permanent college record.

S: OK, I'll try my best.

P: Plus, I'll have higher expectations since you're getting extra time.

S: Um . . . OK.

P: One last thing: Next time, don't wait until the last minute to ask for help—in this or any class. I have office hours every Tuesday. Take advantage of them.

S: OK. Sorry. I will.

P: I'll see you in a week.

S: See ya then. Thanks again.

PAGE 92, SECOND LISTENING

4. *Listen again to part of the conversation. Then answer question 4.*

S: But how would I go about finding out about things like that? I searched the Internet for hours, but the websites that came up were mostly ones that sell luxury cruise vacations!

P: Look—as I say—a lot has been written on this topic. You just need to look for it. The Internet isn't always your best bet.

What is the professor implying?

5. *Listen again to part of the conversation. Then answer question 5.*

S: I was wondering if I could get an extension for my final paper.

P: Vicky, the due date is today! It's right on the syllabus with all of the other assignments. I made it very clear in the first class that I don't give extensions, unless, of course, there are special circumstances.

What is the professor's attitude when he says, "Vicky, the due date is today!"?

6. *Listen again to part of the conversation. Then answer question 6.*

P: Vicky, there's a little more to it than that. In fact, there's a lot out there on the topic. . . . OK, let's focus in on a context. Have you ever taken a vacation?

S: Sure. I went on a cruise to the Caribbean with my family when I was in high school. It was great.

Why does the professor ask, "Have you ever taken a vacation?"

ACADEMIC LISTENING

PAGE 93, FIRST LISTENING

Mayor: OK. Let's start with the first item on our agenda—how to deal with the problems created by too many tourists on Cape Cod during the summer. I'd like to start by identifying some of the problems . . . Yes, Mrs. Green.

Green: Thank you, Mayor. Well for one, the traffic is just terrible in the summer! In winter, it takes me about 15 minutes to drive into town. But in the summer, it can be 45 minutes or more. It's ridiculous!

Mayor: Thank you, Mrs. Green. Yes, you next, sir. Please tell us your name.

Horowitz: Yes, thank you, my name is Frank Horowitz. In my mind the biggest problem is housing. The cost of buying or renting a home here is too high! Pretty much, you can't afford it on a regular salary . . . all the homes are being sold to rich people for vacation homes. And that leaves nothing for the working people who live here. I mean I own a seafood restaurant, OK? And I've got a waitress who's living in her car right now because she can't find any other place to live. Now that's ridiculous!

Keller: Can I say something?

Mayor: One moment, please. Have you finished Mr. Horowitz?

Horowitz: Yes, thank you, Mayor.

Mayor: Very well. Go ahead, ma'am.

Keller: Thank you. My name is Cara Keller. OK, I know it's difficult to have all these tourists around during the summer, but I for one am very happy to have them. I run a souvenir shop, and I do about 80% of my business for the year in the summer. And I'm not the only one. Tourists are essential to our town's economy. We've got to keep them coming.

Mayor: OK . . . Thank you, Ms. Keller. I believe we have time for one or two more people . . . yes, you sir, go ahead . . .

PAGE 94, SECOND LISTENING

4. *Listen again to part of the town meeting. Then answer question 4.*

Green: In winter, it takes me about 15 minutes to drive into town. But in the summer, it can be 45 minutes or more. It's ridiculous!"

What is the speaker's attitude toward tourists when she says, "It's ridiculous!"?

5. *Listen again to part of the town meeting. Then answer question 5.*

Horowitz: I mean I own a seafood restaurant, OK? And I've got a waitress who's living in her car right now because she can't find any other place to live. Now that's ridiculous!

What did Mr. Horowitz mean when he said, "Now that's ridiculous!"?

INTEGRATED TASK

PAGE 101, LISTENING

Good afternoon. My name is Mary Jane Polanco, from the Save Antarctica Foundation. I'm here today to speak with you about the impact tourism has on Antarctica.

Antarctica is important for scientific research, and it *must* be preserved for this purpose. Scientists are now looking at the effects of the ozone hole that was discovered above Antarctica in 1984. They are also trying to understand global warming. For instance, if the earth's temperature continues to increase, the health and safety of every living thing on the planet will be affected. Astronomers are able to see planets and stars very clearly from Antarctica. Biologists have the chance to learn more about the animals that live in this frozen land. Other scientists study the plant life to understand how it can live in such a harsh environment. They also study the Earth to learn more about how it was formed. There are even psychologists who study how people behave when they live and work together in such a remote location.

However, when tourist groups travel to this part of the world, they take scientists away from their research. The work that scientists do there is difficult, and some projects can be damaged by such simple mistakes as opening the wrong door or bumping into a small piece of equipment. In addition, tourists in Antarctica can also hurt the environment. Members of Greenpeace, one of the world's leading environmental organizations, complain that tourists leave trash on beaches and disturb the plants and animals. In a place as frozen as Antarctica, it can take 100 years for a plant to grow back, and tourists taking pictures of baby penguins may not pay close attention to what their feet are stepping on. Oil spills are another problem caused by tourism. In 1989, one cruise ship caused an oil spill that killed many penguins and destroyed a five-year scientific project.

Therefore, I hope that you will support the Save Antarctica Foundation. With your help, we will be able to protect this important resource for the future. Thank you.

Unit 7: Humor

CAMPUS CONVERSATION

PAGE 109, FIRST LISTENING

Student: Excuse me, Professor Watkins? Got a minute?

Professor: Sure. Please—come in. Ah . . . Tell me your name again?

S: Sam Bennett. I'm in your Thursday afternoon chemistry class.

P: Right. Sorry. I'm still trying to put names to faces. It's such a big class. What can I do for you, Sam?

S: It's about chemistry lab, actually.

P: What about it?

S: I didn't do well on the exam last week, well, actually, I think almost everyone didn't.

P: So I noticed. What happened?

S: Um—I, can't speak for anyone else, but I don't think I was ready to take the test.

P: Well, in lab you should have completed chapters 1 through 3.

S: But we only got through chapter 1!

P: What?

S: Bob, the TA, he's great, but he goes off on tangents. He tells jokes and funny stories—even campus gossip. It's interesting and I love going to class and all, but I'm not learning much about chemistry, which is my major—so it's kind of important.

P: I see . . .

S: I don't want Bob to get into trouble—he's such a great guy, but . . .

P: Yeah, no, no. I appreciate your telling me this. I'll have a talk with him.

S: But he won't get into trouble or anything . . .

P: No. Don't worry. This is his first time teaching—it's a learning experience for him as well.

S: What exactly is a teaching assistant supposed to do?

P: Well, at some universities, TAs teach basic courses on their own. At other universities, TAs attend the professor's class and help the professor with grading tests and papers.

S: Uh-huh.

P: And, in a large class, a TA might lead discussion sections, where the students can discuss the professor's lecture and the readings and ask questions.

S: Mmm.

P: In Bob's case, he's supposed to teach the lab sections that correspond to my lectures. He can also answer any questions you have about the lectures or the labs. But if you don't get through the labs, you can't do well on the exams!

S: Again—I don't want to get him into trouble . . . but I do need to get a good grade in this class!

P: No, I'm glad you said something. I need to see that Bob is covering the material.

S: You won't tell him I said anything, will you?

P: No, it'll be between you and me . . . and maybe I'll think about giving a make-up test after you all catch up in lab.

S: That would be great! Thanks.

P: Sure. See you on Thursday, Sam.

S: OK, thanks Professor.

PAGE 109, SECOND LISTENING

5. *Listen again to part of the conversation. Then answer question 5.*

S: You won't tell him I said anything, will you?

P: It'll be between you and me . . . and maybe I'll think about giving a make-up test after you all catch up in lab.

S: That would be great! Thanks.

What is the student's attitude when he says, "You won't tell him I said anything, will you?"

6. *Listen again to part of the conversation. Then answer question 6.*

P: Well, in lab you should have completed chapters 1 through 3.

S: But we only got through chapter 1!

P: What?

What can be inferred when the professor says, "What"?

ACADEMIC LISTENING

PAGE 110, FIRST LISTENING

Professor: Today I want to say a little about Lucille Ball and the creation of the popular 1950s TV show *I Love Lucy*, a program that you can still see on American TV today.

Lucille Ball had been a successful movie actress for many years starting in the late 1930s. Then, in the late 1940s, she became the star of a very popular radio program. Remember that this was all before people had televisions in their homes.

Then, one day someone at the CBS television studios told Desi Arnaz, Lucille's husband, that they wanted to make a TV show about a funny married couple. They wanted Lucille to star in this show and Desi to play her husband. Lucille and Desi couldn't believe it. It was a very busy time for them—they were expecting the birth of their first child—and now they had the opportunity to create their own TV show. Lucille and Desi were confused about what to do. They were radio performers. At that time, TV was still something new, and most Hollywood stars were afraid of it. Lucille knew that if their TV show failed, they might never work in the movies again. But this was also the first chance that Desi and Lucille had to work together, and this was exactly what they wanted to do.

Finally they made the decision to create *I Love Lucy* together. They thought of the characters for the show: Ricky and Lucy Ricardo. Ricky was a Cuban immigrant who worked as a bandleader in a New York night club. Lucy was his wife, a 1950s housewife with a crazy ambition to be in show business—just like her husband.

Desi clearly described and carefully summarized what his ideas for the show were. He told CBS that the show's humor would never be mean or unkind. Ricky and Lucy would be very much in love with each other and would never flirt with other characters. Most of all, Ricky would always keep his dignity as a man. He told the writers not to let Lucy surprise him. "If Lucy's going to play a trick on me, make it clear to the audience that Ricky knows what's going on." It was important to him to be seen as a strong male figure.

After they started making the show, Lucille—and Lucy—looked more and more like an expectant mother. During one of the first shows, Lucy covered herself up with a funny costume: baggy clown pants that she wore while she played the cello. But no matter what she wore, Lucille always played Lucy Ricardo as a very feminine character. She made sure that Lucy always looked soft and pretty, even when someone had thrown a pie in her face. And Lucy was never mean. When she got in trouble, it was usually because she was trying to be a star. Lucille believed this was one reason why the audience liked the show. People in the audience could understand Lucy—because, really, who doesn't want to be a star?

PAGE 111, SECOND LISTENING

3. *Listen again to part of the lecture. Then answer question 3.*

Lucille Ball had been a successful movie actress for many years starting in the late 1930s. Then, in the late 1940s, she became the star of a very popular radio program. Remember that this was all before people had televisions in their homes.

Why does the speaker say, "Remember that this was all before people had televisions in their homes"?

6. Listen again to part of the lecture. Then answer question 6.

When she got in trouble, it was usually because she was trying to be a star. Lucille believed this was one reason why the audience liked the show. People in the audience could understand Lucy—because, really, who doesn't want to be a star?

Why does the speaker say, "People in the audience could understand Lucy—because, really, who doesn't want to be a star"?

INTEGRATED TASK

PAGE 118, LISTENING

Host: Fascinating. OK, let's go to another call. Hi, Joan, you're on "Talk about It."

Joan: Hi, Carmen.

Host: Do you have a joke for us?

Joan: Sure, but first, I want you to know that I'm a lawyer.

Host: So you're going to tell us a lawyer joke?

Joan: Right. Because I know, everyone loves lawyers.

Host: Yeah—OK.

Joan: OK. A man goes to see a famous lawyer. The man asks, "How much do you charge?" The lawyer answers, "I charge $200 to answer three questions." The man says, "Isn't that expensive?" "Yes, it is," replies the lawyer, "Now, what's your third question?"

Host: Ha-ha. Thanks, Joan . . .

Unit 8: Fashion

CAMPUS CONVERSATION

PAGE 127, FIRST LISTENING

David: Hi Mr. Greenwood, How are you?

Advisor: Great, David. How are *you?*

D: Good—I have an appointment with you at 3 o'clock. Can I come in?

A: Let's see, it's 3, so come on in. What can I do for you?

D: Well, I have some job interviews after graduation next week, and I wanted to run something by you.

A: Shoot.

D: Well, OK, I don't exactly know what I want to do after graduation. So I've decided to interview at a couple places—I really need "on the job" experience where I can use my computer science degree.

A: OK. What are some of your options?

D: One is a small hi-tech firm, where I'd be doing software design.

A: Sounds good. And the other?

D: An elementary school. They want me to teach the basic computer class..

A: I thought kids these days were born with computer skills.

D: You're right! They probably know more than I do!

A: So, what's your question?

D: I know I have the skills for both jobs. I have a strong résumé—that internship at Microsoft you helped me get really helps! And I've done my homework—I know a lot about this hi-tech firm and the school, too.

A: But???

D: —But, well, this may sound kind of stupid. But what I'm not sure of is, well, what do I *wear* to an interview?

A: Good question. I guess knowing what to wear is part of the challenge. OK, well, my first suggestion is to dress just a little more formally than the people in that job dress. What do the men wear at the hi-tech firm?

D: The guys wear nice pants, or sometimes jeans, and a dress shirt.

A: Well, jeans are too casual for an interview. Wear some nice pants and a dress shirt, and maybe a suit jacket. A tie might be too formal.

D: What about for the school?

A: When you interview there, you should probably wear a nice shirt and a tie with a suit jacket—not a dark suit, like bankers wear—that would be too much—but something neat and professional.

D: Should I take my earring out when I go for my interview?

A: Ah—well, that's your choice. If you are applying for a job at a conservative place, it might be better to take it out. But you also have to decide if you want to work in a place where you have to make a lot of personal changes.

D: Yeah. Good point. OK—so I should probably cover my tattoos.

A: Tattoos?

D: Yeah . . . See? It's my name written in Chinese characters. I got it when I was in high school. My parents were furious!

A: Well, as long as you wear shirts with sleeves—which I expect you will—there shouldn't be a problem. Just remember you want to put your best foot forward.

D: OK.

A: Both places should be happy to have you.

D: Thanks. So, OK, let's see. Dress neatly—a little better than they do. Think about the earring. Don't mention the tattoo.

A: You've got it. Let me know how your interviews go.

D: I will. Thanks Mr. Greenwood. See you at graduation—if not before.

A: OK. Take care . . . and good luck.

PAGE 127, SECOND LISTENING

4. Listen again to part of the conversation. Then answer question 4.

D: What about for the school?

A: When you interview there, you should probably wear a nice shirt and a tie with a suit jacket—not a dark suit, like bankers wear—that would be too much—but something neat and professional.

What does Mr. Greenwood mean when he says, "not a dark suit, like bankers wear—that would be too much"?

5. Listen again to part of the conversation. Then answer question 5.

D: I know I have the skills for both jobs. I have a strong résumé—that internship at Microsoft you helped me get really helps! And I've done my homework—I know a lot about this hi-tech firm and the school, too.

What is David's attitude when he says, "I know I have the skills for both jobs"?

6. *Listen again to part of the conversation. Then answer question 6.*

A: Well, as long as you wear shirts with sleeves—which I expect you will—there shouldn't be a problem. Just remember you want to put your best foot forward.

D: OK

A: Both places should be happy to have you.

What can be inferred when Mr. Greenwood says, "Both places should be happy to have you"?

ACADEMIC LISTENING

PAGE 129, FIRST LISTENING

Reporter: Hi. This is Sandra Day in New York reporting on "The World of Work" fashion show. With me is designer Marco Bellini. Marco, thanks for joining us!

Marco: My pleasure!

R: Could you tell us about today's show?

M: Well, Sandra, today we'll be seeing the latest styles in men's casual clothing for the workplace.

R: I've heard about this casual trend. Are a lot of businesses doing it?

M: Oh yes. About half of the big companies are allowing employees to dress down, as they say. Some do it once a week or just in the summer. Others do it every day.

R: So, what's a typical outfit in a casual office?

M: OK, comfort is important, but you need to look stylish. No old or torn clothes. No messy hair. You might want to wear a sweater instead of a jacket and tie. And polo shirts with light brown pants are popular. The colors tend to be soft, not flashy, or bright.

R: Now this move to casual . . . has it affected business?

M: Actually business has improved. Companies are finding that if their employees are comfortable, they work longer hours. Also, they don't have to spend so much on clothes, so it's like getting a raise in salary. That makes people want to work for you. Business improves when your employees are happy.

R: What about supervisors? Are they going casual too?

M: Some are. Some people complain that nowadays it's hard to tell the difference between a worker and a supervisor. But most employees like that. It makes everyone feel equal.

R: OK . . . It looks like the show is starting . . . Yes, and here we have the first model. He is wearing . . .

PAGE 129, SECOND LISTENING

6. *Listen again to part of the interview. Then answer question 6.*

Reporter: Hi This is Sandra Day in New York reporting on "The World of Work" fashion show. With me is designer Marco Bellini. Marco, thanks for joining us!"

Marco: My pleasure!

What does Marco Bellini mean when he says, "My pleasure"?

7. *Listen again to part of the interview. Then answer question 7.*

Marco: Actually business has improved. Companies are finding that if their employees are comfortable, they work longer hours. Also, they don't have to spend so much on clothes, so it's like getting a raise in salary. That makes people want to work for you.

What is his tone when Marco Bellini says, "Actually, business has improved"?

INTEGRATED TASK

PAGE 136, LISTENING

Although diet and exercise are still popular ways of improving one's appearance, there are some parts of the body that you cannot change without the help of a cosmetic surgeon.

In the past, American women used to spend weeks repeating words that started with the letter "p" because they wanted to change the shape of their mouths. Today, a cosmetic surgeon can reshape the nose or lips in a few hours. Rhinoplasty, the reshaping of the nose, can greatly improve a person's appearance. People who cannot lose weight in certain areas of their bodies through diet or exercise can use liposuction, which is the surgical removal of body fat, to make their bodies slimmer.

Surprisingly, cosmetic surgery has been used for centuries in China and India. In India, for instance, in the sixth century, noses were actually re-created with plastic surgery after they had been cut off as a punishment. Today, cosmetic surgery is used in many countries to improve the appearance of people who have been hurt in fires or in car accidents. Cosmetic surgery is also used to improve the appearance of children who are born with physical problems.

SKILL FOCUS

PAGE 140, PRACTICE

Ad 1

Hi. I'm Dr. Claudia Crawford. Here at the Dr. Claudia Crawford Total Makeover Clinic we specialize in a wide variety of procedures to help you bring out your own beauty. You can have rhinoplasty to change the shape of your nose, liposuction to get rid of unwanted fat, Botox injections to take away the lines around your eyes. I supervise all procedures right here in my office. You can also speak with our fashion, hair, make-up and exercise specialists, who will help you complete the look you want. Our safe procedures will make you feel and look ten years younger! Let Dr. Claudia Crawford's Total Makeover Clinic show you how beautiful you can be!"

Ad 2

Sunnyvale Community Hospital is the safe place to go for your cosmetic surgery and cosmetic dentistry. Sunnyvale Community Hospital is a *full-service* hospital which also *specializes* in a wide variety of procedures, including rhinoplasty to reshape your nose, liposuction to get rid of unwanted fat, Botox injections to take away the lines around your eyes. Patients at Sunnyvale Community Hospital rest comfortably in private rooms knowing that they are in the hands of a highly certified staff of professional doctors and nurses trained in the latest techniques in cosmetic surgery. Patients here also have the comfort of having all of the resources of a full-service hospital. At Sunnyvale Community Hospital you are safe with us."

Unit 9: Punishment

CAMPUS CONVERSATION

PAGE 145, FIRST LISTENING

Student: Excuse me, professor. You wanted to see me?

Professor: Yes, Andrea. Come in. Have a seat.

S: Thanks. Is there a problem? You didn't give me back my paper in class.

P: Well, Andrea. This is your paper here. And I think you already know there's a problem.

S: Huh? What do you mean?

P: This isn't your writing.

S: Yes, it is!

P: *No*—it's *not*. The first paragraph on page three is almost word-for-word from one of the books on the course syllabus. And the rest of your paper just doesn't sound like you.

S: It doesn't???

P: No, it doesn't. In fact, your concluding paragraphs come directly from the Internet.

S: Well, I was really sick last week . . . *and* I had to visit my brother who is in the hospital because of a serious car accident. But . . .

P: *But* nothing! This is plagiarism, Andrea—and not your first time!

S: Huh?

P: Didn't professor Burton give you a warning after he discovered that you had plagiarized part of your history paper?

S: You spoke with him?

P: Yesterday. And didn't he clearly tell you that you needed to cite every source when you write a paper for his class—or any class?

S: I guess so.

P: So, look Andrea, there is no excuse for plagiarism. I'm sorry if your brother is in the hospital. But you were warned once. There are serious consequences at this university for plagiarism.

S: What do you mean?

P: Well, I need to report this to the ARB.

S: What's the ARB?

P: It's the university's Academic Review Board. They handle cases of academic dishonesty such as this.

S: Oh . . . um . . . so what's going to happen next?

P: Well, you will probably be put on academic probation.

S: Oh.

P: And if you do it again, you could be expelled from the University.

S: Expelled???

P: Perhaps.

S: Well . . . so . . . what do I do now?

P: I imagine someone from the ARB will be in touch with you. That person will tell you the date of the next meeting of the ARB. You know, Andrea you are a bright young woman. You should know better.

S: Um, yeah, you're right. I know. I'm sorry. I'll re-do the paper.

P: All right then. See you in class.

S: All right, see ya in class.

PAGE 146, SECOND LISTENING

5. *Listen again to part of the conversation. Then answer question 5.*

P: And if you do it again, you could be expelled from the university.

S: Expelled???

What is the student's attitude when she says, "Expelled"?

6. *Listen again to part of the conversation. Then answer question 6.*

S: Um, yeah, you're right. I know. I'm sorry. I'll re-do the paper.

P: All right then. See you in class.

S: All right, see ya in class.

Why did the professor say, "All right then. See you in class"?

7. *Listen again to part of the conversation. Then answer question 7.*

P: I imagine someone from the ARB will be in touch with you. That person will tell you the date of the next meeting of the ARB. You know, Andrea you are a bright young woman. You should know better.

S: Um, yeah, you're right. I know. I'm sorry. I'll re-do the paper.

What does the professor mean when she says, "You should know better"?

ACADEMIC LISTENING

PAGE 147, FIRST LISTENING

Announcer: Thank you all for attending this panel discussion on the long-term effects of corporal punishment—specifically spanking or hitting children as a form of discipline. Before we open the discussion up to questions from our audience, I would like to give our expert speakers a chance to summarize their points. The first is Donald Sterling, a lawyer and psychologist who interviews criminals before they go to trial.

Sterling: I've seen it over and over again. Violent criminals were almost always spanked and hit when they were children. This corporal punishment teaches children to be violent when they are very young, so when they are adults, they commit crimes and abuse their wives and children. And then their children grow up to be violent, and the cycle continues.

Announcer: Next is Dr. Phyllis Jones from the Center for Family Research.

Jones: We studied 332 families to see how parents' actions affected teenagers' behavior. We found that teenagers did better when they had clear discipline as a child. Some of these parents used spanking as a form of discipline, and some didn't. It seems that spanking doesn't hurt children if it's done in a loving home, but it's most important to talk to your children and spend time with them. Spanking should be the choice of the parents.

Announcer: And finally, Lois Goldin, a child psychologist.

Goldin: In the United States, the number of parents who spank their kids is decreasing, and people who oppose spanking say that's good because it will make our society less violent. But look at the statistics. Actually, violent crime is rising every year, and the number of teenagers and children that commit crimes is going up the fastest! Parents need to control their children better, and corporal punishment is one way to do that.

Announcer: My thanks to our three speakers. Now our guests will be happy to answer questions from the audience . . .

PAGE 147, SECOND LISTENING

6. Listen again to part of the discussion. Then answer question 6.

Sterling: This corporal punishment teaches children to be violent when they are very young, so when they are adults, they commit crimes and abuse their wives and children. And then their children grow up to be violent, and the cycle continues.

What is the speaker's attitude when he says, "And then their children grow up to be violent, and the cycle continues"?

7. Listen again to part of the discussion. Then answer question 7.

Goldin: In the United States, the number of parents who spank their kids is decreasing, and people who oppose spanking say that's good because it will make our society less violent. But look at the statistics.

Why does Goldin say "But look at the statistics"?

INTEGRATED TASK

PAGE 155, LISTENING

Male speaker: Murder is totally unfair. The victims of murder are gone forever. Take the case of Tammy Thompson for example. Thompson was a twenty-five year-old mother of two who was shot by Gloria Jean Gibson. The two women argued over some money. Out of anger, Gibson shot Thompson to death. Because of Gibson's uncontrollable anger, Tammy Thompson's hopes and plans have ended permanently, and the pleasures she enjoyed in life have been destroyed. This is true of all victims of murder. They will never see their friends again and will never hear the voices of family members who cry, "How could this have happened?" But the murderer is still alive! Without the death penalty, murderers are allowed to live and enjoy life.

There is no reason why a killer should live. Justice demands that each person respect the rights and freedoms of every other person, or be punished for not doing so. People who commit murder give up their rights to citizenship and to life itself. Why should the tax dollars of honest citizens—including the victim's family—be used to keep the killer alive?

The only fair punishment is execution. Execution puts the killer away from society forever, stops him from killing again, and sends a strong message to others who might kill: Killers will not be allowed to live.

Let's give life to people who truly respect it—not those who destroy it.

Unit 10: Marriage

CAMPUS CONVERSATION

PAGE 163, FIRST LISTENING

Student: Excuse me—Is this the reference department?

Librarian: Yes it is. How can I help you?

S: Well, it's my first time in this library, and I'm—ah—I'm doing a paper about marriage and, so, I need a little help doing a search in the library's databases.

L: Well, you've come to the right place. So, what's your topic?

S: Um—*Marriage.*

L: Yes, I know that, but you need to narrow your topic a bit more. *Marriage* is a pretty big category—What course is this for?

S: It's a sociology course...

L: . . . Uh-huh . . .

S: Well, maybe I can research how couples meet, you know, so many people meet on the Internet these days. Or maybe I could research different types of marriages, like same-sex marriages or polygamous marriages. Or how about different marriage customs around the world . . . ?—Wow—it is a big topic. It's hard to narrow it down.

L: Well, some kind of cross-cultural research might be interesting.

S: Um, yeah. I think so too! You know, my brother just got married last summer, and it really got me thinking about marriage. He married this woman he met in graduate school. She's from South America. They tried to incorporate different customs into the wedding, so both families would feel comfortable. It wasn't that easy, but it turned out well in the end. And they're really happy . . .

L: Well, so you have some personal experience with a cross-cultural marriage. So, now let's try to narrow your search a little more. Are there any cultures in particular you would like to study?

S: Well, I think I'd like to learn more about my new sister-in-law's customs. So how about marriage customs in Brazil? That's where she's from.

L: Great. So, have a seat here at the computer.

S: OK. Thanks.

L: Start by entering your search criteria to help locate the information you want—words like *marriage, customs,* and . . . the country, Brazil . . .

S: *Marriage . . . customs . . . Brazil* B-R-A-Z-I-L . . . and . . . Enter. Over 148,000 matches!

L: OK, so let's narrow your search a little more. Do you want to research current traditions or past traditions?

S: Current traditions.

L: OK, so add "current" to your search criteria.

S: OK . . . Still about 130,000! But I can play with this for a little while.

L: Well, it looks like you've got the hang of it now.

S: Yeah, I'm all set for now. Thanks for your help.

L: Sure. I'll be over at the reference desk if you have any questions. Good luck.

S: OK, thanks again.

PAGE 164, SECOND LISTENING

4. Listen again to part of the conversation. Then answer question 4.

L: Well, you've come to the right place. So, what's your topic?

S: Um—*Marriage.*

L: Yes, I know that, but you need to narrow your topic a bit more. *Marriage* is a pretty big category—What course is this for?

What is the student's attitude when she says, "Um—Marriage."?

5. *Listen again to part of the conversation. Then answer question 5.*

L: OK, so add "current" to your search criteria.

S: OK . . . Still about 130,000! But I can play with this for a little while.

L: Well, it looks like you've got the hang of it now.

What is the student's attitude when she says, "Still about 130,000!"?

ACADEMIC LISTENING

PAGE 165, FIRST LISTENING

Professor: OK, class, this week we will be looking at family life around the world. Therefore, today I would like to begin by focusing on marriage.

All societies have their own form of marriage. The ideas that we have about marriage are part of our cultural background. Now, one of the obvious challenges for most people is finding the right person to marry.

As we study marriage, we find that different cultures have solved the problem of finding a marriage partner, or spouse, in different ways. Finding a marriage partner has never been easy for people, no matter when or where they have lived.

In China in the first half of the 1900s, marriage decisions were often made by parents or older family members. This practice is known as arranged marriage. Parents who wanted to find a spouse for their son or daughter asked a matchmaker to find someone with the right characteristics, including age and educational background. According to the Chinese way of thinking at that time, it might be a serious mistake to let two young people choose their own partners. This important decision was made by older family members, who understood that the goal of marriage was to produce healthy sons. Sons were considered to be important because they would take positions of leadership in the family and keep the family name alive.

Today, however, couples in China meet, they fall in love, and then they get married—as couples do in most other cultures around the world. But arranged marriages are not completely a thing of the past. Sometimes, in modern-day India, marriage partners are still matched by their families. Some couples only meet each other two or three times before the wedding day.

In contrast, in some traditions, young people were more involved in choosing a partner. For example, the Hopi, a native people of North America, had a very different idea about finding a marriage partner. The Hopi allowed boys to leave their parents' home at age thirteen to live in a *kiva*, a special home for young males. Here they enjoyed the freedom to go out alone at night and secretly visit young girls. Boys typically left the girl's home before daylight, but a girl's parents usually did not get angry about the night visits. They allowed the visits to continue if they thought the boy would make a good marriage partner. After a few months of visits, most girls became pregnant. In this way, the girls were choosing their favorite boy for a husband.

Now, let me just stop here for a moment and ask if you have any questions before I continue . . . (fade).

PAGE 165, SECOND LISTENING

4. *Listen again to part of the conversation. Then answer question 4.*

In contrast, in some traditions, young people were more involved in choosing a partner.

*Why does the speaker use the expression **in contrast**?*

6. *Listen again to part of the conversation. Then answer question 6.*

After a few months of receiving visits, most girls became pregnant. In this way, the girls were choosing their favorite boy for a husband.

What can be inferred from this statement?

INTEGRATED TASK

PAGE 172, LISTENING

The Mormon View of Marriage

A well-known example of a different style of marriage is found among the early Mormons, a Christian religion that began in the United States.

The group's first leader, Joseph Smith, believed that a man should be allowed to have several wives. As the Mormon Church developed, many of the men followed Smith's teaching and married a number of women. In 1854, one Mormon leader became a father nine times in *one* week when nine of his wives all had babies.

At that time, the Mormons believed that it was a woman's duty to marry at a young age and to raise as many children as possible. The Mormons viewed having children as a way of increasing the number of faithful and making the church stronger.

Today, the Mormon Church, which calls itself the Church of Jesus Christ of Latter-Day Saints, teaches that marriage should be a partnership between one man and one woman who will be together not only during this life but also forever.

Answer Key

UNIT 1

CAMPUS CONVERSATION
Pre-Listening Vocabulary, page 2

1. b
2. h
3. f
4. c
5. a
6. d
7. g
8. i
9. e

First Listening, page 3

1. Infomercials
2. Can we trust the information in infomercials?
3. A friend who bought an ab machine she saw on an infomercial

Second Listening, page 4

1. A
2. A
3. C
4. D
5. A

ACADEMIC LISTENING
First Listening, page 5

	PRODUCT NAME	PROBLEM	EFFECT OF THE PRODUCT
Ad 1	• Thief Buster	• People stealing your car.	• A thief touches the car, and an alarm rings • The engine turns off automatically
Ad 2	• Rinse Away	• Dandruff, white powdery flakes • Embarrassment • Lack of concentration	• Your dandruff will go away • You will feel more confident

Second Listening, page 5

1. C
2. B, D
3. C
4. B
5. A
6. C

READING
Pre-reading, page 6

- Companies selling their products in other countries, including China and Russia
- TV advertising

Reading, page 6

1. A
2. B
3. A
4. B
5. A
6. C
7. C
8. C
9. D
10. A
11. A, D, E

Analysis, page 10

Basic Comprehension: 1, 4, 5, 10, 11

Organization: 9

Inference: 3, 7

Vocabulary and Reference: 2, 6, 8

INTEGRATED TASK
Reading, page 11
Answers will vary.

Listening, page 12

Main Idea: Advertisers use different techniques to persuade us to buy.

Effective Technique: Emotional appeal

Most Popular: Appeal to the sense of humor

Example of an Ad: Doggie's Friend flea collar

Speaking, page 12
Answers will vary.

SKILL FOCUS
Practice, page 15

1. Problems in global advertising related to language and culture.
2. Paragraph 2
3. Star
4. The other side, a competing product
2. *Answers will vary.*

UNIT 2

CAMPUS CONVERSATION
Pre-Listening Vocabulary, page 18

1. d
2. f
3. e
4. g
5. c
6. i
7. a
8. h
9. b

First Listening, page 19

1. The student feels pressure because her parents want her to go to medical school.
2. She wants to become a famous athlete.

Second Listening, page 19

1.	A	3.	C	5.	B
2.	D	4.	C	6.	B

ACADEMIC LISTENING

First Listening, page 20

The passage is about people called: sensation seekers.

These people like:

- strong emotions
- hard rock music
- extreme sports
- frightening horror movies
- danger, risk, excitement

Second Listening, page 21

1.	A	3.	B	5.	B
2.	C	4.	C	6.	A

Analysis, page 22

Basic Comprehension: 1, 2, 6

Organization: 4

Inference: 3, 5

READING

Pre-reading, page 23

1. A gymnast
2. A girl
3. Pressure to lose weight and be a good athlete

Reading, page 23

1.	B	4.	A	7.	C	10.	C
2.	D	5.	C	8.	A	11.	A, D, F
3.	D	6.	D	9.	C		

INTEGRATED TASK

Reading, page 26

Sensation seekers want to have excitement or strong feelings all the time, or they plan activities that will give them this experience. Anorexia nervosa is a condition that results from anxiety. It is an extreme, unhealthy interest in one's weight.

Listening, page 27

Main Idea: Tony Hawk's obsession turned into something positive.

Support:

High point of his career: Writing "skateboarder" as his occupation

1999 Summer X Games: Successfully performing the 900

Problems in school: He dressed differently from other kids. Athletes picked on him. Girls were not interested in him.

Writing, page 27

Step 1:

- skateboarding
- *answers will vary*
- A, B
- *answers will vary*

SKILL FOCUS

Practice, page 30

1

1. A
2. B
3. B
4. D

2

1. A
2. C
3. A

3

Answers will vary.

UNIT 3

CAMPUS CONVERSATION

Pre-Listening Vocabulary, page 34

1.	b	4.	a	7.	a
2.	a	5.	b	8.	a
3.	b	6.	a	9.	a

First Listening, page 35

1. Finding a scholarship
2. He asks about scholarship search agencies.

Second Listening, page 36

1.	D	3.	C	5.	A
2.	A	4.	B	6.	A

ACADEMIC LISTENING

First Listening, page 37

SPEAKERS	WHY DID THE SPEAKER GIVE FRANK MONEY?
Joe	He believes people too easily.
Rosa	She is lonely, and Frank seemed to care about her.
Peter	He hoped to take his wife on a trip with the extra money.
Beth	She felt pressure to decide right away.

Second Listening, page 37

1. B	3. B	5. D
2. C	4. A	6. A

READING

Pre-reading, page 38
Suggested Answers:

PARAGRAPH	WORD IN PASSAGE	YOUR DEFINITION
1	founder	creator, originator
2	cure	treatment, solution
3	qualified	trained, able, skilled
6	testimonials	support, praise

Reading, page 39

1. A	5. A	9. D
2. B	6. C	10. D
3. D	7. B	11. A
4. B	8. B	12. A, C, D

Analysis, page 42

Basic Comprehension: 1, 3, 7, 11, 12

Organization: 6, 10

Inference: 4, 5

Vocabulary and Reference: 2, 8, 9

INTEGRATED TASK

Reading, page 43
Suggested Answers:

- A quack is a person who pretends and gives medical advice.
- Treatments from quacks may be unsafe. These treatments may not work.

Listening, page 43
Suggested Answers:

One year ago: One year ago Matt found out he had cancer.

A few months later: A few months later Matt found out that the cancer was still growing.

Then: Then he became sick and depressed. The doctors gave him more medicine, but it didn't help. The doctors told him that they were unable to do anything more; he had only six months to live.

Today: Today Matt is going to see a doctor who is a quack.

Speaking, page 44

Step 1
Suggested Answers:

Matt's reasons FOR going to a quack:

1. He was afraid of dying.
2. He wanted to find help.
3. His family or friends recommended other treatments.

Matt's friend's reasons AGAINST going to a quack:

1. Treatments are unproven.
2. Treatments can be dangerous.
3. Treatments can be expensive.

SKILL FOCUS

Practice, page 48

1

1. A miracle cure is a treatment or product that solves a problem quickly, easily and completely.
2. That a patient is afraid and will try anything
3. D
4. B
5. Letters written by satisfied customers
6. D
7. Becoming a victim of a quack

2

Answers will vary.

UNIT 4

CAMPUS CONVERSATION

Pre-Listening Vocabulary, page 52

1. c	3. g	5. d	7. f
2. e	4. h	6. a	8. b

First Listening, page 53

1. She wants to know if she can write a paper instead of doing an oral presentation.
2. He tells her that she has to do the oral presentation.
3. He recommends that she use an outline, use visuals, make eye contact and rehearse.

Second Listening, page 53

1. C
2. B
3. A
4. D
5. A, D
6. A

ACADEMIC LISTENING

First Listening, page 54

Torrence's technique for learning a story: Read the story five times.

The first time: Check that you like the story.

The second time: Focus on the images.

The third time: Focus on the words.

Second Listening, page 55

1. A		3. B		5. B		7. D
2. C		4. A		6. B		

Analysis, page 56

Basic Comprehension: 1, 2

Organization: 6, 7

Inference: 3, 4, 5

READING

Pre-reading, page 57

1. A cockroach

2. Two

3. a) Based on Kafka's use of a word meaning "vermin" which can mean a person who is disgusting

   b) Based on Kafka's relationship with his own father

Reading, page 57

1. D	5. B	9. A	13. C, D, E
2. B	6. A	10. B	
3. C	7. D	11. D	
4. C	8. B	12. B	

INTEGRATED TASK

Reading, page 61

Definition: Giving human traits or qualities to something that is not human

Example 1: Greek literature

Example 2: A house plant

Listening, page 62
Suggested Answers:

MAIN IDEAS	DETAILS
Gregor's dream	A bad dream. He realized that he . . . was a cockroach.
Gregor's job	He was a traveling salesman. He hated his job. He had to work hard to support his family.
Gregor's problems	He had overslept. He was a cockroach. He hated his job. He had trouble getting out of bed. He hit his head when he fell on the floor.

Writing, page 62
Answers will vary.

SKILL FOCUS

Practice, page 67

1

1. D	3. A
2. B	4. D

2

Definition

3

Narration

4
Answers will vary.

UNIT 5

CAMPUS CONVERSATION

Pre-Listening Vocabulary, page 70

1. b	4. f	7. e
2. i	5. g	8. a
3. c	6. h	9. d

First Listening, page 71

1. Getting used to living in a big city

2. Don't give up. / Hang in there. Stop by if you want to talk.

Second Listening, page 71

1. D	3. A	5. B
2. C	4. C	6. B

ACADEMIC LISTENING

First Listening, page 72

WORDS	Refer to Men	Refer to Women	Refer to Both
doctor			✓
bachelorette		✓	
policeman	✓		
firefighter			✓
mail carrier			✓

WORDS	Used to Men	Used to Women	Used to Both
purple			✓
lavender		✓	
periwinkle		✓	
mauve		✓	
lovely		✓	
cute		✓	
adorable		✓	

Second Listening, page 73

1.	B	3.	A	5.	B	7.	D
2.	B	4.	A	6.	B		

READING

Pre-reading, page 75

1. Depending on the situation, people who know more than one language might switch or change between languages when speaking to someone who speaks the same languages.

2. **a)** Pamela and Gabriela (social closeness)

   b) Children of immigrant parents (social distance)

   c) Teenaged girl (lack of knowledge about or lack of attention to the language)

Reading, page 75

1.	D	4.	A	7.	A	10.	B
2.	A	5.	C	8.	C	11.	B
3.	B	6.	C, D	9.	D	12.	A, B, D

- Speakers may code switch to show affection or closeness to another speaker.

Analysis, page 79

Basic Comprehension: 1, 5, 6, 11, 12

Organization: 4, 10

Inference: 2, 8, 9

Vocabulary and Reference: 3, 7

INTEGRATED TASK

Reading, page 79

Answers will vary.

Listening, page 80

Suggested Answers:

How do people react to Joseph's accent?

   (+) They think it is musical.

   (-) They think he is not intelligent (bright).

How does Joseph feel about people's reaction to his accent?

- He feels self-conscious.
- He is tired of explaining where he is from.
- He feels that he doesn't fit in sometimes.

Speaking, page 80

Answers will vary.

SKILL FOCUS

Practice, page 85

Main idea: Americans need to learn foreign languages.

Details for support: 1) People from other countries will not respect us if we do not try to understand their languages and cultures.

2) We will have problems in business.

1. B

2. B, E

3. *Answers will vary.*

Main idea: A person who lives in the USA may have problems with language at first.

   Detail 1: You may not understand the local accent.

   Detail 2: Americans may not understand you right away.

   Detail 3: Americans use slang.

   Detail 4: Americans use humor.

   Detail 5: You may not know abbreviations and technical words and phrases.

1. A

2. *Answers will vary.*

3. D

4. *Answers will vary.*

3

Answers will vary.

UNIT 6

CAMPUS CONVERSATION

Pre-Listening Vocabulary, page 90

1.	c	4.	d	7.	e
2.	i	5.	f	8.	b
3.	a	6.	h	9.	g

First Listening, page 91

1. She wants an extension on her paper.

2. He gives her help finding information for her paper.

Second Listening, page 92

1.	B	3.	D	5.	A
2.	B	4.	B	6.	B

ACADEMIC LISTENING

First Listening, page 93

Mrs. Green: Tourism causes traffic jams.

Mr. Horowitz: Tourism causes housing prices to go up.

Ms. Keller: Tourism is important for the town's economy.

Second Listening, page 94

1.	B	3.	C	5.	C
2.	A	4.	D	6.	A, D

Analysis, page 95

Basic Comprehension: 1, 2, 3, 6

Inference: 4, 5

READING

Pre-reading, page 95

Suggested Answers:

1. During her life a woman might wear as many as 25 rings weighing 5-6 kilos around her neck.

2. These women will continue to wear rings around their necks if tourists keep visiting their village.

Reading, page 96

1. C	5. A	9. B	13. A, D, F
2. B	6. D	10. C	
3. C	7. B	11. B	
4. D	8. D	12. A	

INTEGRATED TASK

Reading, page 100

Suggested Answers:

- Going to the Antarctic is an adventure.
- There are many activities.
- It will be an unforgettable educational experience.
- People who experience its beauty will want to work to save it.

Listening, page 101

What scientists study:

- the hole in the ozone
- global warming
- planets and stars
- animals
- plants
- the Earth
- human behavior

Effects of tourism:

- tourists take scientists away from research
- tourists can hurt the environment
- oil spills

Writing, page 101

Answers will vary.

SKILL FOCUS

Practice, page 105

1

1. B
2. B
3. D

2

1. Passport pictures often make us look bad or sick. They are not flattering.

2. The best part of a trip is the planning and remembering it because, during the trip, there are often difficulties.

UNIT 7

CAMPUS CONVERSATION

Pre-Listening Vocabulary, page 108

1. c	4. a	7. d
2. f	5. b	8. g
3. e	6. h	9. i

First Listening, page 109

1. He is concerned about getting a bad grade in his chemistry class because the TA is not covering enough material in lab.

2. The professor is going to check up on the TA and offer a make-up test.

Second Listening, page 109

1. C	3. A	5. B
2. D	4. C	6. A

ACADEMIC LISTENING

First Listening, page 110

In Real Life	On Television
Lucille Ball	*Lucy Ricardo*
• *a successful movie actress in the 1930s*	• a housewife
• a radio star in the 1940s	• had a crazy ambition to be in show business
• was married to Desi Arnaz	• feminine, soft and pretty
• wanted to work with her husband	
Desi Arnaz	*Ricky Ricardo*
• was married to Lucille Ball	• a Cuban immigrant
• a radio performer in the 1940s	• a bandleader
• wanted to work with his wife	• a strong male figure
• described to CBS what kind of humor he wanted on the show	

Second Listening, page 111

1. C	3. A	5. D
2. B	4. C	6. A

READING

Pre-reading, page 112
Suggested Answer:

"The Cosby Show" is a popular, funny TV show about an African-American family.

Reading, page 112

1. C	4. B	7. D	10. A
2. A	5. A	8. D	11. D
3. A	6. B	9. A	12. A, E, F

Analysis, page 117

Basic Comprehension: 1, 2, 6, 11, 12

Organization: 9, 10

Inference: 4, 5, 8

Vocabulary and Reference: 3, 7

INTEGRATED TASK

Reading, page 117

1. Something in the joke is surprising.
2. People want to feel superior to others.

Listening, page 118

1. Carmen, a lawyer
2. a lawyer joke
3. "Now, what's your third question?"
4. Lawyers are only interested in money.

Speaking, page 118
Answers will vary.

SKILL FOCUS

Practice, page 122

Step 1

Her main idea: Humor is important.

The important details: Humor breaks up the repetition of everyday life. Jokes give people confidence to make people laugh.

Step 3
Suggested Answer:

Everyone has a sense of humor and telling jokes is a good way to make other people laugh. People should use their sense of humor because humor makes life more enjoyable.

UNIT 8

CAMPUS CONVERSATION

Pre-Listening Vocabulary, page 126

1. f	4. a	7. b	10. h
2. d	5. c	8. e	
3. g	6. i	9. j	

First Listening, page 127

1. He doesn't know what to wear to his job interviews.
2. Mr. Greenwood tells him to dress a little more formally than the people who work there and to put his best foot forward.

Second Listening, page 127

1. D	3. B	5. D
2. A, C	4. B	6. A

ACADEMIC LISTENING

First Listening, page 129

BENEFITS OF THIS CHANGE	DRAWBACKS OF THIS CHANGE
Employees are more comfortable, spend less money on clothes, work longer, and they feel more equal.	It is hard to tell the difference between workers and supervisors.

Second Listening, page 129

1. A	3. C	5. A	7. A
2. D	4. B	6. D	

Analysis, page 130

Basic Comprehension: 1, 2, 3, 5, 6

Organization: 4

Inference: 7

READING

Pre-reading, page 131

YOUNG WOMEN IN SRI LANKA	
Reasons They Wear Saris	Reasons They Do Not Like To Wear Saris
Saris are more traditional, elegant and formal than Western clothes	Saris are old-fashioned, not practical for everyday life, too warm, difficult to walk in.

Reading, page 132

1. C	4. D	7. B	10. B
2. A	5. C	8. B	11. B, D, E
3. B	6. D	9. D	

INTEGRATED TASK

Reading, page 135

Plastic surgery is risky. For example, patients might receive too much or too little anesthesia or they may receive poor care from clinics.

Listening, page 136

1. Repeating words with the "p" sound
2. Rhinoplasty and liposuction
3. Plastic surgery is used to help people hurt in accidents and children born with physical problems.

Writing, page 136

Answers will vary.

INDEPENDENT TASK

Speaking, page 137

Step 2
Suggested Answers:

	PROS	CONS
Students	Getting dressed is easier.	Student can't express themselves through fashion. There will be too much conformity.
Parents	A dress code gives children discipline. It will teach them the value of rules and conformity.	They have to listen to the complaints of their children.
Teachers / School Admini-strators	It is easier to identify who belongs in the school. It creates a sense of order and community.	They have to listen to the complaints of students.

SKILL FOCUS

Practice, page 140

	DR. CLAUDIA CRAWFORD'S TOTAL MAKEOVER CLINIC	SUNNYVALE COMMUNITY HOSPITAL
What services do they offer?	• Rhinoplasty • Liposuction • Botox injections • Fashion, hair, make-up and exercise consultation	• Rhinoplasty • Liposuction • Botox injections • Cosmetic dentistry
What other information do you learn about these two places?	• Safe procedures • Will help you feel younger	• A safe place • A full-service hospital • Private rooms • Certified staff

UNIT 9

CAMPUS CONVERSATION

Pre-Listening Vocabulary, page 144

1. h	4. d	7. f
2. b	5. g	8. i
3. c	6. e	9. a

First Listening, page 145

1. The student's paper
2. The student plagiarized information in her paper.

Second Listening, page 145

1. B	3. D	5. D	7. A
2. C	4. C	6. A	

ACADEMIC LISTENING

First Listening, page 147

EXPERT	OPINION OF SPANKING	REASONS
Sterling	Against it	Spanking teaches children to be violent. It starts a cycle of violence that the child will pass on to his or her children.
Jones	For it in some cases	Spanking is effective if done in the context of a loving home.
Goldin	For it	Children needs discipline because the number of crimes committed by children and teens is increasing.

Second Listening, page 147

1. D	3. D	5. C	7. A
2. B	4. B	6. B	

READING

Pre-reading, page 148

1. People disagree about spanking.
2. He was arrested for spanking his five-year-old son at a shopping mall. A mall employee called the police.

Reading, page 149

1. B	5. D	9. B
2. B	6. B	10. B
3. D	7. C	11. D
4. C	8. A	12. C

13. Arguments in favor of spanking: A, E, F, J
Arguments against spanking: C, D, G, I
Not used: B, H

Analysis, page 153

Basic Comprehension: 1, 2, 5, 12, 13

Organization: 4, 7, 8, 11

Inference: 3, 9, 10

Vocabulary and Reference: 6

INTEGRATED TASK

Reading, page 154

According to the author, the death penalty is wrong because it is just another type of murder and because it is so expensive.

Listening, page 155

Detailed example for support: The story of Tammy Thompson and Gloria Jean Gibson

Who was involved? Tammy Thompson and Gloria Jean Gibson

What happened? Gibson shot and killed Thompson when they were arguing over some money.

Why did the speaker give this example? To show that it is not fair for a murderer to continue living.

Speaking, page 155
Answer will vary.

SKILL FOCUS

Practice, page 160
Answers will vary.

UNIT 10

CAMPUS CONVERSATION

Pre-Listening Vocabulary, page 162

1. f	4. i	7. h	10. c
2. e	5. a	8. j	11. d
3. k	6. b	9. g	

First Listening, page 163

1. She needs help using the library research databases.

2. The librarian helps the student narrow her topic and shows her how to use the databases.

Second Listening, page 164

1. A	3. D	5. C
2. D	4. C	

ACADEMIC LISTENING

First Listening, page 165

MARRIAGE CUSTOMS	
In China in the First Half of the 1900s	**In Traditional Hopi Culture**
• Marriage partners were chosen by parents or older family members. • Parents used matchmakers.	• Boys visited girls late at night. • After the girl became pregnant, the couple got married.

Second Listening, page 165

1. A	3. B	5. A
2. B	4. C	6. D

Analysis, page 166

Basic Comprehension: 1, 2, 3

Organization: 4, 5

Inference: 6

READING

Pre-reading, page 167

1. Arranged marriage

2. His opinion: Arranged marriage is the best way to find a marriage partner.

   His classmates' opinion: Romantic dating is the best way to find a marriage partner.

Reading, page 167

1. D	4. A	7. C	10. D
2. B	5. D	8. A	11. B
3. A	6. B	9. B	

12. Marriage in Vietnam: A, E, G
Marriage in the United States: B, C, F, H
Not used: D, I

INTEGRATED TASK

Reading, page 171

1. Polygamy is when a man has more than one wife at once.

2. Christianity and Judaism do not permit polygamy. In some countries where Islam is the official religion, polygamy is allowed in some cases.

Listening, page 172

In the Past

- Joseph Smith believed a man should be allowed to have several wives.
- A woman's duty was to get married at an early age and raise as many children as possible.
- Having children was a way of increasing the number of faithful and making the church stronger.

Today

- Today the Mormons are called the Church of Latter Day Saints.
- The church teaches that marriage is between one man and one woman.

Writing, page 172

Answers will vary.

SKILL FOCUS

Practice, page 176

Passage 1: 1. Similar to
2. However
3. and
4. Nevertheless

Passage 2: 1. In addition
2. and
3. however
4. As a result

PART TWO

ETS Practice Sets for the TOEFL® iBT

LISTENING

Listen to the conversations and lectures. Answer the questions based on what is stated or implied by the speakers. You may take notes while you listen. Use your notes to help you answer the questions. (Check the Answer Key on page 231.)

CONVERSATION 1

1. Why does the student go to see the professor?
   (A) To get help with the concepts in a reading assignment
   (B) To ask for more time to complete an assigned report
   (C) To find out important information about course requirements
   (D) To discuss a theory the professor mentioned in class

2. What does the professor say about class assignments? **Choose TWO answers.**
   (A) All projects will include a report.
   (B) Everyone must complete two projects.
   (C) Students have a choice of assignment types.
   (D) All work is due at the end of the semester.

3. According to the professor, what is the advantage of working on a "comprehensive" project?
   (A) It requires less work than the focused project.
   (B) It may be more useful later when looking for a job.
   (C) It gives the students the opportunity to learn more.
   (D) It is usually more interesting than the focused project.

4. What can be inferred about the student's plans?
   (A) He has scheduled a job interview at an advertising firm.
   (B) He will not take any marketing classes next semester.
   (C) He has not yet decided on a possible career.
   (D) He will miss more classes to attend student council meetings.

Listen again to part of the conversation. Then answer question 5.

5. What does the professor mean when he says this?
  (**A**) The student should take his class work more seriously.
  (**B**) Class assignments may help the student in job interviews.
  (**C**) The student should become more involved with some campus sports activities.
  (**D**) An on-campus job would provide the student with valuable experience.

CONVERSATION 2

1. Why does the student go to see his academic adviser?
  (**A**) He needs help with a broken computer.
  (**B**) He wants to talk about which courses he should select.
  (**C**) He wants to ask for advice on a legal issue.
  (**D**) He needs to borrow money for a sick family member.

2. Why did the student attempt to purchase an item via the Internet?
  (**A**) He was having difficulty finding the item in stores.
  (**B**) He always makes his purchases online.
  (**C**) He did not have time to look for the item in stores.
  (**D**) He realized that it was cheaper than the items in the stores.

3. What does the professor imply about the student's problem?
  (**A**) Other students on campus have had the same problem.
  (**B**) The problem should be easy to solve.
  (**C**) The student is to blame for the problem.
  (**D**) A better computer would have prevented the problem.

4. How does the student's academic adviser help him with his problem?
  (**A**) She contacts the police for him.
  (**B**) She gives him the name of a Web site to report his concerns.
  (**C**) She lends him the money he lost.
  (**D**) She suggests that he write a letter to the stereo company requesting a refund.

Listen again to part of the conversation. Then answer question 5.

5. What can be inferred about the professor when she says this?
  (**A**) She would rather not discuss the student's concerns.
  (**B**) She already knew what the student was going to tell her.
  (**C**) She does not feel that the student's problem is valid.
  (**D**) She has a problem similar to the student's.

LECTURE 1

1. What is this lecture mainly about?
   (A) The history of advertising methods
   (B) A study of children's reactions to advertising
   (C) The ways advertisers try to attract consumers
   (D) Research on consumers' spending habits

2. What does the professor imply about the relationship between psychology and business?
   (A) Businesspeople should be more open in expressing their emotions.
   (B) Advertisers need to understand psychological principles.
   (C) Psychologists must learn how to advertise their services.
   (D) Psychology students should take classes in business.

3. Why does the professor talk about blue jeans?
   (A) To comment on historical trends in popular clothing
   (B) To give an example of a product unlikely to be promoted using fear
   (C) To discuss the clothing preferences of college students
   (D) To discuss the importance of finding the right pair

4. According to the professor, what factors influence customers' reactions to advertising? **Choose TWO answers.**
   (A) Their desire to satisfy basic biological needs
   (B) Their opinion of the company that makes the product
   (C) Their hope of building better social relationships
   (D) Their perception of the quality of the product

5. According to the professor, what is the message of some advertising for children's toys?
   (A) Parents should buy toys that are educational.
   (B) New toys are designed better than older toys.
   (C) Parents and children should play with toys together.
   (D) A child with a new toy will have more friends.

Listen again to part of the lecture. Then answer question 6.

6. What does the professor imply when she says this?
   (A) There was a good reason for putting people in the picture.
   (B) She does not remember the main point of her lecture.
   (C) The advertiser forgot to consider basic human instincts.
   (D) She wants students to learn how to develop advertisements correctly.

LECTURE 2

1. What is the purpose of this lecture?
  (A) To persuade the students to become storytellers
  (B) To give instructions on how to tell stories
  (C) To explain the difference between fairy tales and folktales
  (D) To discuss why some people choose to be storytellers

2. According to the professor, why should a storyteller consider the audience before telling a story?
  (A) Some audiences may be more mature than others.
  (B) Some audiences prefer stories filled with physical action.
  (C) Audiences with younger children require more description of imagery.
  (D) Audiences with older children are already familiar with many stories.

3. How does the professor organize her discussion of the parts of storytelling?
  (A) She gives examples of stories for younger children, then stories for older children.
  (B) She explains how to tell shorter stories before how to tell longer stories.
  (C) She describes how to choose a story before how to tell a story.
  (D) She mentions some great stories before naming great storytellers.

4. Why does the professor mention the "Cinderella" story?
  (A) She wants to show why mental imagery can be effective.
  (B) She is trying to illustrate why children prefer fairy tales to folktales.
  (C) She wants to discuss one of her favorite fairy tales.
  (D) She believes "Cinderella" is the best fairy tale for children to hear.

5. Match each of the parts of storytelling delivery with the descriptions below.

mental imagery	physical or body paralanguage	emphasis

  (A) Change the tone in the voice, monitor the volume and rate of speech.
  (B) Use sensory words.
  (C) Use facial expressions and gesture.

Listen again to part of the lecture. Then answer question 6.

6. What is the professor's attitude toward other storytelling instructors?
   (A) She thinks they do not instruct very well.
   (B) She does not understand their writing styles.
   (C) She does not want to criticize them.
   (D) She thinks they do not prepare their students well.

READING

Read the passage and answer the reading comprehension questions. (Check the Answer Key on page 231.)

READING 1

The Rise of Marketing

1   In the 1950s the main focus of competition in United States industry shifted from price to product differentiation and marketing. Production was evolving from a model in which products were mass-produced for a large homogenous group of consumers and were differentiated largely on the basis of price . The new model targeted products to meet the desires of specific groups of consumers. Henry Ford's Model T fits the first pattern. Ford's efficient production methods brought the price of the Model T down, and he resisted making changes in his car so that it would remain affordable for most people. The second pattern is illustrated by the current vast array of automobiles— from small two-seat sports cars to family sedans to sport-utility vehicles—each model with a variety of optional accessories and engine sizes, and each model conveying different images and statuses. It's not that price doesn't matter. Any product must appear to provide good value. It's just that price is often no longer the main arena of competition. This newer approach to marketing requires much more in the way of market research and effort in advertising, as the desires of specific demographic groups need to be shaped, created, or discovered. Then existing products are linked with those desires, products are modified, or new products are created to appeal to public tastes in consumption.

2   The goal of advertising is to identify a product's purpose or usefulness. Use value can be fairly obvious; for example, a car's usefulness is as a form of transportation. But it can also be more subtle, as when a car is also used as a form for representing one's status. Thus, needs and desires may not only be material or practical but psychological and sociological as well. Increasingly, products are sold as much for their indication of a particular lifestyle and social

status as for more practical uses. It is the task of the marketer to package the product in such a way that it symbolizes its usefulness. Thus, a sports car must not only perform like a sports car, it must conform to our ideas about what a sports car should look like, and advertisers must place it in a context where its various use values are apparent; for example, by showing bystanders admiring the car and the person in it.

3   In recent years, advertising has seemed to focus as much or more on the latter aspect of products than on the former; that is, concentrating on symbolizing the product's place in a lifestyle more than on its practical utility. When a sport-utility vehicle is advertised by showing an individual paddling a canoe across a clear lake, the point is not that most potential buyers need a vehicle that can take them into the wilderness. The point is that people who purchase such vehicles like to think of themselves as in touch with the environment, the outdoors, and adventure. Research shows that most of these vehicles never leave the pavement. Similarly, ads such as those for blue jeans mainly create an atmosphere more than they give information about the product.

4   Advertising creates fantasies. The idea is to create a story in which a particular product shows its use in a context appealing to specific types of viewers. A typical strategy is to position the product amid other objects and situations that create associations for the viewer. For example, a manufacturer of a snack food may want to convey that the usefulness of its product is not simply its taste but also that it provides "good times." A fantasy might be created in which a group of young, attractive friends are eating and having a wonderful time. The idea is to link the food, happy attractive friends, and fun together in the consumer's mind.

5   Generally, advertisements take up significant space and time in commercial media. For example, on prime-time network television in the United States in 1996, there were 15 minutes and 21 seconds of advertisements every hour. Daytime network television had more advertising with an average of 20 minutes and 15 seconds per hour. As the cost of obtaining rights to popular programs increases, the networks have compensated by expanding the amount of ad time in those programs.

1. Which of the sentences below best expresses the essential information in the highlighted sentence in the passage? Incorrect choices change the meaning in important ways or leave out essential information.

   Production was evolving from a model in which products were mass-produced for a large homogenous group of consumers and were differentiated largely on the basis of price.

   (**A**) The old model of production assumed that all consumers were the same and that they bought products based primarily on price.
   (**B**) Mass-production methods resulted in products that cost less than they had before.
   (**C**) Most consumers were concerned about the price of products and looked for products that were not expensive.
   (**D**) Similar groups of consumers came together to demand products that were fairly priced.

2. What was the main factor that kept the price of the Model T affordable?
   (**A**) Henry Ford was the manufacturer.
   (**B**) It was designed for people with low incomes.
   (**C**) The style of the car did not change very often.
   (**D**) It had a small engine that did not use much gas.

3. The word **vast** in paragraph 1 is closest in meaning to
   (**A**) amazing
   (**B**) enormous
   (**C**) stylish
   (**D**) colorful

4. According to paragraph 1, what is most important about the price of a product?
   (**A**) The product must be affordable.
   (**B**) The price of similar products should not vary too greatly.
   (**C**) The consumer must want the product enough to pay the set price.
   (**D**) The product must reflect good value for the cost.

5. The word **goal** in paragraph 2 is closest in meaning to
   (**A**) completion
   (**B**) spirit
   (**C**) object
   (**D**) decision

6. The phrase **conform to** in paragraph 2 is closest in meaning to
   (**A**) agree with
   (**B**) enlarge on
   (**C**) confuse
   (**D**) please

7. Why does the author discuss sport-utility vehicles in paragraph 3?
- **(A)** To explain why some people want to buy sport-utility vehicles
- **(B)** To give an example of a product that is advertised for what it suggests about lifestyle
- **(C)** Because sport-utility vehicles have recently become very popular
- **(D)** Because sport-utility vehicles are able to drive off of roads as well as on them

8. According to paragraph 3, what do advertisements for blue jeans emphasize?
- **(A)** Durability
- **(B)** Price
- **(C)** Style
- **(D)** Atmosphere

9. The word *it* in paragraph 4 refers to
- **(A)** manufacturer
- **(B)** usefulness
- **(C)** product
- **(D)** taste

10. The fantasy advertisement described in paragraph 4 creates a positive feeling about all of the following EXCEPT
- **(A)** food
- **(B)** product quality
- **(C)** shared times
- **(D)** friends

11. The word *link* in paragraph 4 is closest in meaning to
- **(A)** limit
- **(B)** connect
- **(C)** modify
- **(D)** prepare

12. The word *significant* in paragraph 5 is closest in meaning to
- **(A)** considerable
- **(B)** desirable
- **(C)** excessive
- **(D)** expensive

13. Look at the four squares ☐ that indicate where the following sentence could be added to the passage. Where would the sentence best fit? Circle the letter that shows the point where you would insert this sentence.

Of the Model T he said, "You can have it in any color you want, as long as it is black."

⬛A Production was evolving from a model in which products were mass-produced for a large homogenous group of consumers, and were differentiated largely on the basis of price, to a model in which products were targeted to meet the desires of specific groups of consumers. ⬛B Henry Ford's Model T fits the first pattern. ⬛C Ford's efficient production methods brought the price of the Model T down and he resisted making changes in his car so that it would remain affordable for most people. ⬛D

14. Read the first sentence of a summary of the passage. Then complete the summary by circling the THREE answer choices that express the most important ideas in the passage. Some sentences do not belong in the summary because they express ideas that are not presented in the passage or are minor ideas in the passage.

In the 1950s the main focus of competition in United States industry shifted from price to product differentiation and marketing.

(A) Products are now marketed toward specific groups of consumers.
(B) The price of a product is no longer important.
(C) Advertising is used to identify a product's purpose or use.
(D) The sports car is seen as an important symbol of status.
(E) Advertising is used to help people create positive images of themselves with particular products.
(F) There has been a decline in the amount of advertising on prime-time television in the last few years.

READING 2

Dreaming and REM Sleep

1   Humans have always been fascinated by dreams. The vivid dreams people remember and talk about are REM dream—the type that occur almost continuously during periods of rapid eye movement (REM) during sleep. But people also have NREM dreams—dreams that occur during periods without rapid eye movement called NREM sleep—although they are typically less frequent and less memorable than REM dreams. REM dreams have a storylike or dreamlike quality and are more visual, vivid, and emotional than NREM dreams. Interestingly, blind people who lose their sight before age five usually do not have visual dreams, but they have vivid dreams involving the other senses. A popular belief about dreams is that an entire dream takes place in an instant, but in fact, it is not true. Sleep researchers have discovered that it takes about as long to dream a dream as it would to experience the same thing in real life.

---

2   Although some people insist that they do not dream at all, researchers say that all people dream unless they consume alcohol or take drugs that suppress REM sleep. Are dreaming and REM sleep essentially one and the same? Some researchers have questioned an assumption long held by some sleep experts that dreaming is simply the brain's effort to make sense of the random firing of neurons that occurs during REM sleep. Are the brain mechanisms responsible for REM sleep the same ones that create the rich dream world we experience? The answer may be no . It is known that dreams do occur outside of REM sleep. Moreover, the REM state can exist without dreams. These two facts suggest that different but complementary brain mechanisms are responsible for REM sleep and the dreaming that normally occurs within it. There is mounting evidence, says British researcher Mark Solms, that dreaming and REM sleep, while normally occurring together, are not one and the same. Rather, the REM state is controlled by neural mechanisms in the brain stem, while areas farther up in the forebrain provide the common pathway that gives us the complex and often vivid mental experiences we call dreams.

3   Other researchers suggest that REM sleep aids in information processing, helping people sift through daily experience to organize and store in memory information that is relevant to them. Animal studies provide strong evidence for a relationship between REM sleep and learning. Some studies have revealed that animals increase their REM sleep following learning sessions. Other studies have indicated that when animals are deprived of REM sleep after new learning, their performance of the learned task is impaired the following day. But depriving subjects of NREM sleep had no such effect in the studies.

4   Research has shown that REM sleep serves an information-processing function in humans and is involved in the consolidation of memories after human learning. Researchers found that research participants learning a new perceptual skill showed an improvement in performance, with no additional practice, eight to ten hours later if they had a normal night's sleep or if the researchers disturbed only their NREM sleep. Performance did not improve, however, in those who were deprived of REM sleep.

5   An opposite view is proposed by Francis Crick and Graeme Mitchison. They suggest that REM sleep functions as mental housecleaning, erasing trivial and unnecessary memories and clearing overloaded neural circuits that might interfere with memory and rational thinking. In other words, they say, people dream in order to forget.

6   There is no doubt that REM sleep serves an important function, even if psychologists do not know precisely what that function is. The fact that newborns have such a high percentage of REM sleep has led to the conclusion that REM sleep is necessary for maturation of the brain in infants. Furthermore, when people are deprived of REM sleep as a result of general sleep loss or illness, they will make up for the loss by getting an increased amount of REM sleep after the deprivation. This increase in the percentage of REM sleep to make up for REM deprivation is called a "REM rebound." Because the intensity of REM sleep is increased during a REM rebound, nightmares often occur.

1. What does the word *it* in paragraph 1 refer to?
   (A) sight
   (B) a popular belief
   (C) an entire dream
   (D) an instant

2. According to paragraph 1, all of the following are characteristics of REM dreams EXCEPT:
   (A) They are easy to remember.
   (B) They occur more often than other dreams.
   (C) They may tell a story.
   (D) They usually take place in an instant.

3. Which of the sentences below best expresses the essential information in the following sentence from paragraph 2? Incorrect choices change the meaning in important ways or leave out essential information.

   Some researchers have questioned an assumption long held by some sleep experts that dreaming is simply the brain's effort to make sense of the random firing of neurons that occurs during REM sleep.

   (A) Some researchers assume dreaming only occurs during REM sleep, while others question the assumption.
   (B) The assumption that dreaming is the processing of random brain activity has been questioned by some researchers.
   (C) For a long time, sleep experts have believed that it is difficult to make logical sense of dreams.
   (D) Sleep experts question how long random brain activity can occur during REM sleep.

4. Why does the author state, "The answer may be no" in paragraph 2?
   (A) To contrast dreaming before and after REM sleep
   (B) To explain why dreaming and REM sleep are essentially the same
   (C) To introduce a theory that REM sleep and dreams are not necessarily connected
   (D) To suggest that more dreams occur inside REM sleep than outside it

5. The word *complementary* in paragraph 2 is closest in meaning to
   (A) corresponding
   (B) complex
   (C) reliable
   (D) unusual

6. According to paragraph 2, which of the following best describes the role of brain activity during the REM state?
   (A) It is not known for sure what kind of brain activity produces the REM state.
   (B) The REM state is caused by activity in the forebrain.
   (C) Several different parts of the brain jointly control the REM state.
   (D) The brain stem regulates the REM state.

7. The word **sift** in paragraph 3 is closest in meaning to
  (**A**) sort
  (**B**) adjust
  (**C**) struggle
  (**D**) wander

8. The animal studies mentioned in paragraph 3 revealed that
  (**A**) the process of learning causes shorter periods of REM sleep
  (**B**) new learning has little effect on REM sleep
  (**C**) REM sleep may improve the ability to learn
  (**D**) depriving animals of NREM sleep prevents them from learning the next day

9. The word **impaired** in paragraph 3 is closest in meaning to
  (A) demonstrated
  (B) inspired
  (C) repeated
  (D) weakened

10. The word **consolidation** in paragraph 4 is closest in meaning to
  (**A**) bringing together
  (**B**) return
  (**C**) disappearance
  (**D**) putting to use

11. What can be inferred from paragraph 4 about the effect of losing NREM sleep?
  (**A**) It may prevent the performance of skills already learned.
  (**B**) It may cause the need for more practice.
  (**C**) It may not affect the performance of newly learned skills.
  (**D**) It may create the need for more REM sleep.

12. According to paragraph 6, a "REM rebound" is best described as
  (**A**) a prolonged sleep loss
  (**B**) a change in brain activity
  (**C**) an increase in REM sleep
  (**D**) a bad dream

13. Look at the four squares ☐ that indicate where the following sentence could be added to the passage. Where would the sentence best fit? Circle the letter that shows the point where you would insert this sentence

Fear and anxiety—often quite extreme—are common in REM dreams.

REM dreams have a storylike or dreamlike quality and are more visual, vivid, and emotional than NREM dreams. **A** Interestingly, blind people who lose their sight before age five usually do not have visual dreams, but they have vivid dreams involving one or more of the other senses. **B** A popular belief about dreaming is that an entire dream takes place in an instant, but in fact, it is not true. **C** Sleep researchers have discovered that it takes about as long to dream a dream as it would to experience the same thing in real life. **D**

14. Read the first sentence of a summary of the passage. Then complete the summary by circling the THREE answer choices that express the most important ideas in the passage. Some sentences do not belong in the summary because they express ideas that are not presented in the passage or are minor ideas in the passage.

Researchers continue to explore the relationship between dreaming and REM sleep.

(**A**) The use of substances like drugs may prevent the occurrence of REM sleep.

(**B**) Research suggests that sleeping and dreaming may use separate brain functions.

(**C**) Large amounts of REM sleep may strengthen both animal and human learning

(**D**) Studies suggest that REM sleep affects learning in animals but not in humans.

(**E**) Studies suggest that REM sleep is important to human brain growth and clearing the mind of unneeded information.

(**F**) Researchers believe that people need equal amounts of REM and NREM sleep.

WRITING

For this task, you will read a passage about an academic topic and you will listen to a lecture about the same topic. Then you will write a response to a question that asks you about the relationship between the lecture you heard and the reading passage. You should allow 3 minutes to read the passage. Then listen to the lecture. Then allow 20 minutes to plan and write your response.

INTEGRATED WRITING TASK 1

READING

Read the passage.

Space Tourism

1   Soon there will be something new for the tourist who has been everywhere and seen everything on Earth. Spacecraft being developed by private commercial companies will soon enable private citizens to buy their own tickets to travel into space, thereby creating a space tourism industry. So far, space travel has been undertaken only by governments, but the new, privatized spaceflight industry will bring great benefits to both science and the public.

2   First, private space travel will benefit serious space exploration by making spaceflight cheaper. Privatization of space technology will bring technological costs down very fast because it will allow competition—and competition is one of the strongest motivators to cut costs. Thus, lowering the cost of space travel will benefit not only space tourists but also scientists, who will be able to use private space flights for research purposes.

3   Furthermore, privatization of space travel will accelerate the rate at which important scientific discoveries occur. The aerospace industry already sponsors a lot of groundbreaking scientific research, and adding private spaceflight companies to it will make the industry as a whole grow in size, thereby employing more scientists than it does now. That increased number of working scientists means not only that more discoveries are likely to be made but also that those discoveries are likely to be made more quickly than in the past.

4   Finally, when governments are the sole providers of space travel, the costs are paid for by the whole taxpaying public, but with privatization, the expenses of space travel will be borne by the customers of the industry. The fact that private spaceflight operators will be able to raise funds through ticket sales means that the financial burden on taxpayers will be eased significantly.

LISTENING

Now listen to part of a lecture on the same topic.

WRITING

Summarize the points made in the lecture, being sure to specifically explain how they cast doubt on points made in the reading passage.

INTEGRATED WRITING TASK 2

READING

Read the passage.

School Uniforms

1   Educators have long recognized that high school can be a difficult experience for many students. Along with the stress of challenging academic work, high school can also be a source of social, emotional, and even financial stress. One effective way of decreasing these nonacademic kinds of stress is to require students to wear a school uniform so that all students wear basically the same clothing.

2   One of the most obvious benefits of such a policy is that it makes high school more affordable for both students and their parents. Clothing, especially trendy, fashionable clothing, is very expensive, and teenagers usually want to have several different outfits in their wardrobes—for some, the more the better. When there is no possibility of dressing fashionably at school, a student's clothing bill will go down drastically.

3   Furthermore, wearing the same school uniform as everyone else eliminates a significant source of discomfort and self-consciousness for many teenagers: the uncertainty that what they are wearing is "right." Such anxiety interferes with a student's ability to act in ways that show his or her personality to advantage.

4   Finally, a mandatory school-uniform policy will reduce the amount of teasing and bullying among students. Currently, many students are teased or put down simply because they dress differently from everyone else or because

they can't afford to dress like the majority. Once all students wear the same uniform, there will be much less opportunity for these kinds of intimidating behaviors.

LISTENING

Now listen to part of a lecture on the same topic.

WRITING

Write a response to the topic.

Summarize the points made in the lecture, being sure to specifically explain how they cast doubt on points made in the reading passage.

SPEAKING

INTEGRATED SPEAKING TASK 1

Read the short text below. Then listen to a talk on the same topic. You will then answer a question about what you have read and heard. You may take notes as you listen. You may use your notes to help you prepare your response. You will need to combine appropriate information from the text and the talk to provide a complete answer to the question. (Check the Answer Key on page 231.)

READING

The university is planning to eliminate its housing program for married students. Read the article from the university newspaper about the plan. You will have 45 seconds to read the article. Begin reading now.

University Reduces Number of Family Housing Units

University officials have announced that they plan to reduce the number of housing units assigned to students with families. In particular, Green Apartments, which are located in the northwest corner of campus and are currently part of the university's family housing program, will no longer be used for student housing. Housing representatives say that many of the apartments have gone uninhabited in recent years. They can no longer afford to maintain the buildings for the few residents currently living there. Officials say the buildings will be renovated and turned into offices for faculty.

LISTENING

Now listen to an excerpt on the same topic.

SPEAKING

Speak on the following topic.

The students are discussing the new housing plan. First describe the plan. Then explain why the woman agrees or disagrees with the plan.

INTEGRATED SPEAKING TASK 2

Listen to part of this conversation. You will then answer a question about what you have heard. You may take notes as you listen. You may use your notes to help you prepare your response. (Check the Answer Key on page 231.)

LISTENING

Listen to two students speaking about a problem.

SPEAKING

Speak on the following topic.

The speakers discuss two possible solutions to the woman's problem. Describe the problem. Then state the solution you recommend and explain why.

Audioscript

LISTENING

PAGE 208, CONVERSATION 1

Student: Hi, umm, Professor Watkins?

Professor: Yes, come in, uh …

S: Fred—from your Introduction to Advertising and Marketing class?

P: Right, Fred. Sorry, I—we've only had two classes, and yesterday weren't you absent …?

S: Yeah, sorry 'bout that. I'm on the student council, and we had a special event—just a one-time thing.

P: It's OK, I'm glad you dropped by. You missed some important course information for the semester yesterday.

S: Right, I heard we went over the advertising project assignments, and I'm not sure what to do. Somebody said we have a choice of doing one assignment or two?

P: Right. Everyone has to do either a longer, "comprehensive" project or two shorter, "focused" projects. The amount of work is the same either way.

S: OK, but, hmmm. I mean, how do I know …uh, how do I decide whether to do the comprehensive assignment or the focused one?

P: It depends on your …probably you would want to think about your reasons for taking the course. If you're not sure of the difference between the two, well …A focused project is a well-researched report on one topic in advertising, such as "identifying a target customer" or "reaching the largest possible audience." And a comprehensive project …well, it includes a well-researched report *also*—but in addition, you're expected to show the development process for an advertisement, from start to finish. In either case—no matter which one you choose to do—you'll have to write a report.

S: Right, umm, OK. I think I'm clear on that, but I'm not sure what you mean by considering my reasons for taking the course.

P: Well, I wanted you think about what your career goal is. Are you interested in going into advertising or marketing?

S: Uh, maybe. I'm not really sure yet.

P: Ah, OK. Knowing what your career goal is will help you determine which project is better for you. So, for instance, the advantage of the comprehensive project is …well, if you're interested in marketing and advertising, it's good to have a portfolio—a collection of previous work to show at job interviews.

S: Oh, OK—and if I did …I could put my class project in my portfolio—if I did the comprehensive project.

P: Absolutely. Of course, a portfolio won't mean as much to potential employers as real-life experience, but at least it's *something* to show you understand how the game is played. But, say if you're sure you *don't* want to go into marketing or advertising and you're taking the class because it fills another requirement, maybe it's better to do the two focused projects—so you can get a broader overview of a greater variety of topics.

S: Hmm. But since I *am* thinking about it, maybe I should do the comprehensive project.

P: Definitely wouldn't hurt. You've got nothing to lose.

S: That makes sense, Professor Watkins. Thanks.

P: No problem, Fred. Let me know if you need advice on finding a topic.

Listen again to part of the conversation. Then answer question 5.

S: Oh, OK—and if I did …I could put my class project in my portfolio—if I did the comprehensive project.

P: Absolutely. Of course, a portfolio won't mean as much to potential employers as real-life experience, but at least it's *something* to show you understand how the game is played.

5. What does the professor mean when he says, " …at least it's *something* to show you understand how the game is played"?

PAGE 209, CONVERSATION 2

Student: Thanks for meeting with me, Professor Mozell. I know you probably thought I wanted to meet with you to discuss my grades this semester or classes for the upcoming semester, but uh well, actually, that's not what I wanted to talk about at all …I trust you and I know that you know a lot about legal matters and to tell the truth, I really didn't know who else I could talk to about this …

Professor: Oh, well, what is it? Is it something serious? I mean, it's nothing serious, I hope.

S: Well, actually, it is, but, well, it's uh a money issue.

P: Oh? OK. Tell me about it then. What seems to be the problem?

S: OK. About three months ago, I saw this ad online for a new stereo system. It caught my eye because I'd been shopping around for quite some time for a stereo just like it. I'd been to every electronics store in town looking for it, and they were always sold out. So, when I saw it on the Internet, it was perfect timing.

P: Well, that sounds great. Is it that the stereo's not as good as you thought it would be and you want your money back?

S: Well, you're partly right. I *do* want my money back, but not because the stereo's not that good. It's because I never got it. They never sent it to me. I sent them $300 for this state-of-the-art stereo system nearly three months ago and it still hasn't arrived!

P: I was hoping you weren't going to tell me that. I had a feeling that was the problem. Believe it or not, you're not the first student to ask me about this. Sorry to say this, but sounds like you're the victim of a cyber crime.

S: Oh no. Cyber crime? Um …

P: You know, those crimes that are committed through the use of the Internet. There's been a lot in the media about them lately. Companies set up online to sell fake products to innocent people like students your age and the elderly. Then it's only after you send them money that you realize it's too late, when the product never arrives, that you've been scammed. And because it's the Internet, you almost never see the people who you're doing business with.

S: OK, so what do I do now?

P: I'm glad you asked … It may not seem like much, but here's *something* … First, you need to report your loss—that is, the amount of money you've lost-to a fraud complaint center. I would recommend going online to the Internet Fraud Complaint Center's website. There, you'll find a place to file your complaint. You're going to need to provide them with as much of the online company's information as you have—name, website, phone numbers—everything. Also, anything about the money—method of payment, how much you paid, when you paid, everything.

S: Sounds like a lot of information.

P: Well, I'd say it's worth it if it means getting your money back.

S: Yeah, I guess you're right. Thanks, Professor Mozell. I'll get right on collecting that information.

Listen again to part of the conversation. Then answer question 5.

P: I was hoping you weren't going to tell me that. I had a feeling that was the problem.

5. What can be inferred about the professor when she says this?

PAGE 210, LECTURE 1

Basically, when we talk about nature versus nurture, we're talking about whether a person's behavior is more influenced by their nature … by their born instinct to satisfy basic needs—such as hunger, thirst, security, or shelter—you know, their biological side, <u>or</u> is it more influenced by other people in their lives—by the people who *nurtured* them, their social side—interaction with family, teachers, maybe friends.

Well, today, we're gonna look at a business application of nature and nurture … at how nature and nurture play a business role in advertising and marketing. Specifically, we're gonna talk about the psychology of advertising.

Now, what does psychology have to do with advertising? Well, basically, advertising is *all* psychology. It's a kind of psychology because it's an attempt to influence people's behavior—in this case, to motivate them to *buy* something.

So, if you're an advertiser, you're always asking yourself, "How can I influence others to buy what I'm selling?" And as an advertiser, you must also come up with a hook to do so. You must find a way to grab people's attention and to persuade them to want to buy a particular product. This is done by trying to create an image that is emotionally appealing—by showing consumers things they desire or want. Now, can you think of a good way to emotionally appeal to consumers through the nature-and-nurture principle?

Man: Through fear? Maybe they could scare people into buying something?

P: Sure, but remember that fear is only one example of an emotion, or rather instinct, and it wouldn't work for every product. I mean, fear might work for something like a home-security alarm, but say you want to sell a pair of blue jeans. Well … just ask yourself, how often does fear motivate <u>you</u> to buy a pair of jeans?

What I want you to think about is some really basic needs.

Well, let me help you out with this one. You all need to eat and drink, don't you? Have a look at this example of an advertisement for bottled water to get a better idea of what I mean.

Have you ever seen an advertisement for a restaurant or some kind of food or drink where it looked so good that you wanted to have it right then and there? In this advertisement, the appeal to instinct is clear: It's hot. You're thirsty. The water will satisfy your natural urge to hydrate yourself. Look at how the designer of the

advertisement has used images that let us know that the temperature of this bottle of water is *cool.*

Hunger and thirst are two of the most basic needs that human beings have. So is the desire for safe shelter. So, appealing to these basic—these built-in urges, or instincts, is one approach to selling things. But it's <u>not</u> the only way. Take this example of an advertisement for living room furniture.

Now, what's the emotional appeal here?

Woman: Well, it looks very comfortable—looks safe, looks warm.

P: Sure, those are part of the shelter instinct that an advertiser might appeal to—but you could show a warm, safe shelter without needing the people in the advertisement, couldn't you? In fact, if all you wanted was to show warmth, safety, and comfort, then the people in the advertisements would just be, uh, a distraction, right?

On one hand, this advertisement appeals to the instinct for a safe environment. On the other, it appeals to our socialization—to our need for companionship, for friendship. You see the family having fun together—the kids playing a game, mom and dad reading—it looks not only like a safe, comfortable place, but it's also saying, If you buy this furniture, your home will be more *social*—you'll spend more time with the people you care about and who care about you. So, that's the *other way* to find an emotional appeal—to appeal to our social side, our tendency to seek relationships. Are there any other examples? Yes?

Woman: How about toy ads, for example, I mean—you know, like a new toy—where the kid who has the new toy is the coolest kid, and everybody wants to play with that kid … you know, everybody wants to be <u>that</u> kid's friend.

P: Good example. Now, the emotional appeal there is the need for social acceptance—to belong to a group—to know that you're accepted.

Now, let's look at some other techniques that advertisers use to get us to buy their goods.

6. *Listen again to part of the lecture. Then answer question 6.*

P: … but you could show a warm, safe shelter without needing the people in the advertisement, couldn't you? In fact, if all you wanted to show was warmth, safety, and comfort, then the people in the advertisements would just be, uh, a distraction, right?

What does the professor imply when she says this? "… if all you wanted to show was warmth, safety, and comfort, then the people in the advertisements would just be, uh, a distraction, right?"?

PAGE 211, LECTURE 2

P: Now, we've already had discussions about great storytellers, but what I want to talk about today is *not* the storytellers, but the stories themselves, uh what goes into telling stories, to be exact. See, storytelling is an oral tradition that's managed to survive hundreds, even thousands of years. And when dealing with children, you'll be able to enliven your lessons with some great stories, but you should at least know what goes into telling a story. And that's what I'm gonna talk about today: two major considerations in storytelling.

First off, you should always start with the selection of a story to tell. And selecting a story always involves considering your audience, whether they are young children or older children. With younger *children* you'd want to select a story that's brief and, uh, easy to grasp, you know, easy to understand. You're going to have to develop the plot relatively early on. And it has to be really engaging, you know, to keep your students interested. Now, with a more *mature audience*, you may be able to spend more time developing the story before you actually reveal the plot, so you can select a story that's a bit lengthier. But don't forget, it still needs to be engaging. No matter how old, everyone likes to be entertained. Now, the story you choose can be from the genre of your choice. But I often enjoy telling folktales. Folktales can range from fairy tales, you know, stories of magic and wonder, to fables, which we could call animal folktales because the animals are the primary characters of the story and there is always a moral to the story. There are other types of stories to tell, but remember, whatever the kind of story, just be mindful of your intended audience. So that's audience and story selection, our first step, but what about *telling* the story itself?

Well, as I said, you should always be prepared when you tell a story. I don't mean in the way that many storytelling instructors say, by writing it out—not that there's anything wrong with that—but I'm saying, you already have your audience ready, you've selected your story, so why not take the time to prepare your delivery? And that brings me to our next part of storytelling: delivery.

Now, delivering the story is probably the hardest part of storytelling—something that often takes lots of practice.… In order to deliver the story you should keep in mind three critical aspects: mental imagery, physical or body paralanguage, and emphasis. For example, let's say you've decided to tell an old tale—a fairy tale—one that everyone's heard of such as … "Cinderella"—that's a pretty well-known story—and your audience is a group of children.

You make the story engaging by talking about the sounds, the smells, the sights, the, uh, tastes, and so on in the imaginary world of the "Cinderella" story. Essentially, you're trying to put the listener *in* the story through these sensory words. This aspect of storytelling is called using *mental imagery*. Mental imagery *alone* has the power to draw in much of your audience, but that's not enough. There's something else that's equally important to use, especially with a live audience.…

Imagine telling a fairy tale or a folktale to a room full of children without showing all of the emotions that come along with a story about hope, sadness, and joy. Pretty boring, right? Well, that's why *physical or body paralanguage* is so important. Physical paralanguage is just a matter of telling the story by *supporting* the oral language with the appropriate gestures. For instance, facial expressions like the down-turned mouth to show sadness, the widened eyes to show surprise, and so on. These elements are critical in storytelling. If you do them right, your audience will love the story even more.

OK, now that I've given you the basics for telling a story, I need to mention one extremely important consideration in storytelling. This is the one thing you absolutely must do when telling a story … particularly if your audience can only hear and not see you … and it's *emphasis*. You *must* emphasize the ideas you want the audience to remember. And you do that by changing the intonation in your voice, by repeating those key ideas, and monitoring your volume and rate of speech. You must combine a flowing tone with repetition and changing volume and rate of speech with those wonderful descriptions and body language. Sounds like a lot to remember, but that's why we're going to practice using these elements today.

6. *Listen again to part of the lecture. Then answer question 6.*

P: Well, as I said, you should always be prepared when you tell a story. I don't mean in the way that many storytelling instructors say, by writing it out—not that there's anything wrong with that—

What is the professor's attitude toward other storytelling instructors?

Writing

INTEGRATED WRITING TASK 1

PAGE 222, LISTENING

Professor: Well, it looks as though we'll soon see private spaceships carrying tourists into space. But will it really provide great benefits for serious science and for the public? I don't think so.

First, privatized space travel, which is extraordinarily expensive, is likely to stay that way. For one thing, commercial space travel will require an elaborate space traffic-control system to prevent collisions—and the development and operation of such a system won't come cheap either. Another thing that'll keep costs high is safety—because each new ship design will have to be safety tested and retested—and that also tends to be a very expensive process. Both of those costs will be reflected in the prices of the spaceflight tickets, so no one should expect the cost of space flights to go down fast.

Second, if commercial spaceflight has *any* effect at all on the rate of scientific discovery and innovation, it will be to delay or even prevent such discovery and innovation. If the best and the brightest engineers get lured away from government space programs by the high salaries offered by private, for-profit companies, they might end up working on commercial stuff that doesn't have much scientific value. And as a result, serious space research might actually suffer.

And finally, will the taxpaying public get off the hook financially? No chance! The fact is that so-called private space tourism isn't possible without huge public tax subsidies. It will take billions and billions of dollars to build space stations, space airports, and so on, and private investors simply cannot raise such huge amounts. So the burden on taxpayers won't be significantly eased with the development of the private spaceflight industry. In fact, all taxpayers'll be paying more to subsidize the vacations of the space tourists.

INTEGRATED WRITING TASK 2

PAGE 224, LISTENING

Professor: What you've just read really is way too optimistic. It's rather easy to poke holes in the reasoning. First off, school uniforms are themselves often quite costly—usually they are only available from certain select stores. Plus, what kind of clothes will students put on after school when they go meet their friends? Well, if you can't dress trendy at school, it's even more likely you'll want to do that after school. So kids will still demand a full wardrobe of fashionable after-school clothes in addition to their uniforms.

To take up another point, doing away with differences in dress can affect some students quite negatively. Many students may feel very uncomfortable—might even feel self-conscious—about how they look when they are not allowed to select the clothes that they wear. For many, choosing clothing is not a matter of making a fashion statement; it is simply a way of presenting themselves in ways they feel will call attention to what they consider their attractive features—plus they feel they can also select clothing to de-emphasize other features they perhaps like less about themselves. So school uniforms can actually end up increasing self-consciousness and discomfort among students.

Finally, students will always pick on other students. Dividing into groups, teasing and bullying others for being different—these are things teenagers everywhere do because they are at that particular stage of life. If students cannot pick on differences in dress, they will surely find other things to pick on—things like choice in music or the kind of backpack brought to school—any of these can easily take on as much importance as clothing.

SPEAKING

INTEGRATED SPEAKING TASK 1

PAGE 225, LISTENING

Man: You must be pretty upset about this new housing plan. That's where you live, right?

Woman: Right. I don't know what we're going to do.

M: You don't want to live off campus?

W: Too expensive. It would be impossible to find a place in town with rent as low as we pay here. Not to mention that we don't have a car, so …

M: You could apply for another building on campus …?

W: Maybe, but they're usually full. And there's a waiting list.

M: That doesn't make sense. Why are there so many sitting empty in Green then?

W: It's because of the condition of the buildings. They need new carpeting … and paint. They're a mess. There probably haven't been any improvements made in 10 years.

M: Well, it's definitely a mess outside of the buildings—it's muddy … no grass ever grows there.

W: Exactly. But if they fixed up the buildings … and the grounds … and maybe put in a play area for kids outside … then I bet lots of married students would want to move in.

M: And they're going to have to renovate anyway.…

W: Right, so why not do it for married students?

M: I guess some professors would be pretty unhappy though.

W: I don't see why faculty would want to be way up there in that area. It's not near any of the class buildings—it's mostly dorms around there.

INTEGRATED SPEAKING TASK 2

PAGE 225, LISTENING

Man: Hey, heard you're expecting company this weekend.

Woman: Yeah. Jane, my best friend from high school, is coming up to visit next week, but I haven't …

M: Sorry … hold on … is this the same Jane I know? The one who got married last year?

W: Yes, that's right. So her husband is coming with her, and I haven't figured out where they're going to stay.… My housemate was going to be away that weekend, so I offered for them to stay in her room. But my housemate just told me that her trip was canceled.…

M: Oh, no. What are you going to do?

W: I don't know. Jane can stay with us. That's not a problem. But there isn't enough room for Jane and her husband and my housemate. So I was thinking, I could ask them to stay in a hotel, … but you know … hotels are so expensive. I'm not sure if they can afford it.

M: Well, there might be a cheap hotel available … though it'll probably be really far away.

W: Hmmm.… Another thought I had is that you live alone, so I was wondering.… I really hate to ask you this, but is there any way Jane's husband could stay with you? I mean, you live right around the corner.

M: Well, I would've offered first thing, but don't forget how small my place is. As long as Jane's husband wouldn't feel like it was too crowded.…

W: Uh, yeah.… I'm not sure.

M: Well, think about it and let me know.…

Answer Key

LISTENING

Conversation 1

1. C	**3.** B	**5.** B
2. A, C	**4.** C	

Conversation 2

1. C	**3.** A	**5.** B
2. A	**4.** B	

Lecture 1

1. C	**3.** B	**5.** D
2. B	**4.** A, C	**6.** A

Lecture 2

1. B
2. A
3. C
4. A
5. A = emphasis; B = mental imagery; C = physical or body paralanguage
6. C

READING

Reading 1

1. A
2. C
3. B
4. D
5. C
6. A
7. B
8. D
9. C
10. B
11. B
12. A
13. D
14. A, C, E

Reading 2

1. B
2. D
3. B
4. C
5. A
6. D
7. A
8. C
9. D
10. A
11. C
12. C
13. A
14. B, C, E

WRITING

Integrated Writing Task 1

Key points

Points made in the lecture counter arguments made by points of the reading passage.

LECTURE POINT	READING PASSAGE POINT
The costs of creating and running a space traffic-control system and of testing new spaceships will keep spaceflight expensive.	Competition in a private spaceflight industry will quickly reduce costs.
Private space travel is likely to prevent or even delay scientific discoveries and innovations by luring top-notch researchers away from serious science into commercial projects.	Privatization of space travel will advance science by increasing the number of scientists working in aerospace projects.
Taxpayers will end up subsidizing the infrastructure of a private space industry because private investors cannot cover the costs.	The costs paid by customers of a private space industry would significantly reduce the burden on taxpayers of government-funded space programs.

Integrated Writing Task 2

Key points

Points made in the lecture counter arguments made by points of the reading passage.

LECTURE POINT	READING PASSAGE POINT
School uniforms are expensive, and students who wear uniforms at school will buy expensive, trendy clothes to wear after school.	If all students wear the same style of uniform, clothing costs will be less.
Being made to wear a school uniform makes many students feel more, not less, self-conscious because they cannot present themselves in a way that makes them comfortable.	With everyone wearing the same uniform, students will not be concerned about whether they are wearing the fashionably correct clothes.
It is impossible to eliminate teenagers' tendency to form groups that exclude or make fun of outsiders.	By eliminating discrimination based on differences in clothing, teasing and bullying of some students by others will be significantly reduced.

SPEAKING

Integrated Speaking Task 1

Key points

1. The university plans to close some of the married housing buildings (Green Apartments). The buildings will be used for faculty offices.

2. The woman is unhappy about/disagrees with the plan because:

   • She wants to continue living on campus. She cannot afford to live off campus (she does not have a car; other campus housing is not currently available).

   • She believes the university should repair the buildings and allow married students to continue living there.

   • She does not believe the buildings are in a good location for faculty offices (they are too far from class buildings, etc.).

Integrated Speaking Task 2

Key points

1. Jane (the woman's best friend) and her husband are visiting next week, but there is a problem. Jane can stay at the woman's place but there isn't enough room for both Jane and her husband.

2. Two solutions are proposed:

   • Ask Jane and her husband to stay at a hotel. The woman is worried that a hotel will be too expensive (and it might be too far from campus).

   • Jane's husband could stay with the man, who lives nearby. However, his place is very small (so it might be too crowded).

Use the TOEFL iBT Scoring Rubrics on the following pages to assess responses to Integrated and Independent Tasks. For more detailed information and explanation of these rubrics, see the *NorthStar: Building Skills for the TOEFL iBT Teacher's Manual.*

TOEFL® iBT Test—Integrated Writing Rubrics

Score	Task Description
5	A response at this level successfully selects the important information from the lecture and coherently and accurately presents this information in relation to the relevant information presented in the reading. The response is well organized, and occasional language errors that are present do not result in inaccurate or imprecise presentation of content or connections.
4	A response at this level is generally good in selecting the important information from the lecture and in coherently and accurately presenting this information in relation to the relevant information in the reading, but it may have minor omission, inaccuracy, vagueness, or imprecision of some content from the lecture or in connection to points made in the reading. A response is also scored at this level if it has more frequent or noticeable minor language errors, as long as such usage and grammatical structures do not result in anything more than an occasional lapse of clarity or in the connection of ideas.
3	A response at this level contains some important information from the lecture and conveys some relevant connection to the reading, but it is marked by one or more of the following: • Although the overall response is definitely oriented to the task, it conveys only vague, global, unclear, or somewhat imprecise connection of the points made in the lecture to points made in the reading. • The response may omit one major key point made in the lecture. • Some key points made in the lecture or the reading, or connections between the two, may be incomplete, inaccurate, or imprecise. • Errors of usage and/or grammar may be more frequent or may result in noticeably vague expressions or obscured meanings in conveying ideas and connections.
2	A response at this level contains some relevant information from the lecture, but is marked by significant language difficulties or by significant omission or inaccuracy of important ideas from the lecture or in the connections between the lecture and the reading; a response at this level is marked by one or more of the following: • The response significantly misrepresents or completely omits the overall connection between the lecture and the reading. • The response significantly omits or significantly misrepresents important points made in the lecture. • The response contains language errors or expressions that largely obscure connections or meaning at key junctures, or that would likely obscure understanding of key ideas for a reader not already familiar with the reading and the lecture.
1	A response at this level is marked by one or more of the following: • The response provides little or no meaningful or relevant coherent content from the lecture. • The language level of the response is so low that it is difficult to derive meaning.
0	A response at this level merely copies sentences from the reading, rejects the topic or is otherwise not connected to the topic, is written in a foreign language, consists of keystroke characters, or is blank.

TOEFL® iBT Test—Independent Writing Rubrics

Score	Task Description
5	**An essay at this level largely accomplishes all of the following:** • effectively addresses the topic and task • is well organized and well developed, using clearly appropriate explanations, exemplifications, and/or details • displays unity, progression, and coherence • displays consistent facility in the use of language, demonstrating syntactic variety, appropriate word choice, and idiomaticity, though it may have minor lexical or grammatical errors
4	**An essay at this level largely accomplishes all of the following:** • addresses the topic and task well, though some points may not be fully elaborated • is generally well organized and well developed, using appropriate and sufficient explanations, exemplifications, and/or details • displays unity, progression, and coherence, though it may contain occasional redundancy, digression, or unclear connections • displays facility in the use of language, demonstrating syntactic variety and range of vocabulary, though it will probably have occasional noticeable minor errors in structure, word form, or use of idiomatic language that do not interfere with meaning
3	**An essay at this level is marked by one or more of the following:** • addresses the topic and task using somewhat developed explanations, exemplifications, and/or details • displays unity, progression, and coherence, though connection of ideas may be occasionally obscured • may demonstrate inconsistent facility in sentence formation and word choice that may result in lack of clarity and occasionally obscure meaning • may display accurate but limited range of syntactic structures and vocabulary
2	**An essay at this level may reveal one or more of the following weaknesses:** • limited development in response to the topic and task • inadequate organization or connection of ideas • inappropriate or insufficient exemplifications, explanations, or details to support or illustrate generalizations in response to the task • a noticeably inappropriate choice of words or word forms • an accumulation of errors in sentence structure and/or usage
1	**An essay at this level is seriously flawed by one or more of the following weaknesses:** • serious disorganization or underdevelopment • little or no detail, or irrelevant specifics, or questionable responsiveness to the task • serious and frequent errors in sentence structure or usage
0	**An essay at this level** merely copies words from the topic, rejects the topic, or is otherwise not connected to the topic, is written in a foreign language, consists of keystroke characters, or is blank.

TOEFL® iBT Test—Integrated Speaking Rubrics

Score	General Description	Delivery	Language Use	Topic Development
4	The response fulfills the demands of the task, with at most minor lapses in completeness. It is highly intelligible and exhibits sustained, coherent discourse. A response at this level is characterized by all of the following:	Speech is generally clear, fluid and sustained. It may include minor lapses or minor difficulties with pronunciation or intonation. Pace may vary at times as speaker attempts to recall information. Overall intelligibility remains high.	The response demonstrates good control of basic and complex grammatical structures that allow for coherent, efficient (automatic) expression of relevant ideas. Contains generally effective word choice. Though some minor (or systematic) errors or imprecise use may be noticeable, they do not require listener effort (or obscure meaning).	The response presents a clear progression of ideas and conveys the relevant information required by the task. It includes appropriate detail, though it may have minor errors or minor omissions.
3	The response addresses the task appropriately, but may fall short of being fully developed. It is generally intelligible and coherent, with some fluidity of expression, though it exhibits some noticeable lapses in the expression of ideas. A response at this level is characterized by at least two of the following:	Speech is generally clear, with some fluidity of expression, but it exhibits minor difficulties with pronunciation, intonation or pacing and may require some listener effort at times. Overall intelligibility remains good, however.	The response demonstrates fairly automatic and effective use of grammar and vocabulary, and fairly coherent expression of relevant ideas. Response may exhibit some imprecise or inaccurate use of vocabulary or grammatical structures or be somewhat limited in the range of structures used. Such limitations do not seriously interfere with the communication of the message.	The response is sustained and conveys relevant information required by the task. However, it exhibits some incompleteness, inaccuracy, lack of specificity with respect to content, or choppiness in the progression of ideas.
2	The response is connected to the task, though it may be missing some relevant information or contain inaccuracies. It contains some intelligible speech, but at times problems with intelligibility and/or overall coherence may obscure meaning. A response at this level is characterized by at least two of the following:	Speech is clear at times, though it exhibits problems with pronunciation, intonation or pacing and so may require significant listener effort. Speech may not be sustained at a consistent level throughout. Problems with intelligibility may obscure meaning in places (but not throughout).	The response is limited in the range and control of vocabulary and grammar demonstrated (some complex structures may be used, but typically contain errors). This results in limited or vague expression of relevant ideas and imprecise or inaccurate connections. Automaticity of expression may only be evident at the phrasal level.	The response conveys some relevant information but is clearly incomplete or inaccurate. It is incomplete if it omits key ideas, makes vague reference to key ideas, or demonstrates limited development of important information. An inaccurate response demonstrates misunderstanding of key ideas from the stimulus. Typically, ideas expressed may not be well connected or cohesive so that familiarity with the stimulus is necessary in order to follow what is being discussed.
1	The response is very limited in content or coherence or is only minimally connected to the task. Speech may be largely unintelligible. A response at this level is characterized by at least two of the following:	Consistent pronunciation and intonation problems cause considerable listener effort and frequently obscure meaning. Delivery is choppy, fragmented, or telegraphic. Speech contains frequent pauses and hesitations.	Range and control of grammar and vocabulary severely limits (or prevents) expression of ideas and connections among ideas. Some very low-level responses may rely on isolated words or short utterances to communicate ideas.	The response fails to provide much relevant content. Ideas that are expressed are often inaccurate, limited to vague utterances, or repetitions (including repetition of prompt).
0	Speaker makes no attempt to respond OR response is unrelated to the topic.			

TOEFL® iBT Test—Independent Speaking Rubrics

Score	General Description	Delivery	Language Use	Topic Development
4	**The response fulfills the demands of the task, with at most minor lapses in completeness. It is highly intelligible and exhibits sustained, coherent discourse. A response at this level is characterized by all of the following:**	Generally well-paced flow (fluid expression). Speech is clear. It may include minor lapses, or minor difficulties with pronunciation or intonation patterns, which do not affect overall intelligibility.	The response demonstrates effective use of grammar and vocabulary. It exhibits a fairly high degree of automaticity with good control of basic and complex structures (as appropriate). Some minor (or systematic) errors are noticeable but do not obscure meaning.	Response is sustained and sufficient to the task. It is generally well developed and coherent; relationships between ideas are clear (or clear progression of ideas).
3	**The response addresses the task appropriately, but may fall short of being fully developed. It is generally intelligible and coherent, with some fluidity of expression though it exhibits some noticeable lapses in the expression of ideas. A response at this level is characterized by at least two of the following:**	Speech is generally clear, with some fluidity of expression, though minor difficulties with pronunciation, intonation, or pacing are noticeable and may require listener effort at times (though overall intelligibility is not significantly affected).	The response demonstrates fairly automatic and effective use of grammar and vocabulary, and fairly coherent expression of relevant ideas. Response may exhibit some imprecise or inaccurate use of vocabulary or grammatical structures or be somewhat limited in the range of structures used. This may affect overall fluency, but it does not seriously interfere with the communication of the message.	Response is mostly coherent and sustained and conveys relevant ideas/information. Overall development is somewhat limited, usually lacks elaboration or specificity. Relationships between ideas may at times not be immediately clear.
2	**The response addresses the task, but development of the topic is limited. It contains intelligible speech, although problems with delivery and/or overall coherence occur; meaning may be obscured in places. A response at this level is characterized by at least two of the following:**	Speech is basically intelligible, though listener effort is needed because of unclear articulation, awkward intonation, or choppy rhythm/pace; meaning may be obscured in places.	The response demonstrates limited range and control of grammar and vocabulary. These limitations often prevent full expression of ideas. For the most part, only basic sentence structures are used successfully and spoken with fluidity. Structures and vocabulary may express mainly simple (short) and/or general propositions, with simple or unclear connections made among them (serial listing, conjunction, juxtaposition).	The response is connected to the task, though the number of ideas presented or the development of ideas is limited. Mostly basic ideas are expressed with limited elaboration (details and support). At times relevant substance may be vaguely expressed or repetitious. Connections of ideas may be unclear.
1	**The response is very limited in content and/or coherence or is only minimally connected to the task, or speech is largely unintelligible. A response at this level is characterized by at least two of the following:**	Consistent pronunciation, stress, and intonation difficulties cause considerable listener effort; delivery is choppy, fragmented, or telegraphic; frequent pauses and hesitations.	Range and control of grammar and vocabulary severely limits (or prevents) expression of ideas and connections among ideas. Some low level responses may rely heavily on practiced or formulaic expressions.	Limited relevant content is expressed. The response generally lacks substance beyond expression of very basic ideas. Speaker may be unable to sustain speech to complete task and may rely heavily on repetition of the prompt.
0	**Speaker makes no attempt to respond OR response is unrelated to the topic.**			

CD 1 TRACKING LIST

CD 2 TRACKING LIST